*not only hearing
but listening*

The
DAILY BIBLE®
30 Days
with Jesus

1. Daily inventory.
   strongest emotions last 24 hrs.
      - feeling anxious, fearful,
        angry
      - write about it.
      - take responsibility for my
        emotions
2. open about my sin w/ friends
      you trust (2-way)

F. LaGard Smith

3. show appreciation for God's
   love + grace + give back to
   others.

Surrender ‖‖ to authority of God
HARVEST HOUSE™ PUBLISHERS   (bible)
EUGENE, OREGON

All Scripture quotations are taken from the Holy Bible: New International Version®. NIV®. Copyright © 1973, 1978, 1984 by the International Bible Society. Used by permission of Zondervan Publishing House. The "NIV" and "New International Version" trademarks are registered in the United States Patent and Trademark Office by International Bible Society.

Cover by Koechel Peterson & Associates, Minneapolis, Minnesota

THE DAILY BIBLE is a registered trademark of The Hawkins Children's LLC. Harvest House Publishers, Inc., is the exclusive licensee of the federally registered trademark THE DAILY BIBLE.

30 DAYS WITH JESUS
Formerly *The Daily Gospels*
Copyright © 2003 by F. LaGard Smith
Published by Harvest House Publishers
Eugene, Oregon 97402
www.harvesthousepublishers.com

Library of Congress Cataloging-in-Publication Data

Smith, F. LaGard (Frank LaGard), 1944-
  [Daily Gospels]
  30 days with Jesus / F. LaGard Smith.
    p. cm.
  Originally published: The daily Gospels. c1988.
  ISBN-13: 978-0-7369-1133-7

  1. Jesus Christ—Biography—Sources, Biblical.   2. Jesus Christ—Biography—Meditations.   3. Christian life.   I. Title: Thirty days with Jesus.   II. Title.
BT299.3 .S65 2003
226'.1—dc21   2002015965

All rights reserved. No part of this publication may be reproduced, stored in a retrieval system, or transmitted in any form or by any means—electronic, mechanical, digital, photocopy, recording, or any other—except for brief quotations in printed reviews, without the prior permission of the publisher.

Printed in the United States of America

09   10   11   12   / BP-MS /   14   13   12   11   10

Contents

As You Begin... 5

Prologue 6

1. Beginnings
   Introductions by the Gospel Writers 9

2. Joy
   The Births of Jesus and John the Baptist 17

3. Growth
   Visit of the Magi and the Flight into Egypt 29

4. Preparation
   The Ministry of John the Baptist 37

5. Insight
   Jesus' Early Work in Judea, Samaria, and Galilee 45

6. Authority
   Beginning of the Great Galilean Ministry 57

7. Deity
   The Rise of Opposition 65

8. Essence
   The Sermon on the Mount 75

9. Rejection
   The Ministry Continues 85

10. Confrontation
    Conflict and Confrontation 95

11. Comparison
    Teaching Through Parables 103

12. Demonstration
    Performing Miracles 111

13. Commission
    Sending Out Apostles 119

14. Nourishment
    Miracles and Multitudes 127

15. Recognition
    Extensive Tour Throughout Galilee 137

16. Questioning
    In Jerusalem for the Feast of Tabernacles 151

17. Giving
    Ministry from Galilee to Judea 165

18. Warning
    The Perean Ministry 175

19. Friendship
    Return to Judea to Raise Lazarus 187

20. Value
    The Final Journey 193

21. Triumph
    The Triumphant—Sunday 203

22. Rebuke
    Final Week—Tuesday Morning 211

23. Prediction
    Discourse on Future Events 223

24. Betrayal
    Final Week—Tuesday Afternoon 233

25. Love
    The Upper Room 241

26. Unity
    Final Discourse 251

27. Denial
    Betrayal and Arrest 259

28. Courage
    Trial Before Pilate 269

29. Forgiveness
    The Crucifixion of Jesus 277

30. Belief
    Jesus' Resurrection and Appearances 285

31. Anticipation
    Final Instructions and Ascension 297

As You Begin...

Welcome to what may be one of the most rewarding experiences you will ever have in reading the Bible! Over the next month (we're actually going to give you an extra day) you will read all four Gospel accounts, interwoven into one sequentially arranged account of the life of Jesus. We believe that you will come to know Jesus like you've never known him before.

Throughout the Scripture text you will find narrative commentary which will give you helpful and interesting background for the section of Scripture you will be reading. The narration will also tie together the readings from one day to the next, so that Jesus' life and ministry will unfold before you like one continuous story.

At the end of each day's reading is a brief insight into the Scriptures you have just read. The reading is easy, and the message is challenging, rewarding and uplifting. Everything has been specially designed for your personal growth.

Just a brief note about the Scripture text itself, which is taken from the highly readable New International Version. In the margin beside the text, you will find a reference to each Gospel account which records a given event. If any portion of that account is actually presented in the text, the reference will appear in bold print. In order to avoid repetition, any account which is a virtual duplication will be cited, but not presented. Our goal has been to give you the most complete account possible, while maintaining a high degree of readability. When more than one Gospel writer contributes to the text presented, you will be alerted to each writer by his abbreviated name appearing as a superscript above the line. It sounds more complicated than it is!

Many books have been written about Jesus, but we hope this book will take you one step beyond. Whether you are reading it alone each day as part of your quiet time, or together with other people in a class or Bible study, we think you will be a changed person as a result.

May God richly bless your reading of the Gospels and may they be a powerful presence in your daily walk with Christ.

—*F. LaGard Smith*

Prologue

This is the story of the most important event in human history. It is an event which was planned even before the creation of the world. It is the keeping of a 2000-year-old promise made to Abraham. It is the fulfillment of a host of prophecies regarding a Messiah who would come to establish his kingdom. Most importantly, it is the beginning of a dynamically new relationship between God and man. The event is the coming of the Savior of the world, the Messiah—or, as referred to in the Greek, the Christ.

This Christ is not to be just another world leader, as Cyrus, Alexander, or Caesar. He is not to be just another great man of God, as Abraham, Moses, or David. He is to be God himself in human flesh! The Lord of heaven is to become a servant of the earth. God, who has previously made himself known through a nation and a law, is now to reveal himself in the most personal way possible—in the form of a man. Until this point in history, God's blessings have been reserved mostly for a chosen people, but now these blessings are to become available to all people in every generation.

Who is this Christ, this Messiah? His name is Jesus. His symbolic name, Immanuel (meaning "God with us"), signifies his deity. He is man, to be sure, but God as well; and he is God—the God of Creation—but man as well. God lowers himself so that man might be elevated. He leaves heaven so that man might enter it. To man, who cannot begin to understand the ways of God, it is clearly a great mystery. But what a marvelous and wonderful mystery it is!

As the Gospel record now begins, the Scriptures proclaim the good news about the salvation of mankind which comes through grace and obedient faith in Jesus the Christ. The good news begins with the miraculous birth of Jesus to a virgin of Galilee in the days of Herod, king of Judea. Then, as Jesus grows into manhood, his coming as the promised Messiah and Savior is announced by John the Baptist. As Jesus begins his own ministry, he confirms his deity with miraculous healings and other signs and wonders, and proclaims the imminent coming of the kingdom of God. His teaching calls men and women to new spiritual heights in their worship of God and in their relationships with one another.

But because his teaching challenges traditional practices of the Jewish religion of his day, and because he claims divine authority, Jesus meets strong opposition from religious leaders. That opposition ultimately leads to arrest and trial before Jewish and Roman authorities. Although falsely accused, Jesus is condemned and sentenced to die by crucifixion—an event which is intended to silence both the man and his message. Instead, the good news comes to a powerful climax when, on the third day after his death, Jesus rises from the grave and shows himself alive, proving his own miraculous resurrection. The Christian hope which derives from the gospel message is that, just as Jesus is raised from the dead, so also the righteous in Christ will be raised to eternal life!

DAY 1 WITH JESUS

BEGINNINGS

Introductions by the Gospel Writers

MARK'S ACCOUNT BEGINS SIMPLY,

Mk. 1:1 | The beginning of the gospel about Jesus Christ, the Son of God.[a]

Mark introduces the reader to the good news about Jesus the Christ which is about to be told. That good news is beautifully summarized by John in a prologue to his account. It begins, as does the first book of Old Testament Scripture, with the creation of man, and shows that the Word (a designation for God as Christ) was not only the source through which all things were made, but also came into this world in human form as the man Jesus. It also shows that, through Jesus, mankind has received the grace of God unto salvation, as attested to during Christ's ministry by John the Baptist, a special messenger of God.

Jn. 1:1-18 | In the beginning was the Word, and the Word was with God, and the Word was God. He was with God in the beginning.

Through him all things were made; without him nothing was made that has been made. In him was life, and that life was the light of men. The light shines in the darkness, but the darkness has not understood[b] it.

There came a man who was sent from God; his name was John. He came as a witness to testify concerning that light, so that through him all men might believe. He himself was not

---

[a]Some manuscripts do not have *the Son of God.*   [b]Or *darkness, and the darkness has not overcome.*

the light; he came only as a witness to the light. The true light that gives light to every man was coming into the world.[c]

He was in the world, and though the world was made through him, the world did not recognize him. He came to that which was his own, but his own did not receive him. Yet to all who received him, to those who believed in his name, he gave the right to become children of God—children born not of natural descent,[d] nor of human decision or a husband's will, but born of God.

The Word became flesh and made his dwelling among us. We have seen his glory, the glory of the One and Only,[e] who came from the Father, full of grace and truth.

John testifies concerning him. He cries out, saying, "This was he of whom I said, 'He who comes after me has surpassed me because he was before me.'" From the fullness of his grace we have all received one blessing after another. For the law was given through Moses; grace and truth came through Jesus Christ. No one has ever seen God, but God the One and Only,[e,f] who is at the Father's side, has made him known.

In his own introduction, Luke writes to a man by the name of Theophilus in order to provide a more complete narrative of the life and work of this incarnate Word, Jesus the Christ, and of the things accomplished by Jesus' followers. Luke points out that, prior to his own account, other writers had already undertaken to record the events surrounding Jesus' coming and the work of his disciples during his ministry. Thus the records of Christ began to be compiled soon after his death and resurrection.

Lk. 1:1-4 | Many have undertaken to draw up an account of the things that have been fulfilled[g] among us, just as they were handed down to us by those who from the first were eyewitnesses and servants of the word. Therefore, since I myself have carefully investigated everything from the beginning, it seemed good also to me to write an orderly account for you, most excellent Theophilus, so that you may know the certainty of the things you have been taught.

[c]Or *This was the true light that gives light to every man who comes into the world.*   [d]Greek of *bloods*   [e]Or *the Only Begotten*   [f]Some manuscripts but *the only* (or *only begotten*) *Son*   [g]Or *been surely believed*

The Genealogies of Jesus

Matthew's account has no formal introduction, but rather begins with a genealogy tracing the descent of Jesus from his ancestor, Abraham, through the royal lineage of David the King. Matthew lists 42 of the known generations and divides these into three groups of 14 each. The genealogy is traced through Jesus' legal father, Joseph, as the husband of the virgin Mary, to whom Jesus was born.

Matthew's genealogy contains several happy surprises. Back in Jesus' early roots are not only such notable righteous men as Abraham and David, but also several who stand out in history as being particularly unrighteous, including wicked King Manasseh. Not only are there Jews, as would be expected, but also Gentiles, including a Canaanite and a Moabite, whose respective countrymen have been notorious enemies of God's people. Also somewhat surprising, in view of their social status at this time, is the listing of women as well as men. Furthermore, at least two of the women are known best for sins which they had committed.

Mt. 1:1-17 | A record of the genealogy of Jesus Christ the son of David, the son of Abraham:
> Abraham was the father of Isaac,
> Isaac the father of Jacob,
> Jacob the father of Judah and his brothers,
> Judah the father of Perez and Zerah, whose mother was Tamar,
> Perez the father of Hezron,
> Hezron the father of Ram,
> Ram the father of Amminadab,
> Amminadab the father of Nahshon,
> Nahshon the father of Salmon,
> Salmon the father of Boaz, whose mother was Rahab,
> Boaz the father of Obed, whose mother was Ruth,
> Obed the father of Jesse,
> and Jesse the father of King David.

> David was the father of Solomon, whose mother had been Uriah's wife,
> Solomon the father of Rehoboam,

Rehoboam the father of Abijah,
Abijah the father of Asa,
Asa the father of Jehoshaphat,
Jehoshaphat the father of Jehoram,
Jehoram the father of Uzziah,
Uzziah the father of Jotham,
Jotham the father of Ahaz,
Ahaz the father of Hezekiah,
Hezekiah the father of Manasseh,
Manasseh the father of Amon,
Amon the father of Josiah,
and Josiah the father of Jeconiah[h] and his brothers at the
time of the exile to Babylon.

After the exile to Babylon:
Jeconiah was the father of Shealtiel,
Shealtiel the father of Zerubbabel,
Zerubbabel the father of Abiud,
Abiud the father of Eliakim,
Eliakim the father of Azor,
Azor the father of Zadok,
Zadok the father of Akim,
Akim the father of Eliud,
Eliud the father of Eleazar,
Eleazar the father of Matthan,
Matthan the father of Jacob,
and Jacob the father of Joseph, the husband of Mary, of
whom was born Jesus, who is called Christ.

Thus there were fourteen generations in all from Abraham to
David, fourteen from David to the exile to Babylon, and fourteen from the exile to the Christ.[i]

Luke also provides a genealogy of Jesus, but his account traces
the lineage directly through Jesus' mother, Mary. This explains the
difference in ancestors from Heli (assumed to be the father-in-law
of Mary's husband, Joseph) to David. Luke's genealogy also goes
beyond Abraham, all the way back through Noah, Enoch, Seth,
and Adam to God himself, who created the human race.

[h]That is, Jehoiachin   [i]Or *Messiah.* "The Christ" (Greek) and "The Messiah" (Hebrew)
both mean "the Anointed One."

Lk.
3:23b-38

He was the son, so it was thought, of Joseph,
    the son of Heli, the son of Matthat,
    the son of Levi, the son of Melki,
    the son of Jannai, the son of Joseph,
    the son of Mattathias, the son of Amos,
    the son of Nahum, the son of Esli,
    the son of Naggai, the son of Maath,
    the son of Mattathias, the son of Semein,
    the son of Josech, the son of Joda,
    the son of Joanan, the son of Rhesa,
    the son of Zerubbabel, the son of Shealtiel,
    the son of Neri, the son of Melki,
    the son of Addi, the son of Cosam,
    the son of Elmadam, the son of Er,
    the son of Joshua, the son of Eliezer,
    the son of Jorim, the son of Matthat,
    the son of Levi, the son of Simeon,
    the son of Judah, the son of Joseph,
    the son of Jonam, the son of Eliakim,
    the son of Melea, the son of Menna,
    the son of Mattatha, the son of Nathan,
    the son of David, the son of Jesse,
    the son of Obed, the son of Boaz,
    the son of Salmon[j], the son of Nahshon,
    the son of Amminadab, the son of Ram,[k]
    the son of Hezron, the son of Perez,
    the son of Judah, the son of Jacob,
    the son of Isaac, the son of Abraham,
    the son of Terah, the son of Nahor,
    the son of Serug, the son of Reu,
    the son of Peleg, the son of Eber,
    the son of Shelah, the son of Cainan,
    the son of Arphaxad, the son of Shem,
    the son of Noah, the son of Lamech,
    the son of Methuselah, the son of Enoch,
    the son of Jared, the son of Mahalalel
    the son of Kenan, the son of Enosh,
    the son of Seth, the son of Adam,
    the son of God.

[j]Some early manuscripts *Sala*   [k]Some manuscripts *Amminadab, the son of Admin, the son of Arni*; other manuscripts vary widely.

Perhaps the most significant aspect of these genealogies is the connection between Jesus and his ancestor, King David. The prophets of old had repeatedly foretold that the Messiah would be of the house of David, and a branch of Jesse, David's father. Therefore, from the Jews' perspective, Jesus is of the royal lineage and worthy to be King of Israel. While this brings comfort to many, it brings confusion to others, who are expecting the Messiah to be the same kind of political king as those who reigned before him.

TODAY'S INSIGHTS

Beginnings

Can you remember the exact words you first spoke to a friend or loved one? Chances are those first words were less than memorable. Even if you do remember the exact words, was there nevertheless a feeling that nothing particularly special was about to happen? Sometimes in human relationships the first words are quite insignificant, hardly noteworthy. Beginnings are often inconsequential.

By contrast, however, our relationship with God is laced through and through with important beginnings. First, Christ comes to us as the Word, to assure us that the God of creation wants to communicate with us. He cares so much about us that he wants to reveal himself to us on the most intimate level possible— through a person we can know and love. A person to whom we can reveal our deepest feelings and darkest secrets. A person with whom we can share joy and triumph as well as sorrow and tragedy.

Second, Christ comes to us as a light which illuminates the darkness of our understanding. It is through his example that we gain the richest insight into how we can best live our lives. And shouldn't we want to follow his light? Can we possibly know our universe—or even ourselves—better than the One who was with God in the beginning and the One through whom we were made? Intelligent though we may be, we're not so bright as to know what is best for our lives on this earth. We need his guiding light.

Third, Christ comes to us as flesh and blood, just as we are flesh and blood. Christ wasn't just some illusion of deity, or an academic concept, or a cold belief system with which we could never possibly identify. Far from it. Jesus Christ was a descendant of Adam, the same as you or I. He was not only the Son of God, but also the Son of man. And the fact of his humanity is as important as his deity, because it is only through his fleshly humanity that he can be for us an example, an intercessor, a brother, and a friend.

The universe itself began in much the same way. In the beginning there was darkness, until God said, "Let there be light." Through his spoken word the worlds were framed, and from his word came light and life. This was his first creation, by which we have our very existence. But Jesus has come that we might become his *new* creation—through the written Word, which is "a lamp to my feet and a light for my path," and through the incarnate Word made flesh, Jesus Christ, who is the Way, the Truth, and the Life.

Word, light, and flesh. Through these characteristics of Christ we have great beginnings in our relationship with God. Through Christ we have communication, insight, and companionship. Through Christ we have God within us.

The written Word reflects the light, but Jesus himself *is* the Light. Which Word do we know best?

JOY

The Births of Jesus and John the Baptist

JESUS IS TO BE BORN IN JUDEA APPROXIMATELY 747 YEARS after the foundation of Rome. Now in the time of Herod the Great, who has been granted the title "King of the Jews" by the Roman senate under Emperor Caesar Augustus, the former land of Palestine is divided into the provinces of Judea, Samaria, and Galilee to the west of the Jordan River, and Perea and Decapolis to the east. The cities of Jerusalem and Bethlehem are both in Judea, while Nazareth is in Galilee. That Jesus is born in the province of Judea is surprising because his family's home is in Nazareth, some 75 miles north. But, due to a decree by Caesar Augustus requiring everyone to return to his own city, Jesus' birth takes place in Bethlehem—the very city named by the prophet Micah over 700 years earlier!

If that fulfillment is not enough to catch the attention of those familiar with earlier prophecies, an even more amazing fulfillment is involved—namely, Jesus' virgin birth. Isaiah had prophesied that the Messiah would be born of a virgin. Certainly there have been miraculous births before, as when couples were beyond the normal age of childbearing. Abraham and Sarah are the foremost example, and Zechariah and Elizabeth are soon to become another. However, never before nor since has a woman conceived without the seed of man. Not only is Mary a virgin in the sense of being a young woman, but, more importantly, she is a virgin in the fact that she has not had sexual relations with either her fiancé, Joseph, or any other man. The Gospel accounts state unequivocally that Jesus is miraculously conceived in Mary by the Holy Spirit of God.

The divine nature of Jesus' birth is both wonderful and exciting, but the human side of the story is touching in and of itself. Although she is told in advance about the miraculous birth, Mary must surely feel the embarrassment of being thought unchaste by her family and friends. She must surely feel the weight of concern in the mind of Joseph. When the two of them find themselves far from home at the time of delivery, they must both feel a terrible isolation and awesome expectation about this special child from God. Yet Mary's confident faith and Joseph's loving support are both rewarded with more celebration than any other human family has ever known at the arrival of a new child. From lowly shepherds on the earth to the highest halls of heaven, the majesty of the occasion is heralded with songs of joy!

As the account of Jesus' birth begins, there is another birth announced as well—that of God's special messenger, John, who, because of his ministry of repentance and baptism, will later be known as John the Baptist. Luke and Matthew tell the story of the two births and of the early events which follow in the young life of Jesus.

Lk. 1:5-17
(Ca. 6-4
B.C.)

JOHN'S BIRTH FORETOLD. In the time of Herod king of Judea there was a priest named Zechariah, who belonged to the priestly division of Abijah; his wife Elizabeth was also a descendant of Aaron. Both of them were upright in the sight of God, observing all the Lord's commandments and regulations blamelessly. But they had no children, because Elizabeth was barren; and they were both well along in years.

Once when Zechariah's division was on duty and he was serving as priest before God, he was chosen by lot, according to the custom of the priesthood, to go into the temple of the Lord and burn incense. And when the time for the burning of incense came, all the assembled worshipers were praying outside.

Then an angel of the Lord appeared to him, standing at the right side of the altar of incense. When Zechariah saw him, he was startled and was gripped with fear. But the angel said to him: "Do not be afraid, Zechariah; your prayer has been heard. Your wife Elizabeth will bear you a son, and you are to give him the name John. He will be a joy and delight to you, and many will rejoice because of his birth, for he will be great in the sight of the Lord. He is never to take wine or other fermented drink, and he will be filled with the Holy Spirit even from birth.[^1] Many of the people of Israel will he bring back to the Lord their God. And he will go on before the Lord, in the spirit and power of Elijah, to turn the hearts of the fathers to their

[^1]: Or *from his mother's womb*

children and the disobedient to the wisdom of the righteous—
to make ready a people prepared for the Lord."

Lk. 1:18-25 ZECHARIAH MADE SPEECHLESS. Zechariah asked the
angel, "How can I be sure of this? I am an old man and my
wife is well along in years."

The angel answered, "I am Gabriel. I stand in the presence
of God, and I have been sent to speak to you and to tell you
this good news. And now you will be silent and not able to
speak until the day this happens, because you did not believe
my words, which will come true at their proper time."

Meanwhile, the people were waiting for Zechariah and
wondering why he stayed so long in the temple. When he
came out, he could not speak to them. They realized he had
seen a vision in the temple, for he kept making signs to them
but remained unable to speak.

When his time of service was completed, he returned home.
After this his wife Elizabeth became pregnant and for five
months remained in seclusion. "The Lord has done this for
me," she said. "In these days he has shown his favor and taken
away my disgrace among the people."

Lk. 1:26-38 MARY TOLD OF CONCEPTION. In the sixth month, God
Nazareth sent the angel Gabriel to Nazareth, a town in Galilee, to a
virgin pledged to be married to a man named Joseph, a
descendant of David. The virgin's name was Mary. The angel
went to her and said, "Greetings, you who are highly favored!
The Lord is with you."

Mary was greatly troubled at his words and wondered what
kind of greeting this might be. But the angel said to her, "Do
not be afraid, Mary, you have found favor with God. You will
be with child and give birth to a son, and you are to give him
the name Jesus. He will be great and will be called the Son of
the Most High. The Lord God will give him the throne of his
father David, and he will reign over the house of Jacob forever; his kingdom will never end."

"How will this be," Mary asked the angel, "since I am a
virgin?"

The angel answered, "The Holy Spirit will come upon you,
and the power of the Most High will overshadow you. So the

holy one to be born will be called[m] the Son of God. Even Elizabeth your relative is going to have a child in her old age, and she who was said to be barren is in her sixth month. For nothing is impossible with God."

"I am the Lord's servant," Mary answered. "May it be to me as you have said." Then the angel left her.

Lk. 1:39-45
A city of
Judah

MARY VISITS ELIZABETH. At that time Mary got ready and hurried to a town in the hill country of Judea, where she entered Zechariah's home and greeted Elizabeth. When Elizabeth heard Mary's greeting, the baby leaped in her womb, and Elizabeth was filled with the Holy Spirit. In a loud voice she exclaimed: "Blessed are you among women, and blessed is the child you will bear! But why am I so favored, that the mother of my Lord should come to me? As soon as the sound of your greeting reached my ears, the baby in my womb leaped for joy. Blessed is she who has believed that what the Lord has said to her will be accomplished!"

Lk. 1:46-56

MARY PRAISES GOD. And Mary said:

> "My soul glorifies the Lord
>> and my spirit rejoices in God my Savior,
> for he has been mindful
>> of the humble state of his servant.
> From now on all generations will call me blessed,
>> for the Mighty One has done great things for me—
>> holy is his name.
> His mercy extends to those who fear him,
>> from generation to generation.
> He has performed mighty deeds with his arm;
>> he has scattered those who are proud in their inmost thoughts.
> He has brought down rulers from their thrones
>> but has lifted up the humble.
> He has filled the hungry with good things
>> but has sent the rich away empty.
> He has helped his servant Israel,
>> remembering to be merciful
> to Abraham and his descendants forever,
>> even as he said to our fathers."

[m]Or So the child to be born will be called holy,

Mary stayed with Elizabeth for about three months and then returned home.

Lk. 1:57-66 | JOHN THE BAPTIST IS BORN. When it was time for Elizabeth to have her baby, she gave birth to a son. Her neighbors and relatives heard that the Lord had shown her great mercy, and they shared her joy.

On the eighth day they came to circumcise the child, and they were going to name him after his father Zechariah, but his mother spoke up and said, "No! He is to be called John."

They said to her, "There is no one among your relatives who has that name."

Then they made signs to his father, to find out what he would like to name the child. He asked for a writing tablet, and to everyone's astonishment he wrote, "His name is John." Immediately his mouth was opened and his tongue was loosed, and he began to speak, praising God. The neighbors were all filled with awe, and throughout the hill country of Judea people were talking about all these things. Everyone who heard this wondered about it, asking, "What then is this child going to be?" For the Lord's hand was with him.

Lk. 1:67-80 | ZECHARIAH PROPHESIES. His father Zechariah was filled with the Holy Spirit and prophesied:

> "Praise be to the Lord, the God of Israel,
>   because he has come and has redeemed his people.
> He has raised up a horn[n] of salvation for us
>   in the house of his servant David
> (as he said through his holy prophets of long ago),
> salvation from our enemies
>   and from the hand of all who hate us—
> to show mercy to our fathers
>   and to remember his holy covenant,
>   the oath he swore to our father Abraham:
> to rescue us from the hand of our enemies,
>   and to enable us to serve him without fear
>   in holiness and righteousness before him all our
>   days.
>
> And you, my child, will be called a prophet of the

[n]*Horn* here symbolizes strength.

Most High;
   for you will go on before the Lord to prepare the way
      for him,
to give his people the knowledge of salvation
  through the forgiveness of their sins,
because of the tender mercy of our God,
  by which the rising sun will come to us from heaven
  to shine on those living in darkness
  and in the shadow of death,
   to guide our feet into the path of peace."

And the child grew and became strong in spirit; and he lived in the desert until he appeared publicly to Israel.

Mt. 1:18-25a

JOSEPH TOLD OF CONCEPTION. This is how the birth of Jesus Christ came about: His mother Mary was pledged to be married to Joseph, but before they came together, she was found to be with child through the Holy Spirit. Because Joseph her husband was a righteous man and did not want to expose her to public disgrace, he had in mind to divorce her quietly.

But after he had considered this, an angel of the Lord appeared to him in a dream and said, "Joseph son of David, do not be afraid to take Mary home as your wife, because what is conceived in her is from the Holy Spirit. She will give birth to a son, and you are to give him the name Jesus,[o] because he will save his people from their sins."

All this took place to fulfill what the Lord had said through the prophet: "The virgin will be with child and will give birth to a son, and they will call him Immanuel"[p]—which means, "God with us."

When Joseph woke up, he did what the angel of the Lord had commanded him and took Mary home as his wife. But he had no union with her until she gave birth to a son.

Lk. 2:1-7 Bethlehem (Ca. 5-3 B.C.)

JESUS THE CHRIST IS BORN. In those days Caesar Augustus issued a decree that a census should be taken of the entire Roman world. (This was the first census that took place while Quirinius was governor of Syria.) And everyone went to his own town to register.

---

[o] *Jesus* is the Greek form of *Joshua*, which means *the LORD saves*.   [p] Isaiah 7:14

So Joseph also went up from the town of Nazareth in Galilee to Judea, to Bethlehem the town of David, because he belonged to the house and line of David. He went there to register with Mary, who was pledged to be married to him and was expecting a child. While they were there, the time came for the baby to be born, and she gave birth to her firstborn, a son. She wrapped him in cloths and placed him in a manger, because there was no room for them in the inn.

Lk. 2:8-14 | ANGELS PROCLAIM BIRTH. And there were shepherds living out in the fields nearby, keeping watch over their flocks at night. An angel of the Lord appeared to them, and the glory of the Lord shone around them, and they were terrified. But the angel said to them, "Do not be afraid. I bring you good news of great joy that will be for all the people. Today in the town of David a Savior has been born to you; he is Christ[q] the Lord. This will be a sign to you: You will find a baby wrapped in cloths and lying in a manger."

Suddenly a great company of the heavenly host appeared with the angel, praising God and saying,

> "Glory to God in the highest,
>   and on earth peace to men on whom his favor
>   rests."

Lk. 2:15-20 | SHEPHERDS VISIT BABY. When the angels had left them and gone into heaven, the shepherds said to one another, "Let's go to Bethlehem and see this thing that has happened, which the Lord has told us about."

So they hurried off and found Mary and Joseph, and the baby, who was lying in the manger. When they had seen him, they spread the word concerning what had been told them about this child, and all who heard it were amazed at what the shepherds said to them. But Mary treasured up all these things and pondered them in her heart. The shepherds returned, glorifying and praising God for all the things they had heard and seen, which were just as they had been told.

Mt. 1:25b
Lk. 2:21 | JESUS CIRCUMCISED AND NAMED. On the eighth day, when it was time to circumcise him, he was named Jesus, the name the angel had given him before he had been conceived.

[q] Or *Messiah*. "The Christ" (Greek) and "the Messiah" (Hebrew) both mean "the Anointed One"

**Lk.
2:22-24
Jerusalem**

JESUS PRESENTED IN TEMPLE. When the time of their purification according to the Law of Moses had been completed, Joseph and Mary took him to Jerusalem to present him to the Lord (as it is written in the Law of the Lord, "Every firstborn male is to be consecrated to the Lord"[r]), and to offer a sacrifice in keeping with what is said in the Law of the Lord: "a pair of doves or two young pigeons."[s]

**Lk.
2:25-35**

SIMEON EXPRESSES HIS JOY. Now there was a man in Jerusalem called Simeon, who was righteous and devout. He was waiting for the consolation of Israel, and the Holy Spirit was upon him. It had been revealed to him by the Holy Spirit that he would not die before he had seen the Lord's Christ. Moved by the Spirit, he went into the temple courts. When the parents brought in the child Jesus to do for him what the custom of the Law required, Simeon took him in his arms and praised God, saying:

> "Sovereign Lord, as you have promised,
>   you now dismiss[t] your servant in peace.
> For my eyes have seen your salvation,
>   which you have prepared in the sight of all people,
> a light for revelation to the Gentiles
>   and for glory to your people Israel."

The child's father and mother marveled at what was said about him. Then Simeon blessed them and said to Mary, his mother: "This child is destined to cause the falling and rising of many in Israel, and to be a sign that will be spoken against, so that the thoughts of many hearts will be revealed. And a sword will pierce your own soul too."

**Lk.
2:36-38**

ANNA THE PROPHETESS. There was also a prophetess, Anna, the daughter of Phanuel, of the tribe of Asher. She was very old; she had lived with her husband seven years after her marriage, and then was a widow until she was eighty-four.[u] She never left the temple but worshiped night and day, fasting and praying. Coming up to them at that very moment, she gave thanks to God and spoke about the child to all who were looking forward to the redemption of Jerusalem.

[r]Exodus 13:2,12   [s]Lev. 12:8   [t]Or *promised, / now dismiss*   [u]Or *widow for eighty-four years*

TODAY'S INSIGHTS

Joy

Is there anything more joyful than the birth of a baby? Not unless it is the birth of a baby who has been born under unusually difficult circumstances, or after previously unsuccessful attempts to create that special new life. Birth announcements are such wonderful occasions! They bring fresh hope and unlimited potential. They bring renewal and excitement. For many parents there is the filling of a void, the satisfaction of a need, perhaps even the answer to a prayer.

For all of us who recognize our spiritual emptiness, the coming of Jesus Christ into our world was just such an event. It would have been joy enough for Joseph and Mary to have a son with whom they could share life and love. But Jesus was meant for the whole family of humankind. He came into *our* lives as well as into theirs. He dares to call us his brothers and sisters! And he shares with us his own personal relationship with God the Father.

The good news of the birth of Christ is the good news that God is with us. The good news of Jesus' coming is the good news that our sins are forgiven through God's grace and our obedient faith in his salvation. The good news is that we have been bought back from the Evil One, to whom we have so many times sold ourselves for paltry pleasures.

The birth of Jesus is not simply a sentimental occasion which is celebrated once each year with extravagant trappings. Jesus' birth is a reminder of our own spiritual rebirth. Jesus' birth by a virgin is a reminder that with God all things are possible. Conception by the Holy Spirit is a reminder that we too have our new life through the working of the Spirit.

Jesus' birth is also the fulfillment of a promise and a reminder that, even in our lives, God, who has promised, is faithful. When he promises us eternal life, we can rest assured that he has indeed prepared a place for us in the world to come. When he promises us a life of joy and peace on this earth, we can rest assured that, even in the rough times, there is in Christ a peace that passes all understanding.

The Christian who does not feel joy daily in his or her own life has missed the message of Jesus' birth. The carols we sing about his birth mean little if they do not bring into our lives the joy of reconciliation with God. And the celebration of the angels has a hollow ring if we fail to find joy in the living of life each day and in the simple sharing with our friends.

For those who *do* know the true meaning of joy, life takes on purpose spiced with pleasure. How about us? Has happiness run its course in our lives? What a wonderful opportunity to embrace a little child and bring him into our hearts! Great joy awaits those who do.

DAY WITH JESUS 3

GROWTH

Visit of the Magi and Flight into Egypt

THE RITE OF PURIFICATION TAKES PLACE 40 DAYS AFTER JESUS' BIRTH and ordinarily would have required the offering of a yearling lamb and a pigeon. However, the law permits poor parents, such as Joseph and Mary are, to offer a second pigeon or dove instead of the lamb, which they cannot afford. Thus, even by his parents' offering of purification, it can be seen that Jesus comes humbly into the world.

Despite these lowly beginnings, news of Jesus' birth spreads quickly throughout Judea and even beyond its borders. Matthew records the account of a visit to Bethlehem by certain philosopher-priests who, interestingly enough, may even be pagan Zoroastrians from Persia. Their presumed contact with Jews of the Dispersion has undoubtedly made them familiar with the Jewish Messiah of prophecy. The Magi are prompted to travel the great distance to Jerusalem because of a star which appeared at the time of Jesus' birth. It is not known how many make the long journey (certainly no compelling evidence exists for the traditional three), but they apparently arrive some six months after Jesus' birth and inquire as to the child's whereabouts. By this time Joseph and Mary have found accommodations in a house, and it is in this house that the Magi's gifts are offered to the newborn "King of the Jews."

King Herod is alarmed by the Magi's visit because he believes Jesus' birth poses a political threat to his reign. Because of this, Herod sends his soldiers to Bethlehem to kill all male children who might have been born within the time frame suggested by the Magi's calculations. By Jewish reckoning, any child over 12 months is considered two years old. Since apparently six months have passed following Jesus' birth, Herod makes his order broad enough to prevent any mistake by including all of the estimated 40 to 50 baby boys in Bethlehem who would be up to 12 or 13 months old at this time.

As will be seen, however, Joseph will be warned about the slaughter and will quickly depart for Egypt, where he and Mary and the child Jesus will stay until after Herod's own death.

Mt. 2:1-8
Jerusalem
(Ca. 4-2
B.C.)

WISE MEN SEEK JESUS. After Jesus was born in Bethlehem in Judea, during the time of King Herod, Magi[v] from the east came to Jerusalem and asked, "Where is the one who has been born king of the Jews? We saw his star in the east[w] and have come to worship him."

When King Herod heard this he was disturbed, and all Jerusalem with him. When he had called together all the people's chief priests and teachers of the law, he asked them where the Christ[x] was to be born. "In Bethlehem in Judea," they replied, "for this is what the prophet has written:

"'But you, Bethlehem, in the land of Judah,
    are by no means least among the rulers of Judah;
for out of you will come a ruler
    who will be the shepherd of my people Israel.'[y]"

Then Herod called the Magi secretly and found out from them the exact time the star had appeared. He sent them to Bethlehem and said, "Go and make a careful search for the child. As soon as you find him, report to me, so that I too may go and worship him."

Mt. 2:9-12
Bethlehem

WISE MEN VISIT JESUS. After they had heard the king, they went on their way, and the star they had seen in the east[z] went ahead of them until it stopped over the place where the child was. When they saw the star, they were overjoyed. On coming to the house, they saw the child with his mother Mary, and they bowed down and worshiped him. Then they opened their treasures and presented him with gifts of gold and of incense and of myrrh. And having been warned in a dream not to go back to Herod, they returned to their country by another route.

Mt.
2:13-15
Egypt

FLIGHT TO EGYPT. When they had gone, an angel of the Lord appeared to Joseph in a dream. "Get up," he said, "take the child and his mother and escape to Egypt. Stay there until I tell you, for Herod is going to search for the child to kill him."

[v]Traditionally *Wise Men*   [w]Or *star when it rose*   [x]Or *Messiah*   [y]Micah 5:2
[z]Or *seen when it rose*

So he got up, took the child and his mother during the night and left for Egypt, where he stayed until the death of Herod. And so was fulfilled what the Lord had said through the prophet: "Out of Egypt I called my son."[a]

Mt.
2:16-18

HEROD ORDERS SLAUGHTER. When Herod realized that he had been outwitted by the Magi, he was furious, and he gave orders to kill all the boys in Bethlehem and its vicinity who were two years old and under, in accordance with the time he had learned from the Magi. Then what was said through the prophet Jeremiah was fulfilled:

"A voice is heard in Ramah,
     weeping and great mourning,
Rachel weeping for her children
     and refusing to be comforted,
because they are no more."[b]

From Infancy to Manhood

After their brief stay in Egypt, Joseph and Mary return to their home in Nazareth of Galilee, where Joseph resumes his trade as a carpenter. Over the next ten years Jesus continues to grow physically, mentally, and spiritually. There is no further record of Jesus until, at the age of 12, he is taken to Jerusalem for the Passover celebration. At age 12, Jesus has reached the point at which a Jewish boy is soon to become a "son of the law," which law he is expected to learn and obey. But Jesus' understanding of the law is far greater than that of other boys his age. After the Passover celebration is completed, Jesus' parents lose track of his whereabouts until they discover him in profound conversation with the learned rabbis. When his parents express their concern about his leaving them, Jesus gives a response which indicates that, even now, he is aware of his divine sonship and role as the Messiah.

Mt. 2:19-23
Lk. 2:39,40
Nazareth

RETURN TO NAZARETH. [Mt]After Herod died, an angel of the Lord appeared in a dream to Joseph in Egypt and said, "Get up, take the child and his mother and go to the land of Israel, for those who were trying to take the child's life are dead."

[a]Hosea 11:1   [b]Jer. 31:15

So he got up, took the child and his mother and went to the land of Israel. But when he heard that Archelaus was reigning in Judea in place of his father Herod, he was afraid to go there. Having been warned in a dream, he withdrew to the district of Galilee, and he went and lived in a town called Nazareth. So was fulfilled what was said through the prophets: "He will be called a Nazarene." ^{Lk}And the child grew and became strong; he was filled with wisdom, and the grace of God was upon him.

Lk. 2:41-50
Jerusalem

JESUS VISITS JERUSALEM. Every year his parents went to Jerusalem for the Feast of the Passover. When he was twelve years old, they went up to the Feast, according to the custom. After the Feast was over, while his parents were returning home, the boy Jesus stayed behind in Jerusalem, but they were unaware of it. Thinking he was in their company, they traveled on for a day. Then they began looking for him among their relatives and friends. When they did not find him, they went back to Jerusalem to look for him. After three days they found him in the temple courts, sitting among the teachers, listening to them and asking them questions. Everyone who heard him was amazed at his understanding and his answers. When his parents saw him, they were astonished. His mother said to him, "Son, why have you treated us like this? Your father and I have been anxiously searching for you."

"Why were you searching for me?" he asked. "Didn't you know I had to be in my Father's house?" But they did not understand what he was saying to them.

Lk. 2:51,52
Nazareth

GROWING UP IN NAZARETH. Then he went down to Nazareth with them and was obedient to them. But his mother treasured all these things in her heart. And Jesus grew in wisdom and stature, and in favor with God and men.

Little more is known of Jesus' first 30 years. It is known that Jesus has at least four brothers—James, Joses, Judas (Jude), and Simon—and also some sisters, who are not named. Because there is no further reference to Joseph, it appears that he probably died while Jesus was still a relatively young man. The support of his mother and younger brothers and sisters, therefore, would naturally fall upon Jesus as the firstborn. For many years, then, Jesus evidently has provided for his family by working as a carpenter, having learned the trade from his father.

Now at about the age of 30—the Jewish age of spiritual leadership—Jesus turns from the work of supporting his earthly family to the task of spiritually feeding the whole family of man.

TODAY'S INSIGHTS

Growth

When was the last time you thought about growth? Was it when you last stepped on the scales, or purchased a new wardrobe? Was it when you had to look up for the first time in order to talk to your son? Or has it been awhile since you gave it any thought? Growth is such a natural part of our world that we sometimes take it for granted. The growth of a child, or of a tree, or even of our mutual funds portfolio, is not likely to cause much concern from day to day.

What really concerns us is when things *stop* growing. If a child fails to gain weight, or a plant withers, or if our savings account dwindles, that's the time we start to take notice.

We like to think at least once a year about the visit of the wise men to Jesus near the time of his birth. We even sing songs about that unique birth which they journeyed so far to celebrate. But do you know any songs written about Jesus' *growth?* Don't we tend merely to assume this particular aspect of Jesus' young life, or simply find it mundane? Yet the Gospels tell us that Jesus' growth is an important part of what we should know about Jesus—not simply his physical and mental growth, which we naturally assume, but his spiritual growth as well.

As a young man in Nazareth, Jesus quickly developed in wisdom and understanding, so much so that even learned scholars were amazed. Did a special measure of wisdom come to Jesus because he was the Son of God and therefore had a head start on his peers? Did he have an inside track that we don't have? Certainly Jesus was deity incarnate. But even from the part of Jesus that was altogether human comes a clue which can help us in our own spiritual growth. With Jesus, spiritual insight was largely a matter of perspective and priorities.

We see this insight when Jesus was asked why he had left his parents in order to participate in the religious discussions in the temple courts. Jesus responded, "Didn't you know I had to be in my Father's house?" What Jesus may be telling us is that we too can experience spiritual growth if we spend time in our Father's house—watching him work, listening to him as he talks to us, absorbing his love for us, letting him pick us up when we stumble and fall.

When it comes to understanding God's will for your life, have you ever had the feeling that you're in the same place where you were a year ago? Can you perhaps look back and see a time when you were even stronger in the Lord? Whether you have merely been stagnant or perhaps have actually slipped backward, now is a time for great growth in your life.

Even now you are headed in that direction. Coming to know Jesus Christ more intimately through the reading of the Gospels will help you grow, just as Jesus did, "in wisdom and stature, and in favor with God and men." If, as Solomon said, "much study is a weariness of the flesh," it is also a doorway to growth.

PREPARATION

The Ministry of John the Baptist

WHEN IT COMES TIME FOR JESUS TO CARRY OUT HIS DIVINE COMMISSION, the ground has already been broken by the successful ministry of John the Baptist, who proclaims Jesus to be "the Lamb of God." John thereby sets the stage for Jesus' own claim that he is the Messiah. As seen so many times before, the Jews have been awaiting the coming of the prophesied Messiah, believing that he will deliver them from political bondage and be an ideal national leader. What they have not expected is a leader arising from among the common people—yet divine in nature—and establishing a spiritual rather than a political kingdom. Perhaps because of this very misconception, John the Baptist is called to prepare the way for Jesus and to testify on his behalf. It is with this announcement of Jesus' special ministry that the gospel message begins its central focus, as seen by the fact that only at this point do Mark and John begin their Gospel accounts.

Jesus' forerunner, John, is a prophet of priestly descent, as were several of the prophets of old. Like Elijah, John is not a writer, but an evangelist and a spokesman for God whose outspoken preaching of repentance and baptism brings him multitudes of disciples. Some of these disciples will be so devoted to John and his teaching that they will not accept even the deity of Jesus, which John is sent to proclaim. As with most of his fellow prophets, John's teaching of spiritual purity is accompanied by strong appeals for practical ethical conduct toward one's fellowman.

Living much of his time in desert areas and existing on a diet of locusts and honey, John strikes an image of being some kind of ascetic wild man. However, his lifestyle is probably dictated more out of necessity than eccentricity, and is by no means offensive to the throngs who come from the cities to hear him. The more intriguing question is why sophisticated city people would go out of their way to be taught by a rough man of the wilderness whose preaching is unusually harsh and demanding. Could it be, ironically, that John's appeal lies in the very strictness of his message, which is in sharp contrast to the soft religiosity peddled by religious leaders seeking popular support? Could it be that John's call for personal purity and individual righteousness is seen as a refreshing change from the ritualistic and institutional religion which has developed over the centuries? Whatever his appeal, John's ministry is given the highest possible honor when even Jesus himself comes to receive John's baptism. Although it is not for sins that Jesus is baptized, his exemplary act of ceremonial washing gives occasion for a dramatic confirmation of his deity.

Mt. 3:1-3
Mk. 1:2-4
Lk. 3:1-6
Wilderness,
Jordan
region
(Oct.,
A.D. 27)

JOHN DECLARES HIS MISSION. In the fifteenth year of the reign of Tiberius Caesar—when Pontius Pilate was governor of Judea, Herod tetrarch of Galilee, his brother Philip tetrarch of Iturea and Traconitis, and Lysanias tetrarch of Abilene—during the high priesthood of Annas and Caiaphas, the word of God came to John son of Zechariah in the desert. He went into all the country around the Jordan, preaching a baptism of repentance for the forgiveness of sins. As is written in the book of the words of Isaiah the prophet:

"A voice of one calling in the desert,
  'Prepare the way for the Lord,
    make straight paths for him.
Every valley shall be filled in,
  every mountain and hill made low
The crooked roads shall become straight,
  the rough ways smooth.
And all mankind will see God's salvation.'"[c]

Mt. 3:4-6
Mk. 1:5,6

JOHN BAPTIZES THE PEOPLE. John's clothes were made of camel's hair, and he had a leather belt around his waist. His food was locusts and wild honey. People went out to him from Jerusalem and all Judea and the whole region of the Jordan. Confessing their sins, they were baptized by him in the Jordan River.

Mt. 3:7-10
Lk. 3:7-14

JOHN PREACHES REPENTANCE. John said to the crowds coming out to be baptized by him, "You brood of vipers! Who warned you to flee from the coming wrath? Produce fruit in keeping with repentance. And do not begin to say to yourselves,

[c]Isaiah 40:3-5

'We have Abraham as our father.' For I tell you that out of these stones God can raise up children for Abraham. The ax is already at the root of the trees, and every tree that does not produce good fruit will be cut down and thrown into the fire."

"What should we do then?" the crowd asked.

John answered, "The man with two tunics should share with him who has none, and the one who has food should do the same."

Tax collectors also came to be baptized. "Teacher," they asked, "what should we do?"

"Don't collect any more than you are required to," he told them.

Then some soldiers asked him, "And what should we do?"

He replied, "Don't extort money and don't accuse people falsely—be content with your pay."

Mt.
3:11,12
Mk. 1:7,8
Lk.
3:15-18

JOHN ANNOUNCES CHRIST. The people were waiting expectantly and were all wondering in their hearts if John might possibly be the Christ.[d] John answered them all, "I baptize you with[e] water. But one more powerful than I will come, the thongs of whose sandals I am not worthy to untie. He will baptize you with the Holy Spirit and with fire. His winnowing fork is in his hand to clear his threshing floor and to gather the wheat into his barn, but he will burn up the chaff with unquenchable fire." And with many other words John exhorted the people and preached the good news to them.

Mt.
3:13-17
Mk.
1:9-11
Lk.
3:21-23a
From
Galilee
to Jordan

JESUS IS BAPTIZED. [Mt]Then Jesus came from Galilee to the Jordan to be baptized by John. But John tried to deter him, saying, "I need to be baptized by you, and do you come to me?"

Jesus replied, "Let it be so now; it is proper for us to do this to fulfill all righteousness." Then John consented.

As soon as Jesus was baptized, he went up out of the water. At that moment heaven was opened, and he saw the Spirit of God descending like a dove and lighting on him. And a voice from heaven said, "This is my Son, whom I love; with him I am well pleased." [Lk]Now Jesus himself was about thirty years old when he began his ministry.

[d]Or *Messiah*   [e]Or *in*

Jesus Faces Temptations

One of the big, as-yet-unanswered questions about Jesus' identity is whether he, as God in the flesh, is vulnerable to the same temptations which all other people face. Although not every temptation which Jesus may encounter will be found in the Gospel accounts, the writers do record a series of temptations which are representative of most of the temptations faced by man. In various encounters with Satan, Jesus must deal with the need to satisfy fleshly appetites, the urge to acquire that which pleases the eye, and the desire to give vent to pride.

This is no academic exercise. As he does with everyone else, Satan confronts Jesus when he is most vulnerable. Jesus has just had a mountaintop spiritual experience: He has been honored by the voice from heaven. How tempting it would be to flaunt his deity in some dramatic way! He is just beginning his mission to a world looking desperately for a leader. How tempting it would be to acquire the whole world's allegiance in one fell swoop! And at the time of the first temptation, Jesus is physically weakened from a 40-day fast. How tempting it would be to produce that which would satisfy normal human hunger!

In every case Jesus' response to temptation is the same. Alone in the desert of temptation, Jesus—divine though he is—recognizes the value of prayer and fasting, and with every temptation he recalls the words of Scripture, which are a reminder of truth and wisdom in the face of Satan's lies.

Mt.
4:1-11
Mk.
1:12,13
Lk. 4:1-13
Mountain
in
wilderness

DEVIL TEMPTS JESUS. Then Jesus was led by the Spirit into the desert to be tempted by the devil. After fasting forty days and forty nights, he was hungry. The tempter came to him and said, "If you are the Son of God, tell these stones to become bread."

Jesus answered, "It is written: 'Man does not live on bread alone, but on every word that comes from the mouth of God.'/"

Then the devil took him to the holy city and had him stand on the highest point of the temple. "If you are the Son of God," he said, "throw yourself down. For it is written:

/Deut. 8:3

"'He will command his angels concerning you,
  and they will lift you up in their hands,
so that you will not strike your foot against a
  stone.'[g]"

Jesus answered him, "It is also written: 'Do not put the Lord
your God to the test.'[h]"

Again, the devil took him to a very high mountain and
showed him all the kingdoms of the world and their splendor.
"All this I will give you," he said, "if you will bow down and
worship me."

Jesus said to him, "Away from me, Satan! For it is written:
'Worship the Lord your God, and serve him only.'[i]"

Then the devil left him, and angels came and attended him.

Throughout his life Jesus will continue to resist all temptation
and remain sinless. It is his perfect righteousness—beyond the
righteousness of even such great prophets as Elijah and now John
the Baptist—that shows Jesus to be the Messiah. By virtue of the
heavenly annunciation which he witnesses, John is convinced that
Jesus is not only incomparably righteous, but also truly God's
Anointed One, the Christ. John therefore repudiates any possibility
of himself being viewed as the Messiah, and forcefully proclaims
Jesus as the messianic Lamb of God.

| Jn. 1:19-28 Bethany | JOHN EXPLAINS HIS MINISTRY. Now this was John's testimony when the Jews of Jerusalem sent priests and Levites to ask him who he was. He did not fail to confess, but confessed freely, "I am not the Christ.[j]" |

They asked him, "Then who are you? Are you Elijah?"

He said, "I am not."

"Are you the Prophet?"

He answered, "No."

Finally they said, "Who are you? Give us an answer to take
back to those who sent us. What do you say about yourself?"

---

[g]Psalm 91:11,12   [h]Deut. 6:16   [i]Deut. 6:13   [j]Or *Messiah*. "The Christ" (Greek)
and "the Messiah" (Hebrew) both mean "the Anointed One"

John replied in the words of Isaiah the prophet, "I am the voice of one calling in the desert, 'Make straight the way for the Lord.'"[k]

Now some Pharisees who had been sent questioned him, "Why then do you baptize if you are not the Christ, nor Elijah, nor the Prophet?"

"I baptize with[l] water," John replied, "but among you stands one you do not know. He is the one who comes after me, the thongs of whose sandals I am not worthy to untie."

This all happened at Bethany on the other side of the Jordan, where John was baptizing.

Jn. 1:29-34 | JOHN SAYS JESUS IS CHRIST. The next day John saw Jesus coming toward him and said, "Look, the Lamb of God, who takes away the sin of the world! This is the one I meant when I said, 'A man who comes after me has surpassed me because he was before me.' I myself did not know him, but the reason I came baptizing with water was that he might be revealed to Israel."

Then John gave this testimony: "I saw the Spirit come down from heaven as a dove and remain on him. I would not have known him, except that the one who sent me to baptize with water told me, 'The man on whom you see the Spirit come down and remain is he who will baptize with the Holy Spirit.' I have seen and I testify that this is the Son of God."

TODAY'S INSIGHTS

Preparation

Have you ever wondered why Jesus did not appear to the first inhabitants of the earth? Or why there was an Old Testament before there was a New Testament? Or why God chose to work through the tiny nation of Israel before showing his grace to the entire world?

Whatever his reasons may have been, God spent over 4000 years preparing the world for the appearance of Jesus Christ. When Jesus finally came to earth, God waited another 30 years before fully revealing Jesus' ministry. And to prepare the people for

[k]Isaiah 40:3 [l]Or *in*

Jesus' teaching, God sent John the Baptist with a message of repentance and baptism.

What we do know is that all things are done in God's own time and for God's own purposes. And it is better that way, of course. How often our own sense of timing is disastrous!

When you think back in your life and remember the times when you were most disappointed, can you not see now where many things have worked out for the best after all? And would you ever in your wildest imagination have predicted the path your life would take? Often we indulge in second-guessing, thinking that our lives might have been so much better had this thing or that thing been different. But it is altogether amazing how even troubles and grief eventually seem to find meaning and fulfillment.

We see it happening early in the ministry of Jesus. Before Jesus preached his first sermon or performed his first miracle, God prepared him through struggle and temptation to be strong and courageous. We often point out that Jesus was tempted immediately following a "mountaintop experience," as is often the case with us as well. But have you stopped to consider that God *gave* Jesus that mountaintop experience just before Jesus was to undergo his temptation? God has a way of preparing us for temptation and trial. That is why, as God promises us, we will never face more temptation than we can endure.

One of the ways in which God prepares us for those weak moments—those times which take us to our spiritual limits—is through his written Word. Remember how Jesus kept telling the Devil: "It is written..." "It is written..." "It is written." That should become our strategy of defense as well. By arming ourselves with "the sword of the Spirit which is the Word of God," we too can fight off temptation, and fear, and moral failure. Preparation is the key. Preparation is God's way.

In our study of the Word, have we dug deeply beyond the shallows of factual knowledge to the depths of understanding and personal application? What a blessing that we can say, "It is written on my heart!"

DAY WITH 5 JESUS

INSIGHT

Jesus' Early Work in Judea, Samaria, and Galilee

THE EARLY MINISTRY OF JESUS IS REPORTED SOLELY BY THE APOSTLE John. His account shows that Jesus' teaching quickly appeals to the common people and results in many faithful disciples. It is during this time that Jesus also performs his first miracles. And just as Nehemiah had done centuries before, Jesus wastes no time in confronting those who profane the sanctity of the temple worship. Jesus also makes it clear from the beginning that his message of salvation will extend beyond the Jewish nation to all people. As if to emphasize the universality of his spiritual kingdom, Jesus takes his ministry to the Samaritans. This people of mixed nationality and religion have been archenemies of the Jews ever since their ancestors were brought in from Assyria to repopulate northern Israel after the first Jews were taken into Assyrian captivity. So Jesus' outreach to Gentiles could not begin more pointedly.

The ministry of John the Baptist will come to an end when he is imprisoned by Herod Antipas, the second son of Herod the Great, who became tetrarch over the provinces of Galilee and Perea upon his father's death. The reason for John's imprisonment will subsequently appear, but for now the Gospel accounts resume with John the Baptist pointing his own disciples to the true Lamb of God.

Jn.
1:35-42

ANDREW AND SIMON PETER. The next day John was there again with two of his disciples. When he saw Jesus passing by, he said, "Look, the Lamb of God!"

When the two disciples heard him say this, they followed Jesus. Turning around, Jesus saw them following and asked, "What do you want?"

They said, "Rabbi" (which means Teacher), "where are you staying?"

"Come," he replied, "and you will see."

So they went and saw where he was staying, and spent that day with him. It was about the tenth hour.

Andrew, Simon Peter's brother, was one of the two who heard what John had said and who had followed Jesus. The first thing Andrew did was to find his brother Simon and tell him, "We have found the Messiah" (that is, the Christ). And he brought him to Jesus.

Jesus looked at him and said, "You are Simon son of John. You will be called Cephas" (which, when translated, is Peter[m]).

Jn. 1:43-51

PHILIP AND NATHANAEL. The next day Jesus decided to leave for Galilee. Finding Philip, he said to him, "Follow me."

Philip, like Andrew and Peter, was from the town of Bethsaida. Philip found Nathanael and told him, "We have found the one Moses wrote about in the Law, and about whom the prophets also wrote—Jesus of Nazareth, the son of Joseph."

"Nazareth! Can anything good come from there?" Nathanael asked.

"Come and see," said Philip.

When Jesus saw Nathanael approaching, he said of him, "Here is a true Israelite, in whom there is nothing false."

"How do you know me?" Nathanael asked.

Jesus answered, "I saw you while you were still under the fig tree before Philip called you."

Then Nathanael declared, "Rabbi, you are the Son of God; you are the King of Israel."

Jesus said, "You believe[n] because I told you I saw you under the fig tree. You shall see greater things than that." He then added, "I tell you the truth, you[o] shall see heaven open, and the angels of God ascending and descending on the Son of Man."

Jn. 2:1-12 Cana

JESUS TURNS WATER INTO WINE. On the third day a wedding took place at Cana in Galilee. Jesus' mother was there, and Jesus and his disciples had also been invited to the wedding. When the wine was gone, Jesus' mother said to him, "They have no more wine."

"Dear woman, why do you involve me?" Jesus replied. "My time has not yet come."

His mother said to the servants, "Do whatever he tells you."

[m]Both *Cephas* (Aramic) and *Peter* (Greek) mean *rock*.   [n]Or *Do you believe...?*
[o]The Greek is plural.

Nearby stood six stone water jars, the kind used by the Jews for ceremonial washing, each holding from twenty to thirty gallons.[p]

Jesus said to the servants, "Fill the jars with water"; so they filled them to the brim.

Then he told them, "Now draw some out and take it to the master of the banquet."

They did so, and the master of the banquet tasted the water that had been turned into wine. He did not realize where it had come from, though the servants who had drawn the water knew. Then he called the bridegroom aside and said, "Everyone brings out the choice wine first and then the cheaper wine after the guests have had too much to drink; but you have saved the best till now."

This, the first of his miraculous signs, Jesus performed in Cana in Galilee. He thus revealed his glory, and his disciples put their faith in him.

After this he went down to Capernaum with his mother and brothers and his disciples. There they stayed for a few days.

[First Passover April, A.D. 27] Jn. 2:13-25 Jerusalem

MERCHANTS DRIVEN FROM TEMPLE. When it was almost time for the Jewish Passover, Jesus went up to Jerusalem. In the temple courts he found men selling cattle, sheep and doves, and others sitting at tables exchanging money. So he made a whip out of cords, and drove all from the temple area, both sheep and cattle; he scattered the coins of the money changers and overturned their tables. To those who sold doves he said, "Get these out of here! How dare you turn my Father's house into a market!"

His disciples remembered that it is written: "Zeal for your house will consume me."[q]

Then the Jews demanded of him, "What miraculous sign can you show us to prove your authority to do all this?"

Jesus answered them, "Destroy this temple, and I will raise it again in three days."

The Jews replied, "It has taken forty-six years to build this temple, and you are going to raise it in three days?" But the temple he had spoken of was his body. After he was raised from the dead, his disciples recalled what he had said. Then

---

[p]Greek *two or three metretes* (probably about 75 to 115 liters)   [q]Psalm 69:9

they believed the Scripture and the words that Jesus had spoken.

Now while he was in Jerusalem at the Passover Feast, many people saw the miraculous signs he was doing and believed in his name.[r] But Jesus would not entrust himself to them, for he knew all men. He did not need man's testimony about man, for he knew what was in a man.

Jn.
3:1-21

JESUS TEACHES NICODEMUS. Now there was a man of the Pharisees named Nicodemus, a member of the Jewish ruling council. He came to Jesus at night and said, "Rabbi, we know you are a teacher who has come from God. For no one could perform the miraculous signs you are doing if God were not with him."

In reply Jesus declared, "I tell you the truth, no one can see the kingdom of God unless he is born again.[s]"

"How can a man be born when he is old?" Nicodemus asked. "Surely he cannot enter a second time into his mother's womb to be born!"

Jesus answered, "I tell you the truth, no one can enter the kingdom of God unless he is born of water and the Spirit. Flesh gives birth to flesh, but the Spirit[t] gives birth to spirit. You should not be surprised at my saying, 'You[u] must be born again.' The wind blows wherever it pleases. You hear its sound, but you cannot tell where it comes from or where it is going. So it is with everyone born of the Spirit."

"How can this be?" Nicodemus asked.

"You are Israel's teacher," said Jesus, "and do you not understand these things? I tell you the truth, we speak of what we know, and we testify to what we have seen, but still you people do not accept our testimony. I have spoken to you of earthly things and you do not believe; how then will you believe if I speak of heavenly things? No one has ever gone into heaven except the one who came from heaven—the Son of Man.[v] Just as Moses lifted up the snake in the desert, so the Son of Man must be lifted up, that everyone who believes in him may have eternal life.[w]

---

[r]Or and believed in him   [s]Or born from above   [t]Or but spirit   [u]The Greek is plural.   [v]Some manuscripts Man, who is in heaven   [w]Or believes may have eternal life in him

"For God so loved the world that he gave his one and only Son,[x] that whoever believes in him shall not perish but have eternal life. For God did not send his Son into the world to condemn the world, but to save the world through him. Whoever believes in him is not condemned, but whoever does not believe stands condemned already because he has not believed in the name of God's one and only Son.[y] This is the verdict: Light has come into the world, but men loved darkness instead of light because their deeds were evil. Everyone who does evil hates the light, and will not come into the light for fear that his deeds will be exposed. But whoever lives by the truth comes into the light, so that it may be seen plainly that what he has done has been done through God."[z]

Jn. 3:22-24 Judea	JESUS AND JOHN BAPTIZE. After this, Jesus and his disciples went out into the Judean countryside, where he spent some time with them, and baptized. Now John also was baptizing at Aenon near Salim, because there was plenty of water, and people were constantly coming to be baptized. (This was before John was put in prison.)
Jn. 3:25-36	JOHN TESTIFIES ABOUT JESUS. An argument developed between some of John's disciples and a certain Jew[a] over the matter of ceremonial washing. They came to John and said to him, "Rabbi, that man who was with you on the other side of the Jordan—the one you testified about—well, he is baptizing, and everyone is going to him."

To this John replied, "A man can receive only what is given him from heaven. You yourselves can testify that I said, 'I am not the Christ[b] but am sent ahead of him.' The bride belongs to the bridegroom. The friend who attends the bridegroom waits and listens for him, and is full of joy when he hears the bridegroom's voice. That joy is mine, and it is now complete. He must become greater; I must become less.

"The one who comes from above is above all; the one who is from the earth belongs to the earth, and speaks as one from the earth. The one who comes from heaven is above all. He testifies to what he has seen and heard, but no one accepts his testimony. The man who has accepted it has certified that God

[x]Or *his only begotten Son*   [y]Or *God's only begotten Son*   [z]Some interpreters end the quotation after verse 15.   [a]Some manuscripts *and certain Jews*   [b]Or *Messiah*

is truthful. For the one whom God has sent speaks the words of God, for God[c] gives the Spirit without limit. The Father loves the Son and has placed everything in his hands. Whoever believes in the Son has eternal life, but whoever rejects the Son will not see life, for God's wrath remains on him."[d]

Jn. 4:1-3 Judea

JESUS LEAVES FOR GALILEE. The Pharisees heard that Jesus was gaining and baptizing more disciples than John, although in fact it was not Jesus who baptized, but his disciples. When the Lord learned of this, he left Judea and went back once more to Galilee.

Jn. 4:4-26 Sychar

WOMAN AT THE WELL. Now he had to go through Samaria. So he came to a town in Samaria called Sychar, near the plot of ground Jacob had given to his son Joseph. Jacob's well was there, and Jesus, tired as he was from the journey, sat down by the well. It was about the sixth hour.

When a Samaritan woman came to draw water, Jesus said to her, "Will you give me a drink?" (His disciples had gone into the town to buy food.)

The Samaritan woman said to him, "You are a Jew and I am a Samaritan woman. How can you ask me for a drink?" (For Jews do not associate with Samaritans.[e])

Jesus answered her, "If you knew the gift of God and who it is that asks you for a drink, you would have asked him and he would have given you living water."

"Sir," the woman said, "you have nothing to draw with and the well is deep. Where can you get this living water? Are you greater than our father Jacob, who gave us the well and drank from it himself, as did also his sons and his flocks and herds?"

Jesus answered, "Everyone who drinks this water will be thirsty again, but whoever drinks the water I give him will never thirst. Indeed, the water I give him will become in him a spring of water welling up to eternal life."

The woman said to him, "Sir, give me this water so that I won't get thirsty and have to keep coming here to draw water."

He told her, "Go, call your husband and come back."

"I have no husband," she replied.

[c]Greek *he* [d]Some interpreters end the quotation after verse 30. [e]Or *do not use dishes Samaritans have used*

Jesus said to her, "You are right when you say you have no husband. The fact is, you have had five husbands, and the man you now have is not your husband. What you have just said is quite true."

"Sir," the woman said, "I can see that you are a prophet. Our fathers worshiped on this mountain, but you Jews claim that the place where we must worship is in Jerusalem."

Jesus declared, "Believe me, woman, a time is coming when you will worship the Father neither on this mountain nor in Jerusalem. You Samaritans worship what you do not know; we worship what we do know, for salvation is from the Jews. Yet a time is coming and has now come when the true worshipers will worship the Father in spirit and truth, for they are the kind of worshipers the Father seeks. God is spirit, and his worshipers must worship in spirit and in truth."

The woman said, "I know that Messiah" (called Christ) "is coming. When he comes, he will explain everything to us."

Then Jesus declared, "I who speak to you am he."

Jn.
4:27-38
(Dec.,
A.D. 27)

SPIRITUAL FOOD. Just then his disciples returned and were surprised to find him talking with a woman. But no one asked, "What do you want?" or "Why are you talking with her?"

Then, leaving her water jar, the woman went back to the town and said to the people, "Come, see a man who told me everything I ever did. Could this be the Christ[f]?" They came out of the town and made their way toward him.

Meanwhile his disciples urged him, "Rabbi, eat something."

But he said to them, "I have food to eat that you know nothing about."

Then his disciples said to each other, "Could someone have brought him food?"

"My food," said Jesus, "is to do the will of him who sent me and to finish his work. Do you not say, 'Four months more and then the harvest'? I tell you, open your eyes and look at the fields! They are ripe for harvest. Even now the reaper draws his wages, even now he harvests the crop for eternal life, so that the sower and the reaper may be glad together. Thus the saying 'One sows and another reaps' is true. I sent you to reap

[f]Or *Messiah*

what you have not worked for. Others have done the hard work, and you have reaped the benefits of their labor."

Jn.
4:39-42

MANY SAMARITANS CONVERTED. Many of the Samaritans from that town believed in him because of the woman's testimony, "He told me everything I ever did." So when the Samaritans came to him, they urged him to stay with them, and he stayed two days. And because of his words many more became believers.

They said to the woman, "We no longer believe just because of what you said; now we have heard for ourselves, and we know that this man really is the Savior of the world."

Jn.
4:43-45
Galilee

JESUS RETURNS TO GALILEE. After the two days he left for Galilee. (Now Jesus himself had pointed out that a prophet has no honor in his own country.) When he arrived in Galilee, the Galileans welcomed him. They had seen all that he had done in Jerusalem at the Passover Feast, for they also had been there.

Jn.
4:46-54
Cana

BOY IN CAPERNAUM HEALED. Once more he visited Cana in Galilee, where he had turned the water into wine. And there was a certain royal official whose son lay sick at Capernaum. When this man heard that Jesus had arrived in Galilee from Judea, he went to him and begged him to come and heal his son, who was close to death.

"Unless you people see miraculous signs and wonders," Jesus told him, "you will never believe."

The royal official said, "Sir, come down before my child dies."

Jesus replied, "You may go. Your son will live."

The man took Jesus at his word and departed. While he was still on the way, his servants met him with the news that his boy was living. When he inquired as to the time when his son get better, they said to him, "The fever left him yesterday at the seventh hour."

Then the father realized that this was the exact time at which Jesus had said to him, "Your son will live." So he and all his household believed.

This was the second miraculous sign that Jesus performed, having come from Judea to Galilee.

Jou 2:13
Zech 14:8

JOHN THE BAPTIST IMPRISONED. But when John rebuked Herod the tetrarch because of Herodias, his brother's wife, and all the other evil things he had done, Herod added this to them all: He locked John up in prison.

TODAY'S INSIGHTS

Insight

Do you ever have the feeling that, if the preacher died in the middle of his sermon, you could figure out the last two points he would have made? Do you ever get tired of people telling you the obvious and proclaiming only the predictable? Those who heard Jesus teach never seemed to encounter that problem. What Jesus taught was always fresh, even surprising. No well-worn sermons for him—no pat phrases or catchy sermon titles. Just simple lessons containing pure gold.

What separated Jesus from other religious teachers was his unique spiritual insight. He was always turning things upside down, but not simply for effect. Nor was Jesus a sophist playing games with words. His ideas were genuinely revolutionary, unheard of, unthinkable yet undeniable.

Imagine his saying to Nicodemus that a person has to be born again! Centuries removed, we have heard that idea so many times that it now seems quite unremarkable. But think what Nicodemus must have thought upon hearing it for the very first time.

What would we think, even today, if someone were to tell us that we need to quit being religious and instead become spiritual? Does that seem somewhat offensive? The woman at the well certainly might have thought so, because her idea of worship was defined by externals. What Jesus came to give us was deeper insight. He came to lead us beyond tradition and custom, beyond the superficial and the external to the invisible.

It is easier to understand things which are outward and visible, and certainly there is security when we are in the grip of the familiar. But Jesus challenges us to reach beyond the borders of our understanding to a realm scarcely within our grasp. For example, what does he mean when he says we will never thirst with the water he gives us? And how is it that Spirit gives birth to spirit? In what way is he to become greater while I become less?

There is so much more to learn from Jesus—always more to learn. But who better to learn from than One who could tell us, as with the Samaritan woman, everything we ever did? Anyone with that power of perception must indeed have the insight to lead us where we have not yet been!

Are we willing to follow Jesus without question, as did Philip? If we want to know the mind of Christ, we must be willing to follow even when the path leads in directions we would never anticipate. Are we ready to heed Mary's advice to the servants: "Do whatever he tells you"? If we want to share in his perfect insight, we must be ready to do for him things that might make little sense to us.

The desire for divine insight is an invitation to be surprised. Lord, lead us into your highest knowledge—even if it takes our breath away!

AUTHORITY

Beginning of the Great Galilean Ministry

APPARENTLY IN ORDER TO EMPHASIZE THE NATURE OF HIS MINISTRY, Jesus does not come as a religious leader in any traditional sense. He holds no official position, nor is he specially trained to be a priest or other cleric. Instead, he takes his ministry to the city streets and roads of Palestine, to homes and fields, and wherever else the common people might be found. He is particularly fond of attending the Jewish synagogues, where the common man is permitted to discuss the meaning of Jewish Scripture.

Rejected by those closest to him in Nazareth, Jesus takes his ministry elsewhere. Surprisingly, though, it is not to Jerusalem and surrounding Judea that Jesus goes, despite the fact that Jerusalem is the Holy City—capital of ancient Israel, site of the temple, and surely, as the Jews anticipate it, the seat of the coming Messiah's government. Contrary to their expectation, Jesus takes his ministry primarily to Galilee. Using the city of Capernaum as a base for his travels, Jesus teaches and performs miracles around the Sea of Galilee (Lake of Gennesaret) and throughout the entire province. It is here that Jesus gains popularity among the people and begins to see the crowds swell. Matthew begins his account of the Galilean ministry by observing that this phase of Jesus' ministry is a fulfillment of Isaiah's prophecy.

Mt. 4:12-17 Mk. 1:14,15 Lk. 4:14,15 Capernaum	COMING OF KINGDOM PREACHED. ᴹᵗWhen Jesus heard that John had been put in prison, he returned to Galilee. Leaving Nazareth, he went and lived in Capernaum, which was by the lake in the area of Zebulun and Naphtali—to fulfill what was said through the prophet Isaiah:

> "Land of Zebulun and land of Naphtali,
>   the way to the sea, along the Jordan,
>   Galilee of the Gentiles—
> the people living in darkness
>   have seen a great light;

on those living in the land of the shadow of death
a light has dawned."[g]

From that time on Jesus began to preach, "Repent, for the
kingdom of heaven is near." [Lk][And] news about him spread
through the whole countryside. He taught in their synagogues, and everyone praised him.

Lk.
4:16-30
Nazareth

JESUS REJECTED AT NAZARETH. He went to Nazareth,
where he had been brought up, and on the Sabbath day he
went into the synagogue, as was his custom. And he stood up
to read. The scroll of the prophet Isaiah was handed to him.
Unrolling it, he found the place where it is written:

"The Spirit of the Lord is on me,
    because he has anointed me
    to preach good news to the poor.
He has sent me to proclaim freedom for the
        prisoners
and recovery of sight for the blind,
to release the oppressed,
    to proclaim the year of the Lord's favor."[h]

Then he rolled up the scroll, gave it back to the attendant
and sat down. The eyes of everyone in the synagogue were
fastened on him, and he began by saying to them, "Today this
scripture is fulfilled in your hearing."

All spoke well of him and were amazed at the gracious words
that came from his lips. "Isn't this Joseph's son?" they asked.

Jesus said to them, "Surely you will quote this proverb to
me: 'Physician, heal yourself! Do here in your hometown what
we have heard that you did in Capernaum.'"

"I tell you the truth," he continued, "no prophet is accepted
in his hometown. I assure you that there were many widows
in Israel in Elijah's time, when the sky was shut for three and
a half years and there was a severe famine throughout the
land. Yet Elijah was not sent to any of them, but to a widow in
Zarephath in the region of Sidon. And there were many in
Israel with leprosy[i] in the time of Elisha the prophet, yet not
one of them was cleansed—only Naaman the Syrian."

[g]Isaiah 9:1,2   [h]Isaiah 61:1,2   [i]The Greek word was used for various diseases
affecting the skin—not necessarily leprosy.

All the people in the synagogue were furious when they heard this. They got up, drove him out of the town, and took him to the brow of the hill on which the town was built, in order to throw him down the cliff. But he walked right through the crowd and went on his way.

Lk.
5:1-10a
Lake of
Gennesaret

GREAT CATCH OF FISH. One day as Jesus was standing by the Lake of Gennesaret,[j] with the people crowding around him and listening to the word of God, he saw at the water's edge two boats, left there by the fishermen, who were washing their nets. He got into one of the boats, the one belonging to Simon, and asked him to put out a little from shore. Then he sat down and taught the people from the boat.

When he had finished speaking, he said to Simon, "Put out into deep water, and let down[k] the nets for a catch."

Simon answered, "Master, we've worked hard all night and haven't caught anything. But because you say so, I will let down the nets."

When they had done so, they caught such a large number of fish that their nets began to break. So they signaled their partners in the other boat to come and help them, and they came and filled both boats so full that they began to sink.

When Simon Peter saw this, he fell at Jesus' knees and said, "Go away from me, Lord; I am a sinful man!" For he and all his companions were astonished at the catch of fish they had taken, and so were James and John, the sons of Zebedee, Simon's partners.

Mt.
4:18-22
Mk.
1:16-20
Lk.
5:10b,11

SIMON, ANDREW, JAMES, AND JOHN. [Lk]Then Jesus said to Simon, "Don't be afraid; from now on you will catch men." [Mt]"Come, follow me," Jesus said, "and I will make you fishers of men." At once they left their nets and followed him.

Going on from there, he saw two other brothers, James son of Zebedee and his brother John. They were in a boat with their father Zebedee, preparing their nets. Jesus called them, and immediately they left the boat and their father and followed him.

Mk.
1:21,22
Lk.
4:31,32
Caper-
naum

JESUS TEACHES AT CAPERNAUM. They went to Capernaum, and when the Sabbath came, Jesus went into the

[j]That is, Sea of Galilee   [k]The Greek verb is plural.

synagogue and began to teach. The people were amazed at his teaching, because he taught them as one who had authority, not as the teachers of the law.

Mk.
1:23-28
Lk.
4:33-37

UNCLEAN SPIRIT HEALED. Just then a man in their synagogue who was possessed by an evil[i] spirit cried out, "What do you want with us, Jesus of Nazareth? Have you come to destroy us? I know who you are—the Holy One of God!"

"Be quiet!" said Jesus sternly. "Come out of him!" The evil spirit shook the man violently and came out of him with a shriek.

The people were all so amazed that they asked each other, "What is this? A new teaching—and with authority! He even gives orders to evil spirits and they obey him." News about him spread quickly over the whole region of Galilee.

Mt.
8:14,15
Mk.
1:29-31
Lk.
4:38,39

PETER'S MOTHER-IN-LAW HEALED. As soon as they left the synagogue, they went with James and John to the home of Simon and Andrew. Simon's mother-in-law was in bed with a fever, and they told Jesus about her. So he went to her, took her hand and helped her up. The fever left her and she began to wait on them.

Mt.
8:16,17
Mk.
1:32-34
Lk.
4:40,41

OTHERS HEALED. That evening after sunset the people brought to Jesus all the sick and demon-possessed. The whole town gathered at the door, and Jesus healed many who had various diseases. He also drove out many demons, but he would not let the demons speak because they knew who he was.

Mk.
1:35-38
Lk.
4:42,43

JESUS GOES OUT TO PRAY. Very early in the morning, while it was still dark, Jesus got up, left the house and went off to a solitary place, where he prayed. Simon and his companions went to look for him, and when they found him, they exclaimed: "Everyone is looking for you!"

Jesus replied, "Let us go somewhere else—to the nearby villages—so I can preach there also. That is why I have come."

Mt.
4:23-25
Mk. 1:39
Lk. 4:44
Galilee

JESUS TRAVELS ABOUT. Jesus went throughout Galilee, teaching in their synagogues, preaching the good news of the kingdom, and healing every disease and sickness among the

[i]Greek *unclean*

people. News about him spread all over Syria, and people brought to him all who were ill with various diseases, those suffering severe pain, the demon-possessed, those having seizures, and the paralyzed, and he healed them. Large crowds from Galilee, the Decapolis,[m] Jerusalem, Judea and the region across the Jordan followed him.

Mt.
8:1-4
Mk.
1:40-45
Lk.
5:12-16

LEPER CLEANSED. A man with leprosy[n] came to him and begged him on his knees, "If you are willing, you can make me clean."

Filled with compassion, Jesus reached out his hand and touched the man. "I am willing," he said. "Be clean!" Immediately the leprosy left him and he was cured.

Jesus sent him away at once with a strong warning: "See that you don't tell this to anyone. But go, show yourself to the priest and offer the sacrifices that Moses commanded for your cleansing, as a testimony to them." Instead he went out and began to talk freely, spreading the news. As a result, Jesus could no longer enter a town openly but stayed outside in lonely places. Yet the people still came to him from everywhere.

Mt.
9:1,2
Mk.
2:1-5
Lk.
5:17-20
Capernaum

PARALYTIC HEALED. A few days later, when Jesus again entered Capernaum, the people heard that he had come home. So many gathered that there was no room left, not even outside the door, and he preached the word to them. Some men came, bringing to him a paralytic, carried by four of them. Since they could not get him to Jesus because of the crowd, they made an opening in the roof above Jesus and, after digging through it, lowered the mat the paralyzed man was lying on. When Jesus saw their faith, he said to the paralytic, "Son, your sins are forgiven."

Mt.
9:3-8
Mk.
2:6-12
Lk.
5:21-26

SCRIBES QUESTION AUTHORITY. Now some teachers of the law were sitting there, thinking to themselves, "Why does this fellow talk like that? He's blaspheming! Who can forgive sins but God alone?"

Immediately Jesus knew in his spirit that this was what they were thinking in their hearts, and he said to them, "Why are you thinking these things? Which is easier: to say to the

---

[m]That is, the Ten Cities   [n]The Greek word was used for various diseases affecting the skin—not necessarily leprosy.

paralytic, 'Your sins are forgiven,' or to say, 'Get up, take your mat and walk'? But that you may know that the Son of Man has authority on earth to forgive sins…." He said to the paralytic, "I tell you, get up, take your mat and go home." He got up, took his mat and walked out in full view of them all. This amazed everyone and they praised God, saying, "We have never seen anything like this!"

Today's Insights

Authority

In a world filled with religious division, do you ever wonder where to turn? When you flip through the channels of your television set on a Sunday night, do you ever wonder where the plethora of conflicting teaching—all done in the name of Jesus Christ—comes from? Do you sometimes feel you are being asked to be a doormat for the latest fashions in religious ideas? Who *can* you trust? Who *can* you believe?

Those who personally heard Jesus speak also had to make tough decisions about genuine and counterfeit spiritual teachers. Yet when Jesus spoke, they almost immediately recognized that he was a teacher apart, someone in his own class. He was not like all the others, who had clamored for their attention and loyalty. Unlike the others, Jesus taught with authority!

His teaching was not the dry, abstract presentation of a theologian, nor the entertaining three-point, nine-illustration sermon of the local minister, nor the emotional appeal of the media evangelist. What Jesus had to say was compelling and from the heart. If simple, it was profound. If reasonable, it was demanding. If seemingly outrageous, it was backed up with a demonstration of miraculous power.

But you don't get the idea that Jesus was a "star performer." Like the apostle Paul, who would boldly proclaim Jesus to a sinful world, Jesus did not come with flair, style, and the "right wardrobe." Even his miracles were not the real power of his teaching; his *teaching* was his real power.

And what was that teaching? Simply good news. The good news that the poor are not disenfranchised in the kingdom of God.

The good news that there is freedom from the chains of sin with which we are bound. The good news that God has given us his own eyes for our spiritual blindness. And the good news that we can overcome our oppression from the tyranny of this world.

Jesus' ministry itself proved the truth of his teaching. It was not enough simply to *talk* about freedom, release, and recovery. The crowds saw Jesus *practicing what he preached*. They saw him walking throughout Galilee, healing every disease and sickness among the people. They saw him, in disregard of his own health, reach out in compassion and touch a man with leprosy in order to heal him. What Jesus did in his teaching and ministry was to make religion real.

He challenged us to leave our comfortable church pews and go out to serve our neighbors—indeed, to serve those who probably are *not* our neighbors because they live in another, less affordable, part of town. It wasn't success-oriented Christianity that was coming from Jesus' lips. And it wasn't a conscience-tickling, lifestyle-verifying message for the "me generation." What Jesus taught with authority was a message of old-fashioned morality and self-sacrificing service. Praise God for a teacher who calls us higher!

DAY 7 WITH JESUS

DEITY

The Rise of Opposition

THIS CONFRONTATION IS BUT THE FIRST OF MANY which will take place between Jesus and the religious leaders of his day. By indicating that he has the divine authority to forgive sins, Jesus naturally arouses immediate reaction from the Scribes and Pharisees. Since they correctly believe that only God can forgive sins, they reject the possibility that Jesus himself is divine and conclude instead that he is guilty of blasphemy.

In addition to the written law given through Moses, the Pharisees accept as equally binding the oral traditions of the rabbis, which traditions have evolved into a highly ritualistic set of religious observances. So when Jesus and his disciples violate some of these traditional rules, the Pharisees are highly offended. Through two parables Jesus tells them that their system of legalistic observances simply will not substitute for the true righteousness which God has always demanded.

John alone records what is apparently a brief trip to Jerusalem, where Jesus attends "a feast of the Jews." Although the exact feast is not indicated, there is strong evidence that it is the Passover of A.D. 28. (Some believe it was Pentecost or the Feast of Tabernacles.) While in Jerusalem, Jesus is once again criticized, this time for healing a man on the Sabbath, the day on which no work is to be done. If there was ever a perfect example of the fallacy of legalism, surely this is it. The incident also raises some fundamental questions: What is at stake—the law itself, or only interpretations of the law? Under what circumstances, if any, may the letter of the law be disregarded in favor of higher concerns consistent with the spirit of the law? Does Jesus consider the law given through Moses to be binding upon his disciples? These quite legitimate questions are clearly on the minds of the religious establishment.

Despite growing opposition, Jesus continues to go about teaching and performing miracles, yet almost consciously without fanfare. As if to underscore the urgency of his mission in the face of opposition, Jesus appoints 12 of his disciples as specially chosen apostles to aid him in his ministry. With their added support, Jesus continues to attract even greater crowds from among the common people.

Mt. 9:9
Mk. 2:13,14
Lk. 5:27,28
Galilee

MATTHEW (LEVI) IS CALLED. Once again Jesus went out beside the lake. A large crowd came to him, and he began to teach them. As he walked along, he saw Levi son of Alphaeus sitting at the tax collector's booth. "Follow me," Jesus told him, and Levi got up and followed him.

Mt. 9:10-13
Mk. 2:15-17
Lk. 5:29-32

EATING WITH SINNERS. LkThen Levi held a great banquet for Jesus at his house, and a large crowd of tax collectors and others were eating with them. But the Pharisees and the teachers of the law who belonged to their sect complained to his disciples, "Why do you eat and drink with tax collectors and 'sinners'?" MtOn hearing this, Jesus said, "It is not the healthy who need a doctor, but the sick. But go and learn what this means: 'I desire mercy, not sacrifice.'o For I have not come to call the righteous, but sinners."

Mt. 9:14-17
Mk. 2:18-22
Lk. 5:33-39

DISCIPLES NOT FASTING. They said to him, "John's disciples often fast and pray, and so do the disciples of the Pharisees, but yours go on eating and drinking."

Jesus answered, "Can you make the guests of the bridegroom fast while he is with them? But the time will come when the bridegroom will be taken from them; in those days they will fast."

He told them this parable: "No one tears a patch from a new garment and sews it on an old one. If he does, he will have torn the new garment, and the patch from the new will not match the old. And no one pours new wine into old wineskins. If he does, the new wine will burst the skins, the wine will run out and the wineskins will be ruined. No, new wine must be poured into new wineskins. And no one after drinking old wine wants the new, for he says, 'The old is better.'"

[Second Passover
April,
A.D. 28]
Jn. 5:1-3,5-9a
Jerusalem

HEALING AT POOL OF BETHESDA. Some time later, Jesus went up to Jerusalem for a feast of the Jews. Now there is in Jerusalem near the Sheep Gate a pool, which in Aramaic is

oHosea 6:6

called Bethesda[p] and which is surrounded by five covered colonnades. Here a great number of disabled people used to lie—the blind, the lame, the paralyzed.[q] One who was there had been an invalid for thirty-eight years. When Jesus saw him lying there and learned that he had been in this condition for a long time, he asked him, "Do you want to get well?"

"Sir," the invalid replied, "I have no one to help me into the pool when the water is stirred. While I am trying to get in, someone else goes down ahead of me."

Then Jesus said to him, "Get up! Pick up your mat and walk." At once the man was cured; he picked up his mat and walked.

n. 5:9b-15

HEALED MAN QUESTIONED. The day on which this took place was a Sabbath, and so the Jews said to the man who had been healed, "It is the Sabbath; the law forbids you to carry your mat."

But he replied, "The man who made me well said to me, 'Pick up your mat and walk.'"

So they asked him, "Who is this fellow who told you to pick it up and walk?"

The man who was healed had no idea who it was, for Jesus had slipped away into the crowd that was there.

Later Jesus found him at the temple and said to him, "See, you are well again. Stop sinning or something worse may happen to you." The man went away and told the Jews that it was Jesus who had made him well.

n. 5:16-29

RESURRECTION AND LIFE. So, because Jesus was doing these things on the Sabbath, the Jews persecuted him. Jesus said to them, "My Father is always at his work to this very day, and I, too, am working." For this reason the Jews tried all the harder to kill him; not only was he breaking the Sabbath, but he was even calling God his own Father, making himself equal with God.

Jesus gave them this answer: "I tell you the truth, the Son can do nothing by himself; he can do only what he sees his Father doing, because whatever the Father does the Son also

---

[p]Some manuscripts *Bethzatha*; other manuscripts *Bethsaida*   [q]Some less important manuscripts *paralyzed—and they waited for the moving of the waters.* [r]*From time to time an angel of the Lord would come down and stir up the waters. The first one into the pool after each such disturbance would be cured of whatever disease he had.*

does. For the Father loves the Son and shows him all he does. Yes, to your amazement he will show him even greater things than these. For just as the Father raises the dead and gives them life, even so the Son gives life to whom he is pleased to give it. Moreover, the Father judges no one, but has entrusted all judgment to the Son, that all may honor the Son just as they honor the Father. He who does not honor the Son does not honor the Father, who sent him.

"I tell you the truth, whoever hears my word and believes him who sent me has eternal life and will not be condemned; he has crossed over from death to life. I tell you the truth, a time is coming and has now come when the dead will hear the voice of the Son of God and those who hear will live. For as the Father has life in himself, so he has granted the Son to have life in himself. And he has given him authority to judge because he is the Son of Man.

"Do not be amazed at this, for a time is coming when all who are in their graves will hear his voice and come out—those who have done good will rise to live, and those who have done evil will rise to be condemned.

Jn. 5:30-47

DISCUSSION OF AUTHORITY. By myself I can do nothing; I judge only as I hear, and my judgment is just, for I seek not to please myself but him who sent me.

"If I testify about myself, my testimony is not valid. There is another who testifies in my favor, and I know that his testimony about me is valid.

"You have sent to John and he has testified to the truth. Not that I accept human testimony; but I mention it that you may be saved. John was a lamp that burned and gave light, and you chose for a time to enjoy his light.

"I have testimony weightier than that of John. For the very work that the Father has given me to finish, and which I am doing, testifies that the Father has sent me. And the Father who sent me has himself testified concerning me. You have never heard his voice nor seen his form, nor does his word dwell in you, for you do not believe the one he sent. You diligently study[r] the Scriptures because you think that by them

[r]Or *Study diligently* (the imperative)

you possess eternal life. These are the Scriptures that testify about me, yet you refuse to come to me to have life.

"I do not accept praise from men, but I know you. I know that you do not have the love of God in your hearts. I have come in my Father's name, and you do not accept me; but if someone else comes in his own name, you will accept him. How can you believe if you accept praise from one another, yet make no effort to obtain the praise that comes from the only God[s]?

"But do not think I will accuse you before the Father. Your accuser is Moses, on whom your hopes are set. If you believed Moses, you would believe me, for he wrote about me. But since you do not believe what he wrote, how are you going to believe what I say?"

Mt.
12:1-8
Mk.
2:23-28
Lk. 6:1-5
Galilee

PLUCKING GRAIN ON SABBATH. [Mt]At that time Jesus went through the grainfields on the Sabbath. His disciples were hungry and began to pick some heads of grain and eat them. When the Pharisees saw this, they said to him, "Look! Your disciples are doing what is unlawful on the Sabbath."

He answered, "Haven't you read what David did when he and his companions were hungry? He entered the house of God, and he and his companions ate the consecrated bread—which was not lawful for them to do, but only for the priests. Or haven't you read in the Law that on the Sabbath the priests in the temple desecrate the day and yet are innocent? I tell you that one[t] greater than the temple is here. If you had known what these words mean, 'I desire mercy, not sacrifice,'[u] you would not have condemned the innocent." [Mk]Then he said to them, "The Sabbath was made for man, not man for the Sabbath. So the Son of Man is Lord even of the Sabbath."

Mt.
12:9-14
Mk.
3:1-6
Lk.
6:6-11

HEALING ON SABBATH. [Lk]On another Sabbath he went into the synagogue and was teaching, and a man was there whose right hand was shriveled. The Pharisees and the teachers of the law were looking for a reason to accuse Jesus, so they watched him closely to see if he would heal on the Sabbath. [Mt]Looking for a reason to accuse Jesus, they asked him, "Is it lawful to heal on the Sabbath?"

---

[s]Some early manuscripts *the Only One*   [t]Or *something*   [u]Hosea 6:6

He said to them, "If any of you has a sheep and it falls into a pit on the Sabbath, will you not take hold of it and lift it out? How much more valuable is a man than a sheep! Therefore it is lawful to do good on the Sabbath." ᴹᵏJesus said to the man with the shriveled hand, "Stand up in front of everyone."

Then Jesus asked them, "Which is lawful on the Sabbath: to do good or to do evil, to save life or to kill?" But they remained silent.

He looked around at them in anger and, deeply distressed at their stubborn hearts, said to the man, "Stretch out your hand." He stretched it out, and his hand was completely restored. ᴸᵏBut they were furious and began to discuss with one another what they might do to Jesus. ᴹᵏThen the Pharisees went out and began to plot with the Herodians how they might kill Jesus.

Mt.
12:15-21
Mk.
3:7-12
By the
sea

JESUS HEALS OTHERS. ᴹᵏJesus withdrew with his disciples to the lake, and a large crowd from Galilee followed. When they heard all he was doing, many people came to him from Judea, Jerusalem, Idumea, and the regions across the Jordan and around Tyre and Sidon. Because of the crowd he told his disciples to have a small boat ready for him, to keep the people from crowding him. For he had healed many, so that those with diseases were pushing forward to touch him.

Whenever the evilᵛ spirits saw him, they fell down before him and cried out, "You are the Son of God." But he gave them strict orders not to tell who he was. ᴹᵗThis was to fulfill what was spoken through the prophet Isaiah:

"Here is my servant whom I have chosen,
the one I love, in whom I delight;
I will put my Spirit on him,
    and he will proclaim justice to the nations.
He will not quarrel or cry out;
no one will hear his voice in the streets.
A bruised reed he will not break,
    and a smoldering wick he will not snuff out,
till he leads justice to victory.
In his name the nations will put their hope."ʷ

ᵛGreek *unclean*   ʷIsaiah 42:1-4

Mk. 3:13-19 Lk. 6:12-16 Hills near sea	JESUS APPOINTS 12 APOSTLES. One of those days Jesus went out to a mountainside to pray, and spent the night praying to God. When morning came, he called his disciples to him and chose twelve of them, whom he also designated apostles: Simon (whom he named Peter), his brother Andrew, James, John, Philip, Bartholomew, Matthew, Thomas, James son of Alphaeus, Simon who was called the Zealot, Judas son of James, and Judas Iscariot, who became a traitor.
Lk. 6:17-19	GREAT CROWD GATHERS. He went down with them and stood on a level place. A large crowd of his disciples was there and a great number of people from all over Judea, from Jerusalem, and from the coast of Tyre and Sidon, who had come to hear him and to be healed of their diseases. Those troubled by evil^x spirits were cured, and the people all tried to touch him, because power was coming from him and healing them all.

TODAY'S INSIGHTS

Deity

What would you think if a person came up to you and said he was God? Or that he knows a way you can live forever? Surely most of us would be extremely skeptical, to say the least. So why are we so critical of the religious leaders of Jesus' day who rejected him? After all, Jesus was actually claiming to be God, and to have the secret to eternal life. Not only that, but he was breaking rules which they held to be sacred. What more proof did they need in order to show that he couldn't be the One he claimed to be? Jesus' claims were unmitigated blasphemy!

Blasphemy, that is, unless he was telling the truth. But that possibility was, and still is, an outrageous thought. That anyone walking around in human form could be God is "unbelievable." That anyone should claim the ability to forgive sins is equally "unbelievable." In fact, not one of Jesus' claims is even remotely "believable" on its face. But there is this problem with what otherwise seems obvious: The power that Jesus had over nature is undeniable.

^xGreek *unclean*

Who but God has the power to heal a man who has been an invalid for 38 years? Who but God has the power to restore a shriveled hand? Who but God would evoke such response from evil spirits? This incredible Man from Nazareth, though seemingly unbelievable, is in every way undeniable. In his own resurrection he would surpass even the prophets of old, who had performed mighty works but had not returned from their own graves.

Instead of dismissing Jesus as either a crazy person or an arrogant fool, we are forced to accept his claims to deity. His life, his humility, his righteousness, and his miraculous power all draw us to that conclusion. Why then were the religious leaders not compelled to accept Jesus? For openers, Jesus didn't match their expectations of what a religious leader ought to be. He didn't fit the institutional mold. He didn't prove loyal to the traditions which they held dear.

But most of all, the religious leaders were so busy doing religious things and talking religious talk that they had missed God in the process. They thought they could find the way to eternal life through their meticulous adherence to the rules contained within Scripture. Rather than using the Scriptures as a guidebook to knowing God, they had turned their own twisted interpretation of Scripture into an object of worship. Having done that, their priorities were all mixed up, with rules taking precedence over persons and human needs.

What Jesus came to tell them—and us—is that rules do not save us from unspirituality, not even rules found in the Scriptures. What makes us spiritual is our relationship with God and with our fellow man. And who better to set us straight about that important distinction than the One who gave us the rules in the first place—God in the flesh, Jesus Christ!

DAY
8
WITH
JESUS

ESSENCE

The Sermon on the Mount

THE "SERMON ON THE MOUNT" IS PERHAPS THE MOST FAMILIAR and instructive sermon ever presented by Jesus. Matthew and Luke may record Jesus' teaching in two different settings, although the content appears much the same. Just as many of Jesus' sermons are apparently never recorded, so too some of his sermons are probably repeated from place to place. In any event, this collection of Jesus' teachings brings one to the heart of his message concerning the kingdom of God.

Covering a broad spectrum of spiritual topics, Jesus speaks of the nature of the kingdom, of repentance, of faith, and of worship—and particularly of prayer and humility. Always demonstrating a concern for human welfare, Jesus deals specifically with family and social relationships and discusses at length the effect of possessions on one's faith and peace of mind. The discourse begins beautifully with the blessings in store for the righteous, and harshly with the woes which will befall those whose lives are spiritually rebellious.

Mt.
5:1-12
Lk.
6:20-23
Mountain
near
Caper-
naum

BEATITUDES PROCLAIMED. Now when he saw the crowds, he went up on a mountainside and sat down. His disciples came to him, and he began to teach them, saying:

> "Blessed are the poor in spirit,
>   for theirs is the kingdom of heaven.
> Blessed are those who mourn,
>   for they will be comforted.
> Blessed are the meek,
>   for they will inherit the earth.
> Blessed are those who hunger and thirst
>   for righteousness,
>   for they will be filled.
> Blessed are the merciful,
>   for they will be shown mercy.
> Blessed are the pure in heart,
>   for they will see God.

Blessed are the peacemakers,
for they will be called sons of God.
Blessed are those who are persecuted because of
righteousness,
for theirs is the kingdom of heaven.

"Blessed are you when people insult you, persecute you and falsely say all kinds of evil against you because of me. Rejoice and be glad, because great is your reward in heaven, for in the same way they persecuted the prophets who were before you.

Lk. 6:24-26 | WOES PRONOUNCED.
"But woe to you who are rich,
for you have already received your comfort.
Woe to you who are well fed now,
for you will go hungry.
Woe to you who laugh now,
for you will mourn and weep.
Woe to you when all men speak well of you,
for that is how their fathers treated the false prophets."

**Mt.
5:13-16** | NATURE OF BELIEVERS. "You are the salt of the earth. But if the salt loses its saltiness, how can it be made salty again? It is no longer good for anything, except to be thrown out and trampled by men.

"You are the light of the world. A city on a hill cannot be hidden. Neither do people light a lamp and put it under a bowl. Instead they put it on its stand, and it gives light to everyone in the house. In the same way, let your light shine before men, that they may see your good deeds and praise your Father in heaven.

**Mt.
5:17-20** | LAW AND GOSPEL. "Do not think that I have come to abolish the Law or the Prophets; I have not come to abolish them but to fulfill them. I tell you the truth, until heaven and earth disappear, not the smallest letter, not the least stroke of a pen, will by any means disappear from the Law until everything is accomplished. Anyone who breaks one of the least of these commandments and teaches others to do the same will be called least in the kingdom of heaven, but whoever practices and teaches these commands will be called great in the kingdom of heaven. For I tell you that unless your righ-

teousness surpasses that of the Pharisees and the teachers of the law, you will certainly not enter the kingdom of heaven.

Mt. 5:21-26 | THE SIXTH COMMANDMENT. "You have heard that it was said to the people long ago, 'Do not murder,[y] and anyone who murders will be subject to judgment.' But I tell you that anyone who is angry with his brother[z] will be subject to judgment. Again, anyone who says to his brother, 'Raca,[a]' is answerable to the Sanhedrin. But anyone who says, 'You fool!' will be in danger of the fire of hell.

"Therefore, if you are offering your gift at the altar and there remember that your brother has something against you, leave your gift there in front of the altar. First go and be reconciled to your brother; then come and offer your gift.

"Settle matters quickly with your adversary who is taking you to court. Do it while you are still with him on the way, or he may hand you over to the judge, and the judge may hand you over to the officer, and you may be thrown into prison. I tell you the truth, you will not get out until you have paid the last penny.[b]

Mt. 5:27-30 | THE SEVENTH COMMANDMENT. "You have heard that it was said, 'Do not commit adultery.'[c] But I tell you that anyone who looks at a woman lustfully has already committed adultery with her in his heart. If your right eye causes you to sin, gouge it out and throw it away. It is better for you to lose one part of your body than for your whole body to be thrown into hell. And if your right hand causes you to sin, cut it off and throw it away. It is better for you to lose one part of your body than for your whole body to go into hell.

Mt. 5:31,32 | MARRIAGE AND DIVORCE. "It has been said, 'Anyone who divorces his wife must give her a certificate of divorce.'[d] But I tell you that anyone who divorces his wife, except for marital unfaithfulness, causes her to become an adulteress, and anyone who marries the divorced woman commits adultery.

Mt. 5:33-37 | HONESTY WITHOUT OATHS. "Again, you have heard that it was said to the people long ago, 'Do not break your oath, but keep the oaths you have made to the Lord.' But I tell you, Do

[y]Exodus 20:13   [z]Some manuscripts *brother without cause*   [a]An Aramaic term of contempt   [b]Greek *kodrantes*   [c]Exodus 20:14   [d]Deut. 24:1

not swear at all: either by heaven, for it is God's throne; or by the earth, for it is his footstool; or by Jerusalem, for it is the city of the Great King. And do not swear by your head, for you cannot make even one hair white or black. Simply let your 'Yes' be 'Yes,' and your 'No,' 'No'; anything beyond this comes from the evil one.

Mt. 5:38-42
Lk. 6:27-31

REGARDING RETALIATION. ᴹᵗ"You have heard that it was said, 'Eye for eye, and tooth for tooth.'ᵉ But I tell you, Do not resist an evil person. If someone strikes you on the right cheek, turn to him the other also. And if someone wants to sue you and take your tunic, let him have your cloak as well. If someone forces you to go one mile, go with him two miles. Give to the one who asks you, and do not turn away from the one who wants to borrow from you. ᴸᵏDo to others as you would have them do to you.

Mt. 5:43-48
Lk. 6:32-36

LOVE FOR ENEMIES. ᴹᵗ"You have heard that it was said, 'Love your neighborᶠ and hate your enemy.' But I tell you: Love your enemiesᵍ and pray for those who persecute you, that you may be sons of your Father in heaven. He causes his sun to rise on the evil and the good, and sends rain on the righteous and the unrighteous. If you love those who love you, what reward will you get? Are not even the tax collectors doing that? And if you greet only your brothers, what are you doing more than others? Do not even pagans do that? ᴸᵏAnd if you lend to those from whom you expect repayment, what credit is that to you? Even 'sinners' lend to 'sinners,' expecting to be repaid in full. But love your enemies, do good to them, and lend to them without expecting to get anything back. Then your reward will be great, and you will be sons of the Most High, because he is kind to the ungrateful and wicked. Be merciful, just as your Father is merciful.

Mt. 6:1-4

ON GIVING. "Be careful not to do your 'acts of righteousness' before men, to be seen by them. If you do, you will have no reward from your Father in heaven.

"So when you give to the needy, do not announce it with trumpets, as the hypocrites do in the synagogues and on the

ᵉExodus 21:24; Lev. 24:20; Deut. 19:21   ᶠLev. 19:18   ᵍSome late manuscripts *enemies, bless those who curse you, do good to those who hate you*

streets, to be honored by men. I tell you the truth, they have received their reward in full. But when you give to the needy, do not let your left hand know what your right hand is doing, so that your giving may be in secret. Then your Father, who sees what is done in secret, will reward you.

Mt. 6:5-15 | ON PRAYING. "And when you pray, do not be like the hypocrites, for they love to pray standing in the synagogues and on the street corners to be seen by men. I tell you the truth, they have received their reward in full. But when you pray, go into your room, close the door and pray to your Father, who is unseen. Then your Father, who sees what is done in secret, will reward you. And when you pray, do not keep on babbling like pagans, for they think they will be heard because of their many words. Do not be like them, for your Father knows what you need before you ask him.

"This, then, is how you should pray:

"'Our Father in heaven,
hallowed be your name,
your kingdom come,
your will be done
　　on earth as it is in heaven.
Give us today our daily bread.
Forgive us our debts,
　　as we also have forgiven our debtors.
And lead us not into temptation,
but deliver us from the evil one.'[h]

For if you forgive men when they sin against you, your heavenly Father will also forgive you. But if you do not forgive men their sins, your Father will not forgive your sins.

Mt. 6:16-18 | ON FASTING. "When you fast, do not look somber as the hypocrites do, for they disfigure their faces to show men they are fasting. I tell you the truth, they have received their reward in full. But when you fast, put oil on your head and wash your face, so that it will not be obvious to men that you are fasting, but only to your Father, who is unseen; and your Father, who sees what is done in secret, will reward you.

[h]Or *from evil*; some late manuscripts *one, / for yours is the kingdom and the power and the glory forever. Amen.*

Mt. 6:19-21 SPIRITUAL TREASURES. "Do not store up for yourselves treasures on earth, where moth and rust destroy, and where thieves break in and steal. But store up for yourselves treasures in heaven, where moth and rust do not destroy, and where thieves do not break in and steal. For where your treasure is, there your heart will be also.

Mt. 6:22,23 VALUE OF SPIRITUAL INSIGHT. "The eye is the lamp of the body. If your eyes are good, your whole body will be full of light. But if your eyes are bad, your whole body will be full of darkness. If then the light within you is darkness, how great is that darkness!

Mt. 6:24 NEED FOR UNDIVIDED LOYALTY. "No one can serve two masters. Either he will hate the one and love the other, or he will be devoted to the one and despise the other. You cannot serve both God and Money.

Mt. 6:25-34 AVOIDING ANXIETY. "Therefore I tell you, do not worry about your life, what you will eat or drink; or about your body, what you will wear. Is not life more important than food, and the body more important than clothes? Look at the birds of the air; they do not sow or reap or store away in barns, and yet your heavenly Father feeds them. Are you not much more valuable than they? Who of you by worrying can add a single hour to his life[i]?

"And why do you worry about clothes? See how the lilies of the field grow. They do not labor or spin. Yet I tell you that not even Solomon in all his splendor was dressed like one of these. If that is how God clothes the grass of the field, which is here today and tomorrow is thrown into the fire, will he not much more clothe you, O you of little faith? So do not worry, saying, 'What shall we eat?' or 'What shall we drink?' or 'What shall we wear?' For the pagans run after all these things, and your heavenly Father knows that you need them. But seek first his kingdom and his righteousness, and all these things will be given to you as well. Therefore do not worry about tomorrow, for tomorrow will worry about itself. Each day has enough trouble of its own.

Mt. 7:1-5 Lk. 6:37-42 HYPOCRITICAL JUDGING. "Do not judge, and you will not be judged. Do not condemn, and you will not be condemned.

[i]Or *single cubit to his height*

Forgive, and you will be forgiven. Give, and it will be given to you. A good measure, pressed down, shaken together and running over, will be poured into your lap. For with the measure you use, it will be measured to you."

He also told them this parable: "Can a blind man lead a blind man? Will they not both fall into a pit? A student is not above his teacher, but everyone who is fully trained will be like his teacher.

"Why do you look at the speck of sawdust in your brother's eye and pay no attention to the plank in your own eye? How can you say to your brother, 'Brother, let me take the speck out of your eye,' when you yourself fail to see the plank in your own eye? You hypocrite, first take the plank out of your eye, and then you will see clearly to remove the speck from your brother's eye.

Mt. 7:6 | INAPPROPRIATE CONCERN. "Do not give dogs what is sacred; do not throw your pearls to pigs. If you do, they may trample them under their feet, and then turn and tear you to pieces.

Mt. 7:7-12 | SEEKING GRACE. "Ask and it will be given to you; seek and you will find; knock and the door will be opened to you. For everyone who asks receives; he who seeks finds; and to him who knocks, the door will be opened.

"Which of you, if his son asks for bread, will give him a stone? Or if he asks for a fish, will give him a snake? If you, then, though you are evil, know how to give good gifts to your children, how much more will your Father in heaven give good gifts to those who ask him! So in everything, do to others what you would have them do to you, for this sums up the Law and the Prophets.

Mt. 7:13,14 | UNPOPULAR DISCIPLESHIP. "Enter through the narrow gate. For wide is the gate and broad is the road that leads to destruction, and many enter through it. But small is the gate and narrow the road that leads to life, and only a few find it.

Mt. 7:15-23 Lk. 6:43-45 | TESTING RELIGIOUS LEADERS. Mt"Watch out for false prophets. They come to you in sheep's clothing, but inwardly they are ferocious wolves. By their fruit you will recognize them. Do people pick grapes from thornbushes, or figs from thistles? Likewise every good tree bears good fruit, but a bad tree bears bad fruit. A good tree cannot bear bad fruit, and a bad tree cannot bear good fruit. Every tree that does not bear good fruit is cut down and thrown into the fire. Thus, by their fruit you will recognize them. ᴸᵏThe good man brings good things out of the good stored up in his heart, and the evil man brings evil things out of the evil stored up in his heart. For out of the overflow of his heart his mouth speaks." ᴹᵗNot everyone who says to me, 'Lord, Lord,' will enter the kingdom of heaven, but only he who does the will of my Father who is in heaven. Many will say to me on that day, 'Lord, Lord, did we not prophesy in your name, and in your name drive out demons and perform many miracles?' Then I will tell them plainly, 'I never knew you. Away from me, you evildoers!'

Mt.
7:24-27
Lk.
6:46-49

FAITH AND DEEDS. ᴸᵏ"Why do you call me, 'Lord, Lord,' and do not do what I say? ᴹᵗTherefore everyone who hears these words of mine and puts them into practice is like a wise man who built his house on the rock. The rain came down, the streams rose, and the winds blew and beat against that house; yet it did not fall, because it had its foundation on the rock. But everyone who hears these words of mine and does not put them into practice is like a foolish man who built his house on sand. The rain came down, the streams rose, and the winds blew and beat against that house, and it fell with a great crash."

Mt.
7:28,29

CROWD IS ASTONISHED. When Jesus had finished saying these things, the crowds were amazed at his teaching, because he taught as one who had authority, and not as their teachers of the law.

TODAY'S INSIGHTS

Essence

Have you ever searched to find the heart, soul, and essence of Jesus' teaching? In the Sermon on the Mount you must surely have found it. Virtually every word of Jesus' sermon is meaningful and memorable. It is eloquent without profusion, profound without seeming so. Beginning with the beatitudes, it rises above all other moral teaching by digging deeply into the human condition. Have you ever been poor in spirit? Jesus says his kingdom is for you. Have you ever been filled with sorrow and grief? His kingdom is for you. Have you ever been persecuted? His kingdom is for you. In his kingdom we receive all the blessings which the God of heaven can give us.

Who is it that God loves? Those who run over others in the business world? Those who blight the nation with moral filth and degradation? Although they may appear to prosper from their actions, Jesus tells us that it is the pure in heart who will truly see God. It is those who search for righteousness, those who are merciful, and those who work to bring about peace to whom God extends his love. To be a success in God's eyes, we don't need to be rich or powerful or popular. We need only cut through the allure of a material world and find the essence of Jesus' teaching in order to be truly successful in this life. The challenge is not to "be successful." Clearly the challenge is: Be salt! Be light!

What is almost shocking about Jesus' teaching is that Jesus is not even saying "Be moral." If his teaching stopped there, the Christian walk would be easy enough to accept. After all, few of us have ever murdered anyone. But Jesus takes us behind the rule and within the heart of the law to its very essence. It is not enough not to kill; we must not even hate. It is not enough not to commit adultery; we must not even wish we could. It is not enough to love the lovable; we must also love those who are unlovable—even those whom we might consider to be enemies! Wanting to know the heart, soul, and essence of Jesus' teaching brings us to a level of human motivation and conduct that may be more than we bargained for.

Nor is Jesus merely saying "Be religious." Again and again Jesus tells us that God is not happy with religious formalism which proceeds from custom, tradition, or hypocritical show. Our religious observances are not meant for others to see and approve; they are for God alone.

Who is the most spiritual person you know? Are you sure about that? Are you basing your judgment on how often he or she worships? Or by an appearance of piety? Or by ecclesiastical language which rolls off the tongue? Or by the frequency with which God is praised in his or her speech? God, who looks at the heart, may see that person quite differently. Wouldn't it be wonderful if we saw people God's way? Who knows—we might find some of God's favorite people in unexpected places!

DAY
WITH
JESUS
9

REJECTION

The Ministry Continues

SUCH PERCEPTIVE AND AUTHORITATIVE TEACHING HAS OBVIOUSLY won the attention of the multitudes, who have long been disillusioned by the empty ritualism and superficiality of their present religious system. As Jesus' fame continues to spread, John the Baptist sends a message to Jesus asking for final confirmation of his messiahship. John is perhaps sensing an impending death and undoubtedly wants to reassure himself that his own ministry has not been in vain. Jesus sends a message of reassurance and praises John for his courage and dedication as a servant of God.

No doubt by this time the religious leaders are also becoming increasingly aware of Jesus' extraordinary power. Instead of accepting it as divine, they accuse Jesus of having power from Satan. This brings a scathing response from Jesus, including reference to a type of sin which Jesus says is unforgivable. The events leading to this confrontation begin to unfold as Jesus makes his way from the mountain back to Capernaum.

Mt.
8:5-13
Lk.
7:1-10
Capernaum

CENTURION'S SLAVE HEALED. LkWhen Jesus had finished saying all this in the hearing of the people, he entered Capernaum. There a centurion's servant, whom his master valued highly, was sick and about to die. The centurion heard of Jesus and sent some elders of the Jews to him, asking him to come and heal his servant. When they came to Jesus, they pleaded earnestly with him, "This man deserves to have you do this, because he loves our nation and has built our synagogue." So Jesus went with them.

He was not far from the house when the centurion sent friends to say to him: "Lord, don't trouble yourself, for I do not deserve to have you come under my roof. That is why I did not even consider myself worthy to come to you. But say the word, and my servant will be healed. For I myself am a man under authority, with soldiers under me. I tell this one, 'Go,' and he goes; and that one, 'Come,' and he comes. I say to my servant, 'Do this,' and he does it."

When Jesus heard this, he was amazed at him, and turning to the crowd following him, he said, "I tell you, I have not found such great faith even in Israel. ^{Mt}I say to you that many will come from the east and the west, and will take their places at the feast with Abraham, Isaac and Jacob in the kingdom of heaven. But the subjects of the kingdom will be thrown outside, into the darkness, where there will be weeping and gnashing of teeth."

Then Jesus said to the centurion, "Go! It will be done just as you believed it would." And his servant was healed at that very hour. ^{Lk}Then the men who had been sent returned to the house and found the servant well.

Lk.
7:11-17
Nain

WIDOW'S SON RAISED. Soon afterward, Jesus went to a town called Nain, and his disciples and a large crowd went along with him. As he approached the town gate, a dead person was being carried out—the only son of his mother, and she was a widow. And a large crowd from the town was with her. When the Lord saw her, his heart went out to her and he said, "Don't cry."

Then he went up and touched the coffin, and those carrying it stood still. He said, "Young man, I say to you, get up!" The dead man sat up and began to talk, and Jesus gave him back to his mother.

They were all filled with awe and praised God, "A great prophet has appeared among us," they said. "God has come to help his people." This news about Jesus spread throughout Judea[j] and the surrounding country.

Mt.
11:2-6
Lk.
7:18-23

JOHN THE BAPTIST QUESTIONS. John's disciples told him about all these things. Calling two of them, he sent them to the Lord to ask, "Are you the one who was to come, or should we expect someone else?"

When the men came to Jesus, they said, "John the Baptist sent us to you to ask, 'Are you the one who was to come, or should we expect someone else?'"

At that very time Jesus cured many who had diseases, sicknesses and evil spirits, and gave sight to many who were blind. So he replied to the messengers, "Go back and report to

^jOr *the land of the Jews*

John what you have seen and heard: The blind receive sight, the lame walk, those who have leprosy[k] are cured, the deaf hear, the dead are raised, and the good news is preached to the poor. Blessed is the man who does not fall away on account of me."

Mt. 11:7-15 Lk. 7:24-30 JESUS PRAISES JOHN. [Lk]After John's messengers left, Jesus began to speak to the crowd about John: "What did you go out into the desert to see? A reed swayed by the wind? If not, what did you go out to see? A man dressed in fine clothes? No, those who wear expensive clothes and indulge in luxury are in palaces. But what did you go out to see? A prophet? Yes, I tell you, and more than a prophet. This is the one about whom it is written:

> "'I will send my messenger ahead of you,
>   who will prepare your way before you.'[l]

I tell you, among those born of women there is no one greater than John; yet the one who is least in the kingdom of God is greater than he."

[Mt]"From the days of John the Baptist until now, the kingdom of heaven has been forcefully advancing, and forceful men lay hold of it. For all the Prophets and the Law prophesied until John. And if you are willing to accept it, he is the Elijah who was to come. He who has ears, let him hear." [Lk](All the people, even the tax collectors, when they heard Jesus' words, acknowledged that God's way was right, because they had been baptized by John. But the Pharisees and experts in the law rejected God's purpose for themselves, because they had not been baptized by John.)

Mt. 11:16-19 Lk. 7:31-35 JESUS REPROVES REJECTION. "To what, then, can I compare the people of this generation? What are they like? They are like children sitting in the marketplace and calling out to each other:

> "'We played the flute for you,
>   and you did not dance;
> we sang a dirge,
>   and you did not cry.'

---

[k]The Greek word was used for various diseases affecting the skin—not necessarily leprosy.   [l]Mal. 3:1

For John the Baptist came neither eating bread nor drinking wine, and you say, 'He has a demon.' The Son of Man came eating and drinking, and you say, 'Here is a glutton and a drunkard, a friend of tax collectors and "sinners."' But wisdom is proved right by all her children."

Lk.
7:36-50

ANOINTING BY SINFUL WOMAN. Now one of the Pharisees invited Jesus to have dinner with him, so he went to the Pharisee's house and reclined at the table. When a woman who had lived a sinful life in that town learned that Jesus was eating at the Pharisee's house, she brought an alabaster jar of perfume, and as she stood behind him at his feet weeping, she began to wet his feet with her tears. Then she wiped them with her hair, kissed them and poured perfume on them.

When the Pharisee who had invited him saw this, he said to himself, "If this man were a prophet, he would know who is touching him and what kind of woman she is—that she is a sinner."

Jesus answered him, "Simon, I have something to tell you."

"Tell me, teacher," he said.

"Two men owed money to a certain moneylender. One owed him five hundred denarii,[m] and the other fifty. Neither of them had the money to pay him back, so he canceled the debts of both. Now which of them will love him more?"

Simon replied, "I suppose the one who had the bigger debt canceled."

"You have judged correctly," Jesus said.

Then he turned toward the woman and said to Simon, "Do you see this woman? I came into your house. You did not give me any water for my feet, but she wet my feet with her tears and wiped them with her hair. You did not give me a kiss, but this woman, from the time I entered, has not stopped kissing my feet. You did not put oil on my head, but she has poured perfume on my feet. Therefore, I tell you, her many sins have been forgiven—for she loved much. But he who has been forgiven little loves little."

Then Jesus said to her, "Your sins are forgiven."

The other guests began to say among themselves, "Who is this who even forgives sins?"

[m]A denarius was a coin worth about a day's wages.

Jesus said to the woman, "Your faith has saved you; go in peace."

Lk.
8:1-3
Galilee

WOMEN PROVIDE SUPPORT. After this, Jesus traveled about from one town and village to another, proclaiming the good news of the kingdom of God. The Twelve were with him, and also some women who had been cured of evil spirits and diseases: Mary (called Magdalene) from whom seven demons had come out; Joanna the wife of Cuza, the manager of Herod's household; Susanna; and many others. These women were helping to support them out of their own means.

Mt.
12:22-30
Mk.
3:20,
22-27
Lk.
11:14-23
Capernaum

JESUS ACCUSED. ᴹᵏThen Jesus entered a house, and again a crowd gathered, so that he and his disciples were not even able to eat. ᴹᵗThen they brought him a demon-possessed man who was blind and mute, and Jesus healed him, so that he could both talk and see. All the people were astonished and said, "Could this be the Son of David?"

But when the Pharisees heard this, they said, "It is only by Beelzebub,ⁿ the prince of demons, that this fellow drives out demons."

Jesus knew their thoughts and said to them, "Every kingdom divided against itself will be ruined, and every city or household divided against itself will not stand. If Satan drives out Satan, he is divided against himself. How then can his kingdom stand? And if I drive out demons by Beelzebub, by whom do your people drive them out? So then, they will be your judges. But if I drive out demons by the Spirit of God, then the kingdom of God has come upon you.

"Or again, how can anyone enter a strong man's house and carry off his possessions unless he first ties up the strong man? Then he can rob his house.

"He who is not with me is against me, and he who does not gather with me scatters.

Mt.
12:31-37
Mk.
3:21,
28-30

BLASPHEMY CONDEMNED. ᴹᵗ"And so I tell you, every sin and blasphemy will be forgiven men, but the blasphemy against the Spirit will not be forgiven. Anyone who speaks a word against the Son of Man will be forgiven, but anyone who speaks against the Holy Spirit will not be forgiven, either in

---

ⁿGreek *Beezeboul* or *Beelzeboul*

this age or in the age to come." ᴹᵏHe said this because they were saying, "He has an evil spirit." ᴹᵗ"Make a tree good and its fruit will be good, or make a tree bad and its fruit will be bad, for a tree is recognized by its fruit. You brood of vipers, how can you who are evil say anything good? For out of the overflow of the heart the mouth speaks. The good man brings good things out of the good stored up in him, and the evil man brings evil things out of the evil stored up in him. But I tell you that men will have to give account on the day of judgment for every careless word they have spoken. For by your words you will be acquitted, and by your words you will be condemned." ᴹᵏWhen his family heard about this, they went to take charge of him, for they said, "He is out of his mind."

Mt.
12:38-42
Lk.
11:29-32

REQUEST FOR PROOF REBUKED. Then some of the Pharisees and teachers of the law said to him, "Teacher, we want to see a miraculous sign from you."

He answered, "A wicked and adulterous generation asks for a miraculous sign! But none will be given it except the sign of the prophet Jonah. For as Jonah was three days and three nights in the belly of a huge fish, so the Son of Man will be three days and three nights in the heart of the earth. The men of Nineveh will stand up at the judgment with this generation and condemn it; for they repented at the preaching of Jonah, and now one° greater than Jonah is here. The Queen of the South will rise at the judgment with this generation and condemn it; for she came from the ends of the earth to listen to Solomon's wisdom, and now one greater than Solomon is here.

Mt.
12:43-45
Lk.
11:24-28

NEED FOR MORAL REFORM. ᴹᵗ"When an evilᵖ spirit comes out of a man, it goes through arid places seeking rest and does not find it. Then it says, 'I will return to the house I left.' When it arrives, it finds the house unoccupied, swept clean and put in order. Then it goes and takes with it seven other spirits more wicked than itself, and they go in and live there. And the final condition of that man is worse than the first. That is how it will be with this wicked generation." ᴸᵏAs Jesus was saying these things, a woman in the crowd called out, "Blessed is the mother who gave you birth and nursed you."

°Or *something*   ᵖGreek *unclean*

He replied, "Blessed rather are those who hear the word of God and obey it."

Mt.
12:46-50
Mk.
3:31-35
Lk.
8:19-21

JESUS TELLS TRUE KINSHIP. While Jesus was still talking to the crowd, his mother and brothers stood outside, wanting to speak to him. Someone told him, "Your mother and brothers are standing outside, wanting to speak to you."[q]

He replied to him, "Who is my mother, and who are my brothers?" Pointing to his disciples, he said, "Here are my mother and my brothers. For whoever does the will of my Father in heaven is my brother and sister and mother."

Lk.
11:33-36

INNER RIGHTEOUSNESS. "No one lights a lamp and puts it in a place where it will be hidden, or under a bowl. Instead he puts it on its stand, so that those who come in may see the light. Your eye is the lamp of your body. When your eyes are good, your whole body also is full of light. But when they are bad, your body also is full of darkness. See to it, then, that the light within you is not darkness. Therefore, if your whole body is full of light, and no part of it dark, it will be completely lighted, as when the light of a lamp shines on you."

TODAY'S INSIGHTS

Rejection

If you had to make a choice as to which person you would believe in a jury trial, would you choose a man who was wearing a business suit, a football jersey, a clerical collar, or baggy overalls? The right answer, of course, is that what one is wearing shouldn't matter. But how often it *does* matter! How often credibility goes with the man in the business suit instead of the longhaired youth in scruffy blue jeans. All too often we reject what people have to say—and sometimes even the people themselves—based on irrelevant considerations.

Sadly, that is the reason why so many people rejected Jesus while he was on the earth. He didn't fit the image they had preconceived about the Messiah. When they looked for a military leader, he showed himself to be a pacifist. When they looked for a political leader, he renounced earthly power.

[q]Some manuscripts do not have verse 47.

For his part, Jesus cut through all levels of social and cultural conditions. It didn't matter to him whether he was ministering to a Gentile, a widow, or even a prostitute. Jesus saw people as individual souls, wholly apart from their backgrounds and outer trappings. And he met them at the point of their need. If they needed healing, he healed them. If they needed encouraging, he encouraged them. If they needed forgiveness, he forgave them.

Perhaps more surprising are the kinds of people who responded to Jesus' teaching. Wouldn't you have thought that the religious leaders would have been the most excited of all at the appearance during their lifetime of the promised Messiah? Yet they kept trying to kill Jesus! The nagging question is, Why did *they*, of all people, reject Jesus? Or reject even John the Baptist, for that matter?

As for John, they thought he took his religion far too seriously. After all, John had told them they needed to change their way of living (surely not!). And as for Jesus, they thought he took religion all too joyfully (heaven forbid!). After all, Jesus was always going to wedding feasts and banquets—even with "sinners." Far be it from the religious leaders to be seen among sinners! Therefore, far be it from them to accept Jesus as a spiritual leader, much less as the promised Messiah.

It's easy to see how his critics rejected Jesus. We too may be rejecting Jesus if we cloister ourselves only among other Christians. Is it possible that we reject his zest for living by putting on sad religious faces? Do we reject his love for the outcast by driving through a ghetto area without thinking how we might alleviate the sad plight of those who must live there? Are there other ways we reject Jesus without ever realizing it? Are we truly part of his spiritual family, or have we rejected his kinship? O God, help us to be *with* Jesus in his ministry of service, and not *against* him.

DAY
10
WITH
JESUS

CONFRONTATION

Conflict and Confrontation

EVEN ON THE HEELS OF JESUS' WARNING THAT HIS DETRACTORS are flirting with an unforgivable sin, they continue to press him regarding his failure to observe their man-imposed traditions. This sets the scene for a scathing rebuke of the Pharisees for their disbelief and hypocrisy, and an urgent call for repentance. The urgency of the call is highlighted when Jesus discusses his second coming and the judgment. It is underscored even more forcefully when Jesus points to the uncertainty of life, with the reminder that no one knows the day of his death. If repentance is in order, says Jesus, then today is the day to do it. And in no uncertain terms Jesus makes it clear that repentance is indeed in order for these self-righteous and legalistic religious leaders.

Lk.
11:37-44
HYPOCRISY CONDEMNED. When Jesus had finished speaking, a Pharisee invited him to eat with him; so he went in and reclined at the table. But the Pharisee, noticing that Jesus did not first wash before the meal, was surprised.

Then the Lord said to him, "Now then, you Pharisees clean the outside of the cup and dish, but inside you are full of greed and wickedness. You foolish people! Did not the one who made the outside make the inside also? But give what is inside the dish[r] to the poor, and everything will be clean for you.

"Woe to you Pharisees, because you give God a tenth of your mint, rue and all other kinds of garden herbs, but you neglect justice and the love of God. You should have practiced the latter without leaving the former undone.

"Woe to you Pharisees, because you love the most important seats in the synagogues and greetings in the marketplaces.

"Woe to you, because you are like unmarked graves, which men walk over without knowing it."

Lk.
11:45-52
LAWYERS CONDEMNED. One of the experts in the law answered him, "Teacher, when you say these things, you insult us also."

[r] Or what you have

Jesus replied, "And you experts in the law, woe to you, because you load people down with burdens they can hardly carry, and you yourselves will not lift one finger to help them.

"Woe to you, because you build tombs for the prophets, and it was your forefathers who killed them. So you testify that you approve of what your forefathers did; they killed the prophets, and you build their tombs. Because of this, God in his wisdom said, 'I will send them prophets and apostles, some of whom they will kill and others they will persecute.' Therefore this generation will be held responsible for the blood of all the prophets that has been shed since the beginning of the world, from the blood of Abel to the blood of Zechariah, who was killed between the altar and the sanctuary. Yes, I tell you, this generation will be held responsible for it all.

"Woe to you experts in the law, because you have taken away the key to knowledge. You yourselves have not entered, and you have hindered those who were entering."

Lk. 11:53,54

LEADERS TRY TO TRAP JESUS. When Jesus left there, the Pharisees and the teachers of the law began to oppose him fiercely and to besiege him with questions, waiting to catch him in something he might say.

Lk. 12:1-3

WARNING AGAINST HYPOCRISY. Meanwhile, when a crowd of many thousands had gathered, so that they were trampling on one another, Jesus began to speak first to his disciples, saying: "Be on your guard against the yeast of the Pharisees, which is hypocrisy. There is nothing concealed that will not be disclosed, or hidden that will not be made known. What you have said in the dark will be heard in the daylight, and what you have whispered in the ear in the inner rooms will be proclaimed from the roofs.

Lk. 12:4-12

FEARING GOD, NOT MAN. "I tell you, my friends, do not be afraid of those who kill the body and after that can do no more. But I will show you whom you should fear: Fear him who, after the killing of the body, has power to throw you into hell. Yes, I tell you, fear him. Are not five sparrows sold for two pennies[s]? Yet not one of them is forgotten by God. Indeed, the very hairs of your head are all numbered. Don't be afraid; you are worth more than many sparrows.

[s]Greek *two assaria*

"I tell you, whoever acknowledges me before men, the Son of Man will also acknowledge him before the angels of God. But he who disowns me before men will be disowned before the angels of God. And everyone who speaks a word against the Son of Man will be forgiven, but anyone who blasphemes against the Holy Spirit will not be forgiven.

"When you are brought before synagogues, rulers and authorities, do not worry about how you will defend yourselves or what you will say, for the Holy Spirit will teach you at that time what you should say."

Lk.
12:13-21

FOOLISH RICH MAN. Someone in the crowd said to him, "Teacher, tell my brother to divide the inheritance with me."

Jesus replied, "Man, who appointed me a judge or an arbiter between you?" Then he said to them, "Watch out! Be on your guard against all kinds of greed; a man's life does not consist in the abundance of his possessions."

And he told them this parable: "The ground of a certain rich man produced a good crop. He thought to himself, 'What shall I do? I have no place to store my crops.'

"Then he said, 'This is what I'll do. I will tear down my barns and build bigger ones, and there I will store all my grain and my goods. And I'll say to myself, "You have plenty of good things laid up for many years. Take life easy; eat, drink and be merry."'

"But God said to him, 'You fool! This very night your life will be demanded from you. Then who will get what you have prepared for yourself?'

"This is how it will be with anyone who stores up things for himself but is not rich toward God."

Lk.
12:22-34

TRUSTING GOD'S PROVIDENCE. Then Jesus said to his disciples: "Therefore I tell you, do not worry about your life, what you will eat; or about your body, what you will wear. Life is more than food, and the body more than clothes. Consider the ravens: They do not sow or reap, they have no storeroom or barn; yet God feeds them. And how much more valuable you are than birds! Who of you by worrying can add a single hour to his life[1]? Since you cannot do this very little thing, why do you worry about the rest?

"Consider how the lilies grow. They do not labor or spin. Yet I tell you, not even Solomon in all his splendor was dressed

[1]Or *single cubit to his height*

like one of these. If that is how God clothes the grass of the field, which is here today, and tomorrow is thrown into the fire, how much more will he clothe you, O you of little faith! And do not set your heart on what you will eat or drink; do not worry about it. For the pagan world runs after all such things, and your Father knows that you need them. But seek his kingdom, and these things will be given to you as well.

"Do not be afraid, little flock, for your Father has been pleased to give you the kingdom. Sell your possessions and give to the poor. Provide purses for yourselves that will not wear out, a treasure in heaven that will not be exhausted, where no thief comes near and no moth destroys. For where your treasure is, there your heart will be also.

Lk.
12:35-40 PARABLE OF WATCHFUL SERVANTS. "Be dressed ready for service and keep your lamps burning, like men waiting for their master to return from a wedding banquet, so that when he comes and knocks they can immediately open the door for him. It will be good for those servants whose master finds them watching when he comes. I tell you the truth, he will dress himself to serve, will have them recline at the table and will come and wait on them. It will be good for those servants whose master finds them ready, even if he comes in the second or third watch of the night. But understand this: If the owner of the house had known at what hour the thief was coming, he would not have let his house be broken into. You also must be ready, because the Son of Man will come at an hour when you do not expect him."

Lk.
12:41-48 EXHORTATION TO WATCHFULNESS. Peter asked, "Lord, are you telling this parable to us, or to everyone?"

The Lord answered, "Who then is the faithful and wise manager, whom the master puts in charge of his servants to give them their food allowance at the proper time? It will be good for that servant whom the master finds doing so when he returns. I tell you the truth, he will put him in charge of all his possessions. But suppose the servant says to himself, 'My master is taking a long time in coming,' and he then begins to beat the menservants and maidservants and to eat and drink and get drunk. The master of that servant will come on a day when he does not expect him and at an hour he is not aware of. He will cut him to pieces and assign him a place with the unbelievers.

"That servant who knows his master's will and does not get ready or does not do what his master wants will be beaten with many blows. But the one who does not know and does things deserving punishment will be beaten with few blows. From everyone who has been given much, much will be demanded; and from the one who has been entrusted with much, much more will be asked.

Lk. 12:49-53 DIVISION PREDICTED. "I have come to bring fire on the earth, and how I wish it were already kindled! But I have a baptism to undergo, and how distressed I am until it is completed! Do you think I came to bring peace on earth? No, I tell you, but division. From now on there will be five in one family divided against each other, three against two and two against three. They will be divided, father against son and son against father, mother against daughter and daughter against mother, mother-in-law against daughter-in-law and daughter-in-law against mother-in-law."

Lk. 12:54-59 TIMELY ACCEPTANCE URGED. He said to the crowd: "When you see a cloud rising in the west, immediately you say, 'It's going to rain,' and it does. And when the south wind blows, you say, 'It's going to be hot,' and it is. Hypocrites! You know how to interpret the appearance of the earth and the sky. How is it that you don't know how to interpret this present time?

"Why don't you judge for yourselves what is right? As you are going with your adversary to the magistrate, try hard to be reconciled to him on the way, or he may drag you off to the judge, and the judge turn you over to the officer, and the officer throw you into prison. I tell you, you will not get out until you have paid the last penny.ᵘ"

Lk. 13:1-5 URGENCY OF REPENTANCE. Now there were some present at that time who told Jesus about the Galileans whose blood Pilate had mixed with their sacrifices. Jesus answered, "Do you think that these Galileans were worse sinners than all the other Galileans because they suffered this way? I tell you, no! But unless you repent, you too will all perish. Or those eighteen who died when the tower in Siloam fell on them—do you think they were more guilty than all the others living in Jerusalem? I tell you, no! But unless you repent, you too will all perish."

ᵘGreek *lepton*

Lk.
13:6-9

UNFRUITFUL FIG TREE. Then he told this parable: "A man had a fig tree, planted in his vineyard, and he went to look for fruit on it, but did not find any. So he said to the man who took care of the vineyard, 'For three years now I've been coming to look for fruit on this fig tree and haven't found any. Cut it down! Why should it use up the soil?'

"'Sir,' the man replied, 'leave it alone for one more year, and I'll dig around it and fertilize it. If it bears fruit next year, fine! If not, then cut it down.'"

Lk.
13:10-17

STOOPED WOMAN HEALED. On a Sabbath Jesus was teaching in one of the synagogues, and a woman was there who had been crippled by a spirit for eighteen years. She was bent over and could not straighten up at all. When Jesus saw her, he called her forward and said to her, "Woman, you are set free from your infirmity." Then he put his hands on her, and immediately she straightened up and praised God.

Indignant because Jesus had healed on the Sabbath, the synagogue ruler said to the people, "There are six days for work. So come and be healed on those days, not on the Sabbath."

The Lord answered him, "You hypocrites! Doesn't each of you on the Sabbath untie his ox or donkey from the stall and lead it out to give it water? Then should not this woman, a daughter of Abraham, whom Satan has kept bound for eighteen long years, be set free on the Sabbath day from what bound her?"

When he said this, all his opponents were humiliated, but the people were delighted with all the wonderful things he was doing.

TODAY'S INSIGHTS

Confrontation

Are you, like most people, reluctant to "tell someone off"? Do you prefer to avoid conflict when possible? Even if there are times when you get angry at others, do you nevertheless shy away from confronting someone when he has done something wrong? Is your approach to religious, doctrinal, or lifestyle differences best described as "live and let live"? You may be on solid ground if you answered yes to those questions. Avoiding a quarrel is a godly trait. Loss of self-control and the angry use of the tongue are subject to condemnation throughout Scripture. Jesus himself said that we are to love our enemies.

But if all of this is true, how are we to explain the crunching confrontation between Jesus and his accusers? Jesus lashes out at hypocritical religionists with a fury uncharacteristic of the "Jesus, meek and gentle" about whom we sometimes sing.

While Jesus would tell us not to judge another person's motives, he himself does just that! Is such judgment proper for Jesus (and not for us) because he was the Son of God? Or is there more at stake? It does seem that his confrontations occur where the issues relate to broad-sweeping matters of principle rather than in response to offenses against him personally.

If those to whom he spoke in outrage were humiliated, it was not because Jesus was deliberately trying to humiliate them.

Jesus was calling them to responsibility. By their ignoring matters of justice while busying themselves with religiosity, the common folk were suffering at their expense. By imposing rules, rules, and more rules upon the people, they were standing in the way between the people and God. By selfishly hoarding the truths of God's Word to themselves, they were hiding the reassuring message of love from those who needed God's love.

Not everyone is called in the role of a prophet to speak out against injustice, religious hypocrisy, and doctrinal error. But all of us are called to defend against evil and to support what is good. Has someone in the office been stealing company property but everyone remains silent? Has a fellow student been cheating but no one says anything about it? Far from being un-Christlike, sometimes the loving thing is to confront another person, or a church fellowship, or an entire society. In view of what Jesus taught about God's righteous judgment, we owe it to others to be concerned about their eternal destiny. And they owe it to us as well. Now. Before it's too late. Before the Son of Man comes again unexpectedly.

Who is in a better position to confront the world about sin than ourselves—sinners who have accepted God's free gift of grace? The words of Jesus still ring clearly: "From everyone who has been given much, much will be demanded." Christlike confrontation— that is the issue. Are we willing to stand up for what Jesus taught? Forcefully, and in love?

DAY
11
WITH
JESUS

COMPARISON

hyperbole - extrava-
gant exageration
"will his re-
pearance"

Teaching Through Parables

BETWEEN THE MANY HEATED CONFRONTATIONS, JESUS CONTINUES to teach his disciples quietly concerning the kingdom of God. As the Great Teacher, Jesus uses numerous methods of instructing his disciples. He employs hyperbole, warnings, laments, and denunciations. He presents truth through beatitudes, proverbs, and dialogue. Of all his methods, however, perhaps the most interesting and distinctive mode of teaching is his use of parables. These illustrations of a moral truth or principle are usually in the form of a simple comparison. As often as not, Jesus' parables are comparisons with things either found in nature or known through human experience.

Although Jesus says the parables will have the effect of concealing truth, he must have in mind those hearers whose hearts are closed to his teaching. Most of the lessons are fairly simple to understand and especially well-suited for the common man, to whom Jesus directs his teaching.

Many parables are recorded by the Gospel writers throughout Jesus' ministry, but a particular series has been collected, principally by Matthew, which gives unique insight into Jesus' use of these simple illustrations.

Mt.
13:1-9
Mk.
4:1-9
Lk.
8:4-8
Sea of
Galilee

PARABLE OF THE SOWER. That same day Jesus went out of the house and sat by the lake. Such large crowds gathered around him that he got into a boat and sat in it, while all the people stood on the shore. Then he told them many things in parables, saying: "A farmer went out to sow his seed. As he was scattering the seed, some fell along the path, and the birds came and ate it up. Some fell on rocky places, where it did not have much soil. It sprang up quickly, because the soil was shallow. But when the sun came up, the plants were scorched, and they withered because they had no root. Other seed fell among thorns, which grew up and choked the plants. Still other seed fell on good soil, where it produced a crop—a hundred, sixty or thirty times what was sown. He who has ears, let him hear."

Mt.
13:10-17
Mk.
4:10-12
Lk. 8:9,10
PURPOSE OF PARABLES. The disciples came to him and asked, "Why do you speak to the people in parables?"

He replied, "The knowledge of the secrets of the kingdom of heaven has been given to you, but not to them. Whoever has will be given more, and he will have an abundance. Whoever does not have, even what he has will be taken from him. This is why I speak to them in parables:

"Though seeing, they do not see;
    though hearing, they do not hear or understand.

In them is fulfilled the prophecy of Isaiah:

"'You will be ever hearing but never understanding;
    you will be ever seeing but never perceiving.
For this people's heart has become calloused;
    they hardly hear with their ears,
    and they have closed their eyes.
Otherwise they might see with their eyes,
    hear with their ears,
        understand with their hearts
and turn, and I would heal them.'[v]

But blessed are your eyes because they see, and your ears because they hear. For I tell you the truth, many prophets and righteous men longed to see what you see but did not see it, and to hear what you hear but did not hear it.

Mt.
13:18-23
Mk.
4:13-20
Lk. 8:11-15
PARABLE OF SOWER EXPLAINED. "Listen then to what the parable of the sower means: When anyone hears the message about the kingdom and does not understand it, the evil one comes and snatches away what was sown in his heart. This is the seed sown along the path. The one who received the seed that fell on rocky places is the man who hears the word and at once receives it with joy. But since he has no root, he lasts only a short time. When trouble or persecution comes because of the word, he quickly falls away. The one who received the seed that fell among the thorns is the man who hears the word, but the worries of this life and the deceitfulness of wealth choke it, making it unfruitful. But the one who received the seed that fell on good soil is the man who hears the word and understands it. He produces a crop, yielding a hundred, sixty or thirty times what was sown."

[v]Isaiah 6:9,10

Mt.
13:24-30

PARABLE OF THE WEEDS. Jesus told them another parable: "The kingdom of heaven is like a man who sowed good seed in his field. But while everyone was sleeping, his enemy came and sowed weeds among the wheat, and went away. When the wheat sprouted and formed heads, then the weeds also appeared.

"The owner's servants came to him and said, 'Sir, didn't you sow good seed in your field? Where then did the weeds come from?'

"'An enemy did this,' he replied.

"The servants asked him, 'Do you want us to go and pull them up?'

"'No,' he answered, 'because while you are pulling the weeds, you may root up the wheat with them. Let both grow together until the harvest. At that time I will tell the harvesters: First collect the weeds and tie them in bundles to be burned; then gather the wheat and bring it into my barn.'"

Mt.
13:36-43

PARABLE OF THE WEEDS EXPLAINED. Then he left the crowd and went into the house. His disciples came to him and said, "Explain to us the parable of the weeds in the field."

He answered, "The one who sowed the good seed is the Son of Man. The field is the world, and the good seed stands for the sons of the kingdom. The weeds are the sons of the evil one, and the enemy who sows them is the devil. The harvest is the end of the age, and the harvesters are angels.

"As the weeds are pulled up and burned in the fire, so it will be at the end of the age. The Son of Man will send out his angels, and they will weed out of his kingdom everything that causes sin and all who do evil. They will throw them into the fiery furnace, where there will be weeping and gnashing of teeth. Then the righteous will shine like the sun in the kingdom of their Father. He who has ears, let him hear."

Mk.
4:21-25
Lk.
8:16-18

PARABLE OF THE LIGHTED LAMP. He said to them, "Do you bring in a lamp to put it under a bowl or a bed? Instead, don't you put it on its stand? For whatever is hidden is meant to be disclosed, and whatever is concealed is meant to be brought out into the open. If anyone has ears to hear, let him hear.

"Consider carefully what you hear," he continued. "With the measure you use, it will be measured to you—and even more. Whoever has will be given more; whoever does not have, even what he has will be taken from him."

Mk.
4:26-29

PARABLE OF THE SEED GROWING. He also said, "This is what the kingdom of God is like. A man scatters seed on the ground. Night and day, whether he sleeps or gets up, the seed sprouts and grows, though he does not know how. All by itself the soil produces grain—first the stalk, then the head, then the full kernel in the head. As soon as the grain is ripe, he puts the sickle to it, because the harvest has come."

Mt.
13:31,32
Mk.
4:30-32
Lk.
13:18,19

PARABLE OF THE MUSTARD SEED. He told them another parable: "The kingdom of heaven is like a mustard seed, which a man took and planted in his field. Though it is the smallest of all your seeds, yet when it grows, it is the largest of garden plants and becomes a tree, so that the birds of the air come and perch in its branches."

Mt.
13:33
Lk.
13:20,21

PARABLE OF THE YEAST. He told them still another parable: "The kingdom of heaven is like yeast that a woman took and mixed into a large amount[w] of flour until it worked all through the dough."

Mt.
13:44

PARABLE OF HIDDEN TREASURE. "The kingdom of heaven is like treasure hidden in a field. When a man found it, he hid it again, and then in his joy went and sold all he had and bought that field.

Mt.
13:45,46

PARABLE OF VALUABLE PEARL. "Again, the kingdom of heaven is like a merchant looking for fine pearls. When he found one of great value, he went away and sold everything he had and bought it.

Mt.
13:47-50

PARABLE OF THE NET. "Once again, the kingdom of heaven is like a net that was let down into the lake and caught all kinds of fish. When it was full, the fishermen pulled it up on the shore. Then they sat down and collected the good fish in baskets, but threw the bad away. This is how it will be at the end of the age. The angels will come and separate the wicked from the righteous and throw them into the fiery furnace, where there will be weeping and gnashing of teeth.

[w]Greek *three satas* (probably about ½ bushel or 22 liters)

| Mt.
13:51,52 | PARABLE OF TREASURES. "Have you understood all these things?" Jesus asked.

"Yes," they replied.

He said to them, "Therefore every teacher of the law who has been instructed about the kingdom of heaven is like the owner of a house who brings out of his storeroom new treasures as well as old." |

| Mt.
13:34,35
Mk.
4:33,34 | PARABLES FULFILL PROPHECY. MkWith many similar parables Jesus spoke the word to them, as much as they could understand. He did not say anything to them without using a parable. But when he was alone with his own disciples, he explained everything. MtSo was fulfilled what was spoken through the prophet: |

> "I will open my mouth in parables,
> I will utter things hidden since the creation of
> the world."[x]

TODAY'S INSIGHTS

Comparison

Who was the best teacher you ever had? Or the best preacher you ever heard? Can you remember anything that distinguished him and made him special? It may have been his humor, or his care for students or an audience. Perhaps it was his enthusiasm about the lessons or messages he shared. If it was the clarity with which he taught, the chances are good that he used helpful illustrations. Illustrations are bridges from the known to the unknown. They are mental matchmakers, introducing old understandings to new understandings. In his use of parables, Jesus knew the value of illustration and comparison. He was, after all, the Master Teacher.

Yet isn't it odd that Jesus suggested his parables would not be readily understood by all his listeners? Indeed, isn't it odd that even his disciples needed detailed explanations for some of the parables? How could such simple stories be misunderstood? Jesus said that simple teachings have a way of helping some but acting as a stumbling block to others, depending on the attitude with which they hear the story.

[x]Psalm 78:2

To the person of pride and scholarship, sometimes a simple lesson is lost in the subterranean wasteland lying far below his elevated dignity. To the simpleminded, sometimes a profound application is lost in the very simplicity of the story. Simple is all he sees. But for those who are humble enough to accept simple comparisons, and for those who are wise enough to look beyond the obvious, Jesus' parables are a source of great truth and insight.

In modern times, when the economy is based on urban industry and commerce rather than on rural agriculture, Jesus' comparisons may hit home with less force. Today we know little about sowing and reaping. But who could miss the point in any event, except perhaps those who *want* to miss the point! And isn't that the lesson of the sower? The seed of God's Word sometimes falls on hearts that don't care to hear what God has to say. Sometimes it falls on hearts that fully understand what God wants in their lives but cannot take root because the heart is more inclined toward materialistic concerns.

The beauty of the parables is found in the unity between what we can observe in God's wonderful creation and what we are striving to know about the spiritual realm. For anyone seeking truth and understanding, God has given endless natural illustrations.

The ultimate comparison, of course, is Jesus Christ himself. Have you ever thought about Jesus' life itself as being a parable? By comparing our life with his, we know the direction in which we ought to proceed. Hearing him, we can hear the voice of God for our own lives. Seeing him, we can perceive the wonderful meaning and purpose of our existence. What a source of spiritual strength—Jesus, the *living* Word!

DAY
12
WITH
JESUS

DEMONSTRATION

Performing Miracles

IT IS ONE THING FOR A MAN TO TEACH WHAT HE CLAIMS IS TRUTH; it is quite another thing to demonstrate one's authority to claim that truth. That is why the miracles which Jesus performs are such a vital part of his ministry. They are not being performed merely to entertain, or to show off his divine power, or even to convince the skeptical. Nor does Jesus heal the sick and raise the dead simply because of his great compassion for those who suffer.

More than this, the miracles are a means of confirming the message that the kingdom of God is now being established with power! God is establishing his rule through Christ, and proving it with the miraculous power which Jesus exercises over the forces of nature, over the spirit world, and over death and disease. Mark's account takes Jesus from his teaching in parables and follows him throughout Galilee as he confirms the authority of his teaching with miraculous works.

Mt.
8:18-22
Lk.
9:57-62

CHALLENGING FOLLOWERS. ^{Mt}When Jesus saw the crowd around him, he gave orders to cross to the other side of the lake. Then a teacher of the law came to him and said, "Teacher, I will follow you wherever you go." ^{Lk}Jesus replied, "Foxes have holes and birds of the air have nests, but the Son of Man has no place to lay his head."

He said to another man, "Follow me."

But the man replied, "Lord, first let me go and bury my father."

Jesus said to him, "Let the dead bury their own dead, but you go and proclaim the kingdom of God."

Still another said, "I will follow you, Lord; but first let me go back and say good-by to my family."

Jesus replied, "No one who puts his hand to the plow and looks back is fit for service in the kingdom of God."

Mt.
8:23-27
Mk.
4:35-41
Lk.
8:22-25
Sea of
Galilee

JESUS CALMS THE SEA. That day when evening came, he said to his disciples, "Let us go over to the other side." Leaving the crowd behind, they took him along, just as he was, in the boat. There were also other boats with him. A furious squall came up, and the waves broke over the boat, so that it was nearly swamped. Jesus was in the stern, sleeping on a cushion. The disciples woke him and said to him, "Teacher, don't you care if we drown?"

He got up, rebuked the wind and said to the waves, "Quiet! Be still!" Then the wind died down and it was completely calm.

He said to his disciples, "Why are you so afraid? Do you still have no faith?"

They were terrified and asked each other, "Who is this? Even the wind and the waves obey him!"

Mt.
8:28-34
Mk.
5:1-20
Lk.
8:26-39
Gerasa

DEMON-POSSESSED GERASENE. They went across the lake to the region of the Gerasenes.ʸ When Jesus got out of the boat, a man with an evilᶻ spirit came from the tombs to meet him. This man lived in the tombs, and no one could bind him any more, not even with a chain. For he had often been chained hand and foot, but he tore the chains apart and broke the irons on his feet. No one was strong enough to subdue him. Night and day among the tombs and in the hills he would cry out and cut himself with stones.

When he saw Jesus from a distance, he ran and fell on his knees in front of him. He shouted at the top of his voice, "What do you want with me, Jesus, Son of the Most High God? Swear to God that you won't torture me!" For Jesus had said to him, "Come out of this man, you evil spirit!"

Then Jesus asked him, "What is your name?"

"My name is Legion," he replied, "for we are many." And he begged Jesus again and again not to send them out of the area.

A large herd of pigs was feeding on the nearby hillside. The demons begged Jesus, "Send us among the pigs; allow us to go into them." He gave them permission, and the evil spirits came out and went into the pigs. The herd, about two thousand in number, rushed down the steep bank into the lake and were drowned.

ʸSome manuscripts *Gadarenes*; other manuscripts *Gergesenes*   ᶻGreek *unclean*

Those tending the pigs ran off and reported this in the town and countryside, and the people went out to see what had happened. When they came to Jesus, they saw the man who had been possessed by the legion of demons, sitting there, dressed and in his right mind; and they were afraid. Those who had seen it told the people what had happened to the demon-possessed man—and told about the pigs as well. Then the people began to plead with Jesus to leave their region.

As Jesus was getting into the boat, the man who had been demon-possessed begged to go with him. Jesus did not let him, but said, "Go home to your family and tell them how much the Lord has done for you, and how he has had mercy on you." So the man went away and began to tell in the Decapolis[a] how much Jesus had done for him. And all the people were amazed.

Mt. 9:18,19
Mk. 5:21-24a
Lk. 8:40-42

JAIRUS BEGS JESUS TO HEAL. When Jesus had again crossed over by boat to the other side of the lake, a large crowd gathered around him while he was by the lake. Then one of the synagogue rulers, named Jairus, came there. Seeing Jesus, he fell at his feet and pleaded earnestly with him, "My little daughter is dying. Please come and put your hands on her so that she will be healed and live." So Jesus went with him.

Mt. 9:20-22
Mk. 5:24b-34
Lk. 8:43-48

WOMAN TOUCHES GARMENT. A large crowd followed and pressed around him. And a woman was there who had been subject to bleeding for twelve years. She had suffered a great deal under the care of many doctors and had spent all she had, yet instead of getting better she grew worse. When she heard about Jesus, she came up behind him in the crowd and touched his cloak, because she thought, "If I just touch his clothes, I will be healed." Immediately her bleeding stopped and she felt in her body that she was freed from her suffering.

At once Jesus realized that power had gone out from him. He turned around in the crowd and asked, "Who touched my clothes?"

"You see the people crowding against you," his disciples answered, "and yet you can ask, 'Who touched me?'"

But Jesus kept looking around to see who had done it. Then the woman, knowing what had happened to her, came and

[a]That is, the Ten Cities

fell at his feet and, trembling with fear, told him the whole truth. He said to her, "Daughter, your faith has healed you. Go in peace and be freed from your suffering."

Mt.
9:23-26
Mk.
5:35-43
Lk.
8:49-56
Caper-
naum

JAIRUS' DAUGHTER RAISED. While Jesus was still speaking, some men came from the house of Jairus, the synagogue ruler. "Your daughter is dead," they said. "Why bother the teacher any more?"

Ignoring what they said, Jesus told the synagogue ruler, "Don't be afraid; just believe."

He did not let anyone follow him except Peter, James and John the brother of James. When they came to the home of the synagogue ruler, Jesus saw a commotion, with people crying and wailing loudly. He went in and said to them, "Why all this commotion and wailing? The child is not dead but asleep." But they laughed at him.

After he put them all out, he took the child's father and mother and the disciples who were with him, and went in where the child was. He took her by the hand and said to her, *"Talitha koum!"* (which means, "Little girl, I say to you, get up!"). Immediately the girl stood up and walked around (she was twelve years old). At this they were completely astonished. He gave strict orders not to let anyone know about this, and told them to give her something to eat.

Mt.
9:27-31

TWO BLIND MEN HEALED. As Jesus went on from there, two blind men followed him, calling out, "Have mercy on us, Son of David!"

When he had gone indoors, the blind men came to him, and he asked them, "Do you believe that I am able to do this?"

"Yes, Lord," they replied.

Then he touched their eyes and said, "According to your faith will it be done to you"; and their sight was restored. Jesus warned them sternly, "See that no one knows about this." But they went out and spread the news about him all over that region.

Mt.
9:32-34

MUTE MADE TO SPEAK. While they were going out, a man who was demon-possessed and could not talk was brought to Jesus. And when the demon was driven out, the man who had been mute spoke. The crowd was amazed and said, "Nothing like this has ever been seen in Israel."

But the Pharisees said, "It is by the prince of demons that he drives out demons."

| Mt. 13:53-58 Mk. 6:1-6a Nazareth | JESUS REJECTED AGAIN. Jesus left there and went to his hometown, accompanied by his disciples. When the Sabbath came, he began to teach in the synagogue, and many who heard him were amazed. |

"Where did this man get these things?" they asked, "What's this wisdom that has been given him, that he even does miracles! Isn't this the carpenter? Isn't this Mary's son and the brother of James, Joseph,[b] Judas and Simon? Aren't his sisters here with us?" And they took offense at him.

Jesus said to them, "Only in his hometown, among his relatives and in his own house is a prophet without honor." He could not do any miracles there, except lay his hands on a few sick people and heal them. And he was amazed at their lack of faith.

TODAY'S INSIGHTS

Demonstration

Do you believe in miracles? Can you perform miracles? If not, are there people today who can? Certainly many claim that power, and many more claim they have been the recipients of miraculous power exercised on their behalf. Some claim miraculous power in the name of Jesus Christ, while others claim to be able to achieve supernatural feats through the exercise of mind over matter.

Whatever might be the truth about miracles today, can anyone come anywhere close to demonstrating the power over nature which Jesus had? If there are those today who believe they are able to make the blind to see, the deaf to hear, and the mute to talk, is there anyone who can show proof of bringing someone back from the dead? Not simply on the operating table, but *days* following the person's death (as soon will be seen)? The ability to do that puts Jesus in a category all his own. And what about calming rough ocean waves? Has anyone been able to do that since Jesus calmed the sea? With his disciples, we too must exclaim, "Who is this that even the waves obey him!"

[b]Greek *Joses*, a variant of *Joseph*

Any miraculous gifts that God may give to his disciples in the furtherance of his ministry are far overshadowed by the power of Jesus Christ. And that is for a reason. Jesus' unique power demonstrates his unique lordship. His divine power excels all other power, whether economic, political, atomic, or demonic. There is none like him in heaven or on earth.

But to what purpose are we to know this fact? Merely to affirm that we have a powerful God? His creation alone should tell us that. To seek miraculous power for ourselves? The apostle Paul would later warn us that self-interest has an insidious way of getting involved in the exercise of spiritual gifts.

Jesus' miracles were, first and foremost, a demonstration of his *truth*, because in his *truth* there is the power to change lives. What good is it to raise a person from the dead if his soul remains spiritually dead? What good is it to exorcise a demon from a man's body if you can give him no truth to fill the void? Why give a man sight without insight? Why hearing without understanding?

Can you perform miracles? There's no doubt about it. Each of us can be an instrument in the miraculous changing of lives. It will not be through our own power, of course, but through the power of the Holy Spirit, working and renewing, transforming and liberating.

Through godly lives and the sharing of the Word, we can show others the power of God and the way to Christ. We can help the fearful to "touch the hem of his garment." We can bring Jesus to those who are spiritually dying. We can open the eyes of the spiritually blind and watch them leap for joy at their new understanding of life's meaning.

What miracle will happen because of you today?

COMMISSION

Sending Out Apostles

AFTER HIS SECOND REJECTION IN HIS HOMETOWN OF NAZARETH, Jesus gains renewed encouragement as he is met by crowds in other parts of Galilee. Keenly aware of their need for spiritual guidance, Jesus calls for those who are willing to work among the multitudes for the sake of his kingdom. The time is especially appropriate, then, for sending out the 12 apostles on a special mission of teaching and performing miracles with the power he gives them. He warns them that they, like all who would work in the Lord's name, will be persecuted and will face the need for sacrifice.

Perhaps for that reason, or perhaps to provide a stronger witness of his messiahship, Jesus sends the apostles out in pairs. Interestingly, Jesus does not appear to place particular emphasis on organization, methods of evangelism, or academic religious training. The 12 apostles are mostly of simple education, but the power of Christ is with them.

As the apostles are away carrying out their mission, Jesus will hear that John the Baptist has been put to death by Herod.

Mt. 9:35-38 Mk. 6:6b	NEED FOR WORKERS. Jesus went through all the towns and villages, teaching in their synagogues, preaching the good news of the kingdom and healing every disease and sickness. When he saw the crowds, he had compassion on them, because they were harassed and helpless, like sheep without a shepherd. Then he said to his disciples, "The harvest is plentiful but the workers are few. Ask the Lord of the harvest, therefore, to send out workers into his harvest field."
Mt. 10:1-4 Mk. 6:7 Lk. 9:1,2	APOSTLES GIVEN POWER TO HEAL. MkCalling the Twelve to him, he sent them out two by two...Mtand gave them authority to drive out evilc spirits and to heal every disease and sickness.

cGreek unclean

119

Mt.
10:5-15
Mk.
6:8-11
Lk.
9:3-5

APOSTLES INSTRUCTED. These twelve Jesus sent out with the following instructions: "Do not go among the Gentiles or enter any town of the Samaritans. Go rather to the lost sheep of Israel. As you go, preach this message: 'The kingdom of heaven is near.' Heal the sick, raise the dead, cleanse those who have leprosy,[d] drive out demons. Freely you have received, freely give. Do not take along any gold or silver or copper in your belts; take no bag for the journey, or extra tunic, or sandals or a staff; for the worker is worth his keep.

"Whatever town or village you enter, search for some worthy person there and stay at his house until you leave. As you enter the home, give it your greeting. If the home is deserving, let your peace rest on it; if it is not, let your peace return to you. If anyone will not welcome you or listen to your words, shake the dust off your feet when you leave that home or town. I tell you the truth, it will be more bearable for Sodom and Gomorrah on the day of judgment than for that town.

Mt.
10:16-33

APOSTLES WARNED. I am sending you out like sheep among wolves. Therefore be as shrewd as snakes and as innocent as doves.

"Be on your guard against men; they will hand you over to the local councils and flog you in their synagogues. On my account you will be brought before governors and kings as witnesses to them and to the Gentiles. But when they arrest you, do not worry about what to say or how to say it. At that time you will be given what to say, for it will not be you speaking, but the Spirit of your Father speaking through you.

"Brother will betray brother to death, and a father his child; children will rebel against their parents and have them put to death. All men will hate you because of me, but he who stands firm to the end will be saved. When you are persecuted in one place, flee to another. I tell you the truth, you will not finish going through the cities of Israel before the Son of Man comes.

"A student is not above his teacher, nor a servant above his master. It is enough for the student to be like his teacher, and the servant like his master. If the head of the house has been called Beelzebub,[e] how much more the members of his household!

[d]The Greek word was used for various diseases affecting the skin—not necessarily leprosy. [e]Greek *Beezeboul* or *Beelzeboul*

"So do not be afraid of them. There is nothing concealed that will not be disclosed, or hidden that will not be made known. What I tell you in the dark, speak in the daylight; what is whispered in your ear, proclaim from the roofs. Do not be afraid of those who kill the body but cannot kill the soul. Rather, be afraid of the One who can destroy both soul and body in hell. Are not two sparrows sold for a penny[f]? Yet not one of them will fall to the ground apart from the will of your Father. And even the very hairs of your head are all numbered. So don't be afraid; you are worth more than many sparrows.

"Whoever acknowledges me before men, I will also acknowledge him before my Father in heaven. But whoever disowns me before men, I will disown him before my Father in heaven.

Mt. 10:34-39

CONFLICT AND SACRIFICE. "Do not suppose that I have come to bring peace to the earth. I did not come to bring peace, but a sword. For I have come to turn

"'a man against his father,
  a daughter against her mother,
  a daughter-in-law against her mother-in-law—
  a man's enemies will be the members of his own
    household.'[g]

"Anyone who loves his father or mother more than me is not worthy of me; anyone who loves his son or daughter more than me is not worthy of me; and anyone who does not take his cross and follow me is not worthy of me. Whoever finds his life will lose it, and whoever loses his life for my sake will find it.

Mt. 10:40-42

RECEIVING APOSTLES. "He who receives you receives me, and he who receives me receives the one who sent me. Anyone who receives a prophet because he is a prophet will receive a prophet's reward, and anyone who receives a righteous man because he is a righteous man will receive a righteous man's reward. And if anyone gives even a cup of cold water to one of these little ones because he is my disciple, I tell you the truth, he will certainly not lose his reward."

[f]Greek an assarion   [g]Micah 7:6

Mt.
11:1
Mk.
6:12,13
Lk. 9:6

APOSTLES IN ACTION. ^{Mt}After Jesus had finished instructing his twelve disciples, he went on from there to teach and preach in the towns of Galilee.^h ^{Lk}So they set out and went from village to village, preaching the gospel and healing people everywhere.

Mt.
14:1,2
Mk.
6:14-16
Lk.
9:7-9
Perea

HEROD CURIOUS ABOUT JESUS. ^{Mk}King Herod heard about this, for Jesus' name had become well known. Some were saying,ⁱ "John the Baptist has been raised from the dead, and that is why miraculous powers are at work in him."

Others said, "He is Elijah."

And still others claimed, "He is a prophet, like one of the prophets of long ago."

But when Herod heard this, he said, "John, the man I beheaded, has been raised from the dead!" ^{Lk}..."I beheaded John. Who, then, is this I hear such things about?" And he tried to see him.

Mt.
14:3-12a
Mk.
6:17-29

DEATH OF JOHN THE BAPTIST. ^{Mk}For Herod himself had given orders to have John arrested, and he had him bound and put in prison. He did this because of Herodias, his brother Philip's wife, whom he had married. For John had been saying to Herod, "It is not lawful for you to have your brother's wife." So Herodias nursed a grudge against John and wanted to kill him. But she was not able to, because Herod feared John and protected him, knowing him to be a righteous and holy man. When Herod heard John, he was greatly puzzled^j; yet he liked to listen to him.

Finally the opportune time came. On his birthday Herod gave a banquet for his high officials and military commanders and the leading men of Galilee. When the daughter of Herodias came in and danced, she pleased Herod and his dinner guests.

The king said to the girl, "Ask me for anything you want, and I'll give it to you," And he promised her with an oath, "Whatever you ask I will give you, up to half my kingdom."

She went out and said to her mother, "What shall I ask for?"

"The head of John the Baptist," she answered.

^hGreek *in their towns*   ⁱSome early manuscripts *He was saying*   ^jSome early manuscripts *he did many things*

At once the girl hurried in to the king with the request: "I want you to give me right now the head of John the Baptist on a platter."

The king was greatly distressed, but because of his oaths and his dinner guests, he did not want to refuse her. So he immediately sent an executioner with orders to bring John's head. The man went, beheaded John in the prison, and brought back his head on a platter. He presented it to the girl, and she gave it to her mother. [Mt]John's disciples came and took his body and buried it.

Mt.
14:12b,13
Mk.
6:30-33
Lk.
9:10,11a
Jn. 6:1

APOSTLES RETURN AND REPORT. [Lk]When the apostles returned, they reported to Jesus what they had done. [Mk]Then, because so many people were coming and going that they did not even have a chance to eat, he said to them, "Come with me by yourselves to a quiet place and get some rest."

So they went away by themselves in a boat...[Jn]to the far shore of the Sea of Galilee (that is, the Sea of Tiberias), [Mk]to a solitary place. But many who saw them leaving recognized them and ran on foot from all the towns and got there ahead of them.

TODAY'S INSIGHTS

Commission

Do you feel a sense of mission in your life? Is there something special you are supposed to accomplish before you die? Not everyone can be a special ambassador for Christ (as the apostle Paul would later become), or even one of the original 12 whom Jesus chose as his specially designated messengers to the world.

Perhaps we have no special appointment with destiny. But don't you ever wonder how God is using you through your life? Don't you feel as if there surely must be some mission, some special purpose for your existence?

Jesus seems to agree with such a feeling when he looks with compassion on the millions of spiritually empty people in the world who go about like lost sheep searching desperately for a shepherd to lead them—somewhere, anywhere, to anything.

Changing the metaphor, Jesus says the harvest is so plentiful that all available hands are welcome. If the mission is unlimited, so is the need for people who understand that mission and want to be a part of it. Have you ever thought of yourself as a missionary? "Freely you have received, freely give."

But the mission is not without risks. There is personal rejection just around the corner—perhaps ridicule, even abuse. Around the sheep lurk many wolves of discouragement, doubt, and fear. Ours is by no means a mission impossible, but neither are we assured of instant or lasting success.

And are we to assume that the mission is always, in every case, evangelism? Perhaps in some cases it is the lawyer who makes a corrupt and inefficient legal system more just and fair for the forgotten people in society. Perhaps it is the scientist who discovers an elusive cure, or the grocery clerk whose exemplary life permits him to be a spiritual shepherd in his local congregation.

The highest calling of all may be the mother who raises her children in the nurture and admonition of the Lord. Who knows the impact of one Christian mother! And fathers are not left out in that regard. Did not Jesus send out his disciples two by two?

When God gave us life and breath, he commissioned us to be his messengers to the world. When we became Christians we eagerly accepted that commission. Have we stopped to think about our mission lately? Do we really understand how giving up our lives in his service will result in truly fulfilled lives?

What will we do today in carrying out what God has planned for us to do? Will anyone give us a cup of cold water in appreciation for our having brought spiritual refreshment his or her way?

The rewards of Christian service are often great, though by no means assured. Yet even if we are unrewarded in this life, we have Jesus' own invitation to his faithful disciples: "Come with me by yourselves to a quiet place and get some rest."

DAY
14
WITH
JESUS

NOURISHMENT

Miracles and Multitudes

AS HIS MINISTRY NEARS ITS SECOND YEAR, JESUS REACHES A PEAK of popularity among the multitudes. He amazes a crowd of over 5000 by feeding them all, using just a few loaves of bread and some fish. Upon that demonstration they are ready to make him king, but of course they have misunderstood the nature of his kingdom. When Jesus says that he is the true bread of life and that they must eat his flesh, many are offended and turn away. They can accept Jesus as a popular hero who works wonders, but they are unwilling to accept the demands of discipleship.

Jesus continues his dialogue with the Pharisees, pointing out the danger of legalism, especially regarding traditional doctrinal rules which are not a part of the law. Naturally, Jesus' condemnation of their institutionalized religion, as well as his threat to their political power base, evokes their hostility. Opposition in Judea grows to such a point that the political and religious leaders there are seeking to kill Jesus. Therefore Jesus remains in Galilee for a while longer, apparently not even leaving to attend the Passover Feast in Jerusalem, which takes place during this time.

Despite his opposition, what is so impressive about Jesus is the extent to which he has won the hearts of the common people. The prophets of old had also preached righteousness and brought judgment against false religious leaders, but none of them ever had the popular following of Jesus. Which of the prophets could match Jesus' insight? Which of the prophets could approach Jesus' personal righteousness? And which of the prophets did the people want to make their king? This Jesus is not just another prophet, but rather the Messiah about whom all the other prophets have prophesied.

Mt. 14:14 Mk. 6:34 Lk. 9:11b Jn. 6:2-4	JESUS TEACHES MULTITUDE. MkWhen Jesus landed and saw a large crowd, he had compassion on them, because they were like sheep without a shepherd. So he began teaching

127

them many things. LkHe welcomed them and spoke to them about the kingdom of God, and healed those who needed healing. JnThe Jewish Passover Feast was near.

[Third Passover April, A.D. 29] Mt. 14:15-21 Mk. 6:35-44 Lk. 9:12-17 Jn. 6:5-14

FIVE THOUSAND FED. MkBy this time it was late in the day, so his disciples came to him "This is a remote place," they said, "and it's already very late. Send the people away so they can go to the surrounding countryside and villages and buy themselves something to eat." JnWhen Jesus looked up and saw a great crowd coming toward him, he said to Philip, "Where shall we buy bread for these people to eat?" He asked this only to test him, for he already had in mind what he was going to do.

Philip answered him, "Eight months' wagesk would not buy enough bread for each one to have a bite!"

Another of his disciples, Andrew, Simon Peter's brother, spoke up, "Here is a boy with five small barley loaves and two small fish, but how far will they go among so many?" MkThen Jesus directed them to have all the people sit down in groups on the green grass. So they sat down in groups of hundreds and fifties. Taking the five loaves and the two fish and looking up to heaven, he gave thanks and broke the loaves. Then he gave them to his disciples to set before the people. He also divided the two fish among them all. They all ate and were satisfied, and the disciples picked up twelve basketfuls of broken pieces of bread and fish. The number of the men who had eaten was five thousand. JnAfter the people saw the miraculous sign that Jesus did, they began to say, "Surely this is the Prophet who is to come into the world."

Mt. 14:22,23a Mk. 6:45,46 Jn. 6:15-17a

KINGSHIP AVOIDED. MkImmediately Jesus made his disciples get into the boat and go on ahead of him to Bethsaida, while he dismissed the crowd. JnJesus, knowing that they intended to come and make him king by force, withdrew again to a mountain by himself.

Mt. 14:23b-27 Mk. 6:47-50 Jn. 6:17b-21

JESUS WALKS ON WATER. JnBy now it was dark, and Jesus had not yet joined them. A strong wind was blowing and the waters grew rough. MkHe saw the disciples straining at the oars, because the wind was against them. About the fourth

kGreek two hundred denarii

watch of the night he went out to them, walking on the lake. JnWhen they had rowed three or three and a half miles[j], they saw Jesus approaching the boat, walking on the water…MkHe was about to pass by them, but when they saw him walking on the lake, they thought he was a ghost. They cried out, because they all saw him and were terrified.

Immediately he spoke to them and said, "Take courage! It is I. Don't be afraid."

Mt. 14:28-33 Mk. 6:51,52 Sea of Galilee	PETER WALKS ON WATER. Mt"Lord, if it's you," Peter replied, "tell me to come to you on the water."

"Come," he said.

Then Peter got down out of the boat, walked on the water and came toward Jesus. But when he saw the wind, he was afraid and, beginning to sink, cried out, "Lord, save me!"

Immediately Jesus reached out his hand and caught him. "You of little faith," he said, "why did you doubt?"

And when they climbed into the boat, the wind died down. MkThey were completely amazed, for they had not understood about the loaves; their hearts were hardened. MtThen those who were in the boat worshiped him, saying, "Truly you are the Son of God."

Mt. 14:34-36 Mk. 6:53-56 Plain of Gennesaret	MIRACLES AT GENNESARET. When they had crossed over, they landed at Gennesaret and anchored there. As soon as they got out of the boat, people recognized Jesus. They ran throughout that whole region and carried the sick on mats to wherever they heard he was. And wherever he went—into villages, towns or countryside—they placed the sick in the marketplaces. They begged him to let them touch even the edge of his cloak, and all who touched him were healed.

Jn. 6:22-24	JESUS' CROSSING IS MYSTERY. The next day the crowd that had stayed on the opposite shore of the lake realized that only one boat had been there, and that Jesus had not entered it with his disciples, but that they had gone away alone. Then some boats from Tiberias landed near the place where the people had eaten the bread after the Lord had given thanks. Once the crowd realized that neither Jesus nor his disciples were there, they got into the boats and went to Capernaum in search of Jesus.

[j]Greek rowed twenty-five or thirty stadia (about 5 or 6 kilometers)

Jn.
6:25-40
Caper-
naum
DISCOURSE ON BREAD OF LIFE. When they found him on the other side of the lake, they asked him, "Rabbi, when did you get here?"

Jesus answered, "I tell you the truth, you are looking for me, not because you saw miraculous signs but because you ate the loaves and had your fill. Do not work for food that spoils, but for food that endures to eternal life, which the Son of Man will give you. On him God the Father has placed his seal of approval."

Then they asked him, "What must we do to do the works God requires?"

Jesus answered, "The work of God is this: to believe in the one he has sent."

So they asked him, "What miraculous sign then will you give that we may see it and believe you? What will you do? Our forefathers ate the manna in the desert; as it is written: 'He gave them bread from heaven to eat.'*m*"

Jesus said to them, "I tell you the truth, it is not Moses who has given you the bread from heaven, but it is my Father who gives you the true bread from heaven. For the bread of God is he who comes down from heaven and gives life to the world."

"Sir," they said, "from now on give us this bread."

Then Jesus declared, "I am the bread of life. He who comes to me will never go hungry, and he who believes in me will never be thirsty. But as I told you, you have seen me and still you do not believe. All that the Father gives me will come to me, and whoever comes to me I will never drive away. For I have come down from heaven not to do my will but to do the will of him who sent me. And this is the will of him who sent me, that I shall lose none of all that he has given me, but raise them up at the last day. For my Father's will is that everyone who looks to the Son and believes in him shall have eternal life, and I will raise him up at the last day."

Jn.
6:41-51
JEWS CHALLENGE JESUS' CLAIM. At this the Jews began to grumble about him because he said, "I am the bread that came down from heaven." They said, "Is this not Jesus, the son of Joseph, whose father and mother we know? How can he now say, 'I came down from heaven'?"

---

*m*Exodus 16:4; Neh. 9:15; Psalm 78:24,25

"Stop grumbling among yourselves," Jesus answered. "No one can come to me unless the Father who sent me draws him, and I will raise him up at the last day. It is written in the Prophets: 'They will all be taught by God.'[n] Everyone who listens to the Father and learns from him comes to me. No one has seen the Father except the one who is from God; only he has seen the Father. I tell you the truth, he who believes has everlasting life. I am the bread of life. Your forefathers ate the manna in the desert, yet they died. But here is the bread that comes down from heaven, which a man may eat and not die. I am the living bread that came down from heaven. If anyone eats of this bread, he will live forever. This bread is my flesh, which I will give for the life of the world."

Jn.
6:52-59

JEWS QUESTION EATING FLESH. Then the Jews began to argue sharply among themselves, "How can this man give us his flesh to eat?"

Jesus said to them "I tell you the truth, unless you eat the flesh of the Son of Man and drink his blood, you have no life in you. Whoever eats my flesh and drinks my blood has eternal life, and I will raise him up at the last day. For my flesh is real food and my blood is real drink. Whoever eats my flesh and drinks my blood remains in me, and I in him. Just as the living Father sent me and I live because of the Father, so the one who feeds on me will live because of me. This is the bread that came down from heaven. Your forefathers ate manna and died, but he who feeds on this bread will live forever." He said this while teaching in the synagogue in Capernaum. *metaphor*

Jn.
6:60-66

OFFENDED DISCIPLES TURN AWAY. On hearing it, many of his disciples said, "This is a hard teaching. Who can accept it?"

Aware that his disciples were grumbling about this, Jesus said to them, "Does this offend you? What if you see the Son of Man ascend to where he was before! The Spirit gives life; the flesh counts for nothing. The words I have spoken to you are spirit[o] and they are life. Yet there are some of you who do not believe." For Jesus had known from the beginning which of them did not believe and who would betray him. He went on

[n]Isaiah 54:13   [o]Or Spirit

to say, "This is why I told you that no one can come to me unless the Father has enabled him."

From this time many of his disciples turned back and no longer followed him.

Jn
6:67-71
Caper-
naum

PETER AFFIRMS FAITH. "You do not want to leave too, do you?" Jesus asked the Twelve.

Simon Peter answered him, "Lord, to whom shall we go? You have the words of eternal life. We believe and know that you are the Holy One of God."

Then Jesus replied, "Have I not chosen you, the Twelve? Yet one of you is a devil!" (He meant Judas, the son of Simon Iscariot, who, though one of the Twelve, was later to betray him.)

Mt.
15:1-9
Mk.
7:1-13
(Spring,
A.D. 29)

TRADITION CONDEMNED. The Pharisees and some of the teachers of the law who had come from Jerusalem gathered around Jesus and saw some of his disciples eating food with hands that were "unclean," that is, unwashed. (The Pharisees and all the Jews do not eat unless they give their hands a ceremonial washing, holding to the tradition of the elders. When they come from the marketplace they do not eat unless they wash. And they observe many other traditions, such as the washing of cups, pitchers and kettles.ᵖ)

So the Pharisees and teachers of the law asked Jesus, "Why don't your disciples live according to the tradition of the elders instead of eating their food with 'unclean' hands?"

He replied, "Isaiah was right when he prophesied about you hypocrites; as it is written:

"'These people honor me with their lips,
    but their hearts are far from me!
They worship me in vain;
    their teachings are but rules taught by men.' q

You have let go of the commands of God and are holding on to the traditions of men."

And he said to them: "You have a fine way of setting aside the commands of God in order to observeʳ your own traditions! For Moses said, 'Honor your father and your mother,'ˢ

ᵖSome early manuscripts *pitchers, kettles and dining couches*   qIsaiah 29:13
ʳSome manuscripts *set up*   ˢExodus 20:12; Deut. 5:16

and, 'Anyone who curses his father or mother must be put to death.'[t] But you say that if a man says to his father or mother: 'Whatever help you might otherwise have received from me is Corban' (that is, a gift devoted to God), then you no longer let him do anything for his father or mother. Thus you nullify the word of God by your tradition that you have handed down. And you do many things like that."

DEFILEMENT CONTRASTED. [Mk]Again Jesus called the crowd to him and said, "Listen to me, everyone, and understand this. Nothing outside a man can make him 'unclean' by going into him. Rather, it is what comes out of a man that makes him 'unclean.'[u]" [Mt]Then the disciples came to him and asked, "Do you know that the Pharisees were offended when they heard this?"

Mt.
15:10-20
Mk.
7:14-23

He replied, "Every plant that my heavenly Father has not planted will be pulled up by the roots. Leave them; they are blind guides.[v] If a blind man leads a blind man, both will fall into a pit."

Peter said, "Explain the parable to us."

"Are you still so dull?" Jesus asked them. [Mk]"Don't you see that nothing that enters a man from the outside can make him 'unclean'? For it doesn't go into his heart but into his stomach, and then out of his body." (In saying this, Jesus declared all foods "clean.")

He went on: "What comes out of a man is what makes him 'unclean.' For from within, out of men's hearts, come evil thoughts, sexual immorality, theft, murder, adultery, greed, malice, deceit, lewdness, envy, slander, arrogance and folly. All these evils come from inside and make a man 'unclean.'"

Jn. 7:1

MINISTRY ONLY IN GALILEE. After this, Jesus went around in Galilee, purposely staying away from Judea because the Jews there were waiting to take his life.

---

[t]Exodus 21:17; Lev. 20:9   [u]Some early manuscripts 'unclean.' [16]If anyone has ears to hear, let him hear.   [v]Some manuscripts guides of the blind

TODAY'S INSIGHTS

Nourishment

Have you ever heard someone ask why God would allow millions of people to starve? Have you ever answered that, quite to the contrary, it is *we* who let them starve by our overconsumption and apathy toward their need? When Jesus saw the multitudes hungry, he used his miraculous power to feed them. But feeding their bodies was the easy part. The people *wanted* to receive the loaves and the fish. Feeding them spiritually was another matter altogether. (Try feeding a panhandler and then talk to him about his soul, and you might experience something of the problem which Jesus encountered.)

God made food for the body, to nourish and sustain it. For the soul, he has given us Christ. So when Jesus said that one could have eternal life by eating his flesh and drinking his blood, he appeared to be quite mad to those who heard him. But anyone who truly knew the character of Jesus would instantly have known that he was not talking about cannibalism. In fact, Jesus spelled out the truth for them: It is the *Spirit* that gives life.

Jesus was telling them that his words, his example, his teaching, and his power are the nourishment which he gives us. Physical food lasts only until the next meal, but a life lived in Christ truly sustains. It gives health to the outlook, strength to the character, and vitality to one's purpose.

Are we missing out on true spiritual nourishment because we are too busy worrying about food? How to afford it, where to find it, how to prepare it, what kind to eat, or what kind *not* to eat? Literally hours each day are consumed in the pursuit of consumption. Imagine what might result if we spent anywhere near as much time each day getting to know Christ!

How ironic it is that man-imposed religious rules about eating often take the focus away from "the bread of life" who has been sent down like manna to draw us away from the emptiness of rule-keeping. As Jesus pointed out to the Pharisees, rule-keeping rarely satisfies the hunger for moral uprightness, and even has a way of impeding it.

NOURISHMENT

Every now and then someone gets our attention and organizes dramatic relief for the starving people of Africa. It doesn't happen often enough. But have you ever stopped to think that the person next to you in that fancy restaurant last week was starving to death? Or that there is a famine at the office, factory, or school where you go every day? If Jesus alone is true spiritual nourishment, the world is literally wasting away.

When it comes to answering the spiritual needs of a sinful world, a person-to-person relief effort is God's primary solution to the problem. Is there some starving soul you can feed today? Who is the person you can help?

DAY
15
WITH
JESUS

RECOGNITION

Extensive Tour Throughout Galilee

PERHAPS IN AN ACT OF WITHDRAWAL FROM THE JEWS, OR PERHAPS as part of a plan for wider evangelism, Jesus turns his ministry now to Phoenicia and the area around Tyre and Sidon. Here he encounters a Canaanite woman who begs Jesus to heal her daughter. As descendants of Noah's son Ham, against whom a curse had been directed, the Canaanites are looked down upon by the Jews as unworthy of God's blessings. So the woman's request is an excellent opportunity for Jesus to teach his disciples once again about the universality of his kingdom. At first it appears that Jesus rebuffs the woman, but the end result demonstrates Jesus' concern for all people, and also provides an excellent example of persistent faith on the part of a believer.

Returning to the Sea of Galilee, Jesus will perform more miracles and chastise the Pharisees for demanding signs of his deity. After that Jesus will continue his extensive tour by going north into Caesarea Philippi.

Mt. 15:21-28 Mk. 7:24-30 Tyre and Sidon	CANAANITE WOMAN PLEADS. ^{Mt}Leaving that place, Jesus withdrew to the region of Tyre and Sidon. ^{Mk}He entered a house and did not want anyone to know it; yet he could not keep his presence secret. ^{Mt}A Canaanite woman from that vicinity came to him, crying out, "Lord, Son of David, have mercy on me! My daughter is suffering terribly from demon-possession."

Jesus did not answer a word. So his disciples came to him and urged him, "Send her away, for she keeps crying out after us."

He answered, "I was sent only to the lost sheep of Israel."

The woman came and knelt before him. "Lord, help me!" she said.

He replied, "It is not right to take the children's bread and toss it to their dogs."

"Yes, Lord," she said, "but even the dogs eat the crumbs that fall from their master's table."

Then Jesus answered, "Woman, you have great faith! Your request is granted." And her daughter was healed from that very hour.

Mt.
15:29-31
Mk.
7:31-37

DEAF MUTE HEALED. ^{Mk}Then Jesus left the vicinity of Tyre and went through Sidon, down to the Sea of Galilee and into the region of the Decapolis.^w There some people brought to him a man who was deaf and could hardly talk, and they begged him to place his hand on the man.

After he took him aside, away from the crowd, Jesus put his fingers into the man's ears. Then he spit and touched the man's tongue. He looked up to heaven and with a deep sigh said to him, *"Ephphatha!"* (which means, "Be opened!"). At this, the man's ears were opened, his tongue was loosened and he began to speak plainly.

Jesus commanded them not to tell anyone. But the more he did so, the more they kept talking about it. People were overwhelmed with amazement. "He has done everything well," they said. "He even makes the deaf hear and the mute speak." ^{Mt}Great crowds came to him, bringing the lame, the blind, the crippled, the mute and many others, and laid them at his feet; and he healed them. The people were amazed when they saw the mute speaking, the crippled made well, the lame walking and the blind seeing. And they praised the God of Israel.

Mt.
15:32-39
Mk.
8:1-10
Hills
by sea

FOUR THOUSAND FED. During those days another large crowd gathered. Since they had nothing to eat, Jesus called his disciples to him and said, "I have compassion for these people; they have already been with me three days and have nothing to eat. If I send them home hungry, they will collapse on the way, because some of them have come a long distance."

His disciples answered, "But where in this remote place can anyone get enough bread to feed them?"

"How many loaves do you have?" Jesus asked.

"Seven," they replied.

He told the crowd to sit down on the ground. When he had taken the seven loaves and given thanks, he broke them and gave them to his disciples to set before the people, and they did so. They had a few small fish as well; he gave thanks for

^wThat is, the Ten Cities

them also and told the disciples to distribute them. The people ate and were satisfied. Afterward the disciples picked up seven basketfuls of broken pieces that were left over. About four thousand men were present. And having sent them away, he got into the boat with his disciples and went to the region of Dalmanutha.

Mt.
16:1-4
Mk.
8:11-13
Magadan

PHARISEES ASK FOR SIGN. ^{Mt}The Pharisees and Sadducees came to Jesus and tested him by asking him to show them a sign from heaven.

He replied,^x "When evening comes, you say, 'It will be fair weather, for the sky is red,' and in the morning, 'Today it will be stormy, for the sky is red and overcast.' You know how to interpret the appearance of the sky, but you cannot interpret the signs of the times. A wicked and adulterous generation looks for a miraculous sign, but none will be given it except the sign of Jonah." ^{Mk}Then he left them, got back into the boat and crossed to the other side.

Mt.
16:5-12
Mk.
8:14-21

WARNING ABOUT LEADERS. ^{Mk}The disciples had forgotten to bring bread, except for one loaf they had with them in the boat. ^{Mt}"Be careful," Jesus said to them. "Be on your guard against the yeast of the Pharisees and Sadducees." ^{Mk}They discussed this with one another and said, "It is because we have no bread."

Aware of their discussion, Jesus asked them: "Why are you talking about having no bread? Do you still not see or understand? Are your hearts hardened? Do you have eyes but fail to see, and ears but fail to hear? And don't you remember? When I broke the five loaves for the five thousand, how many basketfuls of pieces did you pick up?"

"Twelve," they replied.

"And when I broke the seven loaves for the four thousand, how many basketfuls of pieces did you pick up?"

They answered, "Seven."

He said to them, "Do you still not understand? ^{Mt}How is it you don't understand that I was not talking to you about bread? But be on your guard against the yeast of the Pharisees and Sadducees." Then they understood that he was not telling them to guard against the yeast used in bread, but against the teaching of the Pharisees and Sadducees.

^xSome early manuscripts do not have the rest of verse 2 and all of verse 3.

Mk.
8:22-26
Beth-
saida

BLIND MAN NEAR BETHSAIDA. They came to Bethsaida, and some people brought a blind man and begged Jesus to touch him. He took the blind man by the hand and led him outside the village. When he had spit on the man's eyes and put his hands on him, Jesus asked, "Do you see anything?"

He looked up and said, "I see people; they look like trees walking around."

Once more Jesus put his hands on the man's eyes. Then his eyes were opened, his sight was restored, and he saw everything clearly. Jesus sent him home, saying, "Don't go into the village.ʸ"

Preparation of Apostles for the End

As Jesus now continues his extensive tour north through Caesarea Philippi and then south again into Galilee, he uses this time to prepare his chosen disciples for his death and to strengthen their ministry in carrying on his work. At this point in Jesus' ministry, the apostles are truly convinced that Jesus is the Messiah, but apparently they too have notions of a political Messiah. Realizing that their understanding of his messiahship is still very limited, and that their somewhat simplistic faith will be tested, Jesus begins to tell the apostles about his death, as well as the burdens which they themselves will face. Talk of their Leader's imminent death must surely confuse these men, who have hopes of playing key roles in a wholly different kind of kingdom.

The highlight of this period of preparation comes when Jesus takes Peter, James, and John (who seem to be the inner circle of the disciples) to (apparently) Mount Hermon. There Jesus is transfigured. In what is evidently more than a mere vision, Moses and Elijah appear with Jesus as representatives of the law and the prophets. The subsequent disappearance of Moses and Elijah, as well as words of confirmation spoken from heaven, indicate to the three disciples the demise of the former dispensation and the supremacy of the kingdom of God in Christ Jesus.

Even with this demonstration to the inner three, and despite Jesus' warning about humility in the use of their miraculous

ʸSome manuscripts *Don't go and tell anyone in the village*

power, it is not long before all the disciples begin to dispute among themselves as to who among them is the greatest. Jesus sets a young child before them as an example of humility and teaches them about temptation, discipline, and forgiveness.

The Gospel accounts record here a confession by Peter that Jesus is the Christ. Using the word "rock" symbolically (since Peter's name means "rock"), Jesus says that it is upon the rock of Peter's confession of Christ that Jesus' kingdom will be established.

Mt. 16:13-20 Mk. 8:27-30 Lk. 9:18-21 Caesarea Philippi	PETER ACKNOWLEDGES CHRIST. When Jesus came to the region of Caesarea Philippi, he asked his disciples, "Who do people say the Son of Man is?" They replied, "Some say John the Baptist; others say Elijah; and still others, Jeremiah or one of the prophets." "But what about you?" he asked. "Who do you say I am?" Simon Peter answered, "You are the Christ^z, the Son of the living God." Jesus replied, "Blessed are you, Simon son of Jonah, for this was not revealed to you by man, but by my Father in heaven. And I tell you that you are Peter^a, and on this rock I will build my church, and the gates of Hades^b will not overcome it.^c I will give you the keys of the kingdom of heaven; whatever you bind on earth will be bound in heaven, and whatever you loose on earth will be^d loosed in heaven." Then he warned his disciples not to tell anyone that he was the Christ.
Mt. 16:21-23 Mk. 8:31-33 Lk. 9:21,22	SUFFERING FORETOLD. From that time on Jesus began to explain to his disciples that he must go to Jerusalem and suffer many things at the hands of the elders, chief priests and teachers of the law, and that he must be killed and on the third day be raised to life. Peter took him aside and began to rebuke him. "Never, Lord!" he said. "This shall never happen to you!" Jesus turned and said to Peter, "Get behind me, Satan! You are a stumbling block to me; you do not have in mind the things of God, but the things of men."
Mt. 16:24-27 Mk. 8:34-38 Lk. 9:23-26	BURDENS OF DISCIPLESHIP. Then he called the crowd to him along with his disciples and said: "If anyone would come

^zOr *Messiah*   ^a*Peter* means *rock*   ^bOr *hell*   ^cOr *not prove stronger than it*   ^dOr *have been*

after me, he must deny himself and take up his cross and follow me. For whoever wants to save his life[e] will lose it, but whoever loses his life for me and for the gospel will save it. What good is it for a man to gain the whole world, yet forfeit his soul? Or what can a man give in exchange for his soul? If anyone is ashamed of me and my words in this adulterous and sinful generation, the Son of Man will be ashamed of him when he comes in his Father's glory with the holy angels."

Mt.
16:28
Mk. 9:1
Lk. 9:27

KINGDOM WITHIN LIFETIME. And he said to them, "I tell you the truth, some who are standing here will not taste death before they see the kingdom of God come with power."

Mt. 17:1-8
Mk. 9:2-8
Lk.
9:28-36a
Mount
Hermon?

JESUS IS TRANSFIGURED. After six days Jesus took with him Peter, James and John the brother of James, and led them up a high mountain by themselves. There he was transfigured before them. His face shone like the sun, and his clothes became as white as the light. Just then there appeared before them Moses and Elijah, talking with Jesus.

Peter said to Jesus, "Lord, it is good for us to be here. If you wish, I will put up three shelters—one for you, one for Moses and one for Elijah."

While he was still speaking, a bright cloud enveloped them, and a voice from the cloud said, "This is my Son, whom I love; with him I am well pleased. Listen to him!"

When the disciples heard this, they fell facedown to the ground, terrified. But Jesus came and touched them. "Get up," he said. "Don't be afraid." When they looked up, they saw no one except Jesus.

Mt.
17:9-13
Mk.
9:9-13
Lk. 9:36b

APOSTLES ASK ABOUT ELIJAH. [Mt]As they were coming down the mountain, Jesus instructed them, "Don't tell anyone what you have seen, until the Son of Man has been raised from the dead."

The disciples asked him, "Why then do the teachers of the law say that Elijah must come first?"

Jesus replied, "To be sure, Elijah comes and will restore all things. But I tell you, Elijah has already come, and they did not recognize him, but have done to him everything they wished. In the same way the Son of Man is going to suffer at their

[e]The Greek word means either *life* or *soul*

hands." Then the disciples understood that he was talking to them about John the Baptist. ^{Lk}The disciples kept this to themselves, and told no one at that time what they had seen.

Mt.
17:14-21
Mk.
9:14-29
Lk.
9:37-43a;
17:5,6
Near the
mountain

EPILEPTIC BOY HEALED. ^{Mk}When they came to the other disciples, they saw a large crowd around them and the teachers of the law arguing with them. As soon as all the people saw Jesus, they were overwhelmed with wonder and ran to greet him.

"What are you arguing with them about?" he asked.

A man in the crowd answered, "Teacher, I brought you my son, who is possessed by a spirit that has robbed him of speech. Whenever it seizes him, it throws him to the ground. He foams at the mouth, gnashes his teeth and becomes rigid. I asked your disciples to drive out the spirit, but they could not."

"O unbelieving generation," Jesus replied, "how long shall I stay with you? How long shall I put up with you? Bring the boy to me."

So they brought him. When the spirit saw Jesus, it immediately threw the boy into a convulsion. He fell to the ground and rolled around, foaming at the mouth.

Jesus asked the boy's father, "How long has he been like this?"

"From childhood," he answered. "It has often thrown him into fire or water to kill him. But if you can do anything, take pity on us and help us."

"'If you can'?" said Jesus. "Everything is possible for him who believes."

Immediately the boy's father exclaimed, "I do believe; help me overcome my unbelief!"

When Jesus saw that a crowd was running to the scene, he rebuked the evil^f spirit. "You deaf and mute spirit," he said, "I command you, come out of him and never enter him again."

The spirit shrieked, convulsed him violently and came out. The boy looked so much like a corpse that many said, "He's dead." But Jesus took him by the hand and lifted him to his feet, and he stood up.

^fGreek unclean

After Jesus had gone indoors, his disciples asked him privately, "Why couldn't we drive it out?" [Mt]He replied, "Because you have so little faith. I tell you the truth, if you have faith as small as a mustard seed, you can say to this mountain, 'Move from here to there' and it will move. Nothing will be impossible for you.[g]" [Mk]"This kind can come out only by prayer.[h]"

Mt. 17:22,23 Mk. 9:30-32 Lk. 9:43b-45 Galilee	DEATH AGAIN FORETOLD. They left that place and passed through Galilee. Jesus did not want anyone to know where they were, because he was teaching his disciples. He said to them, "The Son of Man is going to be betrayed into the hands of men. They will kill him, and after three days he will rise." But they did not understand what he meant and were afraid to ask him about it.
Mt. 17:24-27 Capernaum	COIN FROM FISH'S MOUTH. After Jesus and his disciples arrived in Capernaum, the collectors of the two-drachma tax came to Peter and asked, "Doesn't your teacher pay the temple tax[i]?" "Yes, he does," he replied. When Peter came into the house, Jesus was the first to speak. "What do you think, Simon?" he asked. "From whom do the kings of the earth collect duty and taxes—from their own sons or from others?" "From others," Peter answered. "Then the sons are exempt," Jesus said to him. "But so that we may not offend them, go to the lake and throw out your line. Take the first fish you catch; open its mouth and you will find a four-drachma coin. Take it and give it to them for my tax and yours."
Mt. 18:1-4 Mk. 9:33-35 Lk. 9:46-48 17:7-10	APOSTLES DISPUTE ABOUT RANK. [Mk]They came to Capernaum. When he was in the house, he asked them, "What were you arguing about on the road?" But they kept quiet because on the way they had argued about who was the greatest. Sitting down, Jesus called the Twelve and said, "If anyone wants to be first, he must be the very last, and the servant of all." [Lk]"Suppose one of you had a servant plowing or looking after the sheep. Would he say to the servant when he comes in from

[g]Some manuscripts you. [21]But this kind does not go out except by prayer and fasting. [h]Some manuscripts prayer and fasting [i]Greek the two drachmas

the field, 'Come along now and sit down to eat'? Would he not rather say, 'Prepare my supper, get yourself ready and wait on me while I eat and drink; after that you may eat and drink'? Would he thank the servant because he did what he was told to do? So you also, when you have done everything you were told to do, should say, 'We are unworthy servants; we have only done our duty.'" MtHe called a little child and had him stand among them. And he said: "I tell you the truth, unless you change and become like little children, you will never enter the kingdom of heaven. Therefore, whoever humbles himself like this child is the greatest in the kingdom of heaven."

Mt.
18:5,6,
10-14
Mk.
9:36,
37,42
Lk.
17:2,3a
CONCERN FOR THE YOUNG. Mk"Whoever welcomes one of these little children in my name welcomes me; and whoever welcomes me does not welcome me but the one who sent me. Mt"But if anyone causes one of these little ones who believe in me to sin, it would be better for him to have a large millstone hung around his neck and to be drowned in the depths of the sea.

"See that you do not look down on one of these little ones. For I tell you that their angels in heaven always see the face of my Father in heaven.j

"What do you think? If a man owns a hundred sheep, and one of them wanders away, will he not leave the ninety-nine on the hills and go to look for the one that wandered off? And if he finds it, I tell you the truth, he is happier about that one sheep than about the ninety-nine that did not wander off. In the same way your Father in heaven is not willing that any of these little ones should be lost."

Mt.
18:7-9
Mk.
9:43-50
Lk. 17:1
WARNING ABOUT TEMPTATION. Mt"Woe to the world because of the things that cause people to sin! Such things must come, but woe to the man through whom they come! If your hand or your foot causes you to sin, cut it off and throw it away. It is better for you to enter life maimed or crippled than to have two hands or two feet and be thrown into eternal fire. MkAnd if your eye causes you to sin, pluck it out. It is better for you to enter the kingdom of God with one eye than to have two eyes and be thrown into hell, where

---

jSome manuscripts *heaven.* 11*The Son of Man came to save what was lost.*

"'their worm does not die,
and the fire is not quenched.'[k]

Everyone will be salted with fire.

"Salt is good, but if it loses its saltiness, how can you make it salty again? Have salt in yourselves, and be at peace with each other."

Mk.
9:38-41
Lk.
9:49,50

WORKS DONE IN JESUS' NAME. "Teacher," said John, "we saw a man driving out demons in your name and we told him to stop, because he was not one of us."

"Do not stop him," Jesus said. "No one who does a miracle in my name can in the next moment say anything bad about me, for whoever is not against us is for us. I tell you the truth, anyone who gives you a cup of water in my name because you belong to Christ will certainly not lose his reward."

Mt.
18:15-17

REBUKE AND DISCIPLINE. "If your brother sins against you,[l] go and show him his fault, just between the two of you. If he listens to you, you have won your brother over. But if he will not listen, take one or two others along, so that 'every matter may be established by the testimony of two or three witnesses.'[m] If he refuses to listen to them, tell it to the church; and if he refuses to listen even to the church, treat him as you would a pagan or a tax collector.

Mt.
18:18-20

APOSTLES GIVEN AUTHORITY. "I tell you the truth, whatever you bind on earth will be[n] bound in heaven, and whatever you loose on earth will be[n] loosed in heaven.

"Again, I tell you that if two of you on earth agree about anything you ask for, it will be done for you by my Father in heaven. For where two or three come together in my name, there am I with them."

Mt.
18:21,22
Lk.
17:3b,4

PETER ASKS ABOUT FORGIVENESS. [Mt]Then Peter came to Jesus and asked, "Lord, how many times shall I forgive my brother when he sins against me? Up to seven times?"

Jesus answered, "I tell you, not seven times, but seventy-seven times.[o] [Lk]If your brother sins, rebuke him, and if he repents, forgive him. If he sins against you seven times in a day, and seven times comes back to you and says, 'I repent,' forgive him."

[k]Isaiah 66:24   [l]Some manuscripts do not have *against you*.   [m]Deut. 19:15
[n]Or *have been*   [o]Or *seventy times seven*

<table>
<tr><td>Mt.
18:23-35</td><td>PARABLE OF SERVANTS IN DEBT. "Therefore, the kingdom of heaven is like a king who wanted to settle accounts with his servants. As he began the settlement, a man who owed him ten thousand talents^p was brought to him. Since he was not able to pay, the master ordered that he and his wife and his children and all that he had be sold to repay the debt.</td></tr>
</table>

Mt. 18:23-35 | PARABLE OF SERVANTS IN DEBT. "Therefore, the kingdom of heaven is like a king who wanted to settle accounts with his servants. As he began the settlement, a man who owed him ten thousand talents[p] was brought to him. Since he was not able to pay, the master ordered that he and his wife and his children and all that he had be sold to repay the debt.

"The servant fell on his knees before him. 'Be patient with me,' he begged, 'and I will pay back everything.' The servant's master took pity on him, canceled the debt and let him go.

"But when that servant went out, he found one of his fellow servants who owed him a hundred denarii.[q] He grabbed him and began to choke him. 'Pay back what you owe me!' he demanded.

"His fellow servant fell to his knees and begged him, 'Be patient with me, and I will pay you back.'

"But he refused. Instead, he went off and had the man thrown into prison until he could pay the debt. When the other servants saw what had happened, they were greatly distressed and went and told their master everything that had happened.

"Then the master called the servant in. 'You wicked servant,' he said, 'I canceled all that debt of yours because you begged me to. Shouldn't you have had mercy on your fellow servant just as I had on you?' In anger his master turned him over to the jailers to be tortured, until he should pay back all he owed.

"This is how my heavenly Father will treat each of you unless you forgive your brother from your heart."

TODAY'S INSIGHTS

Recognition

If you were to walk into a crowd of strangers, would they recognize you? Would anyone ask you for your autograph or point you out to others? When was the last time you were singled out for some special honor? Not many of us even get near the shadow of the limelight. But Jesus stole the show! From an unnamed Canaanite woman who called him "Lord, Son of David," to Peter, who acknowledged Jesus as "the Christ, the Son of the living God,"

^pThat is, millions of dollars   ^qThat is, a few dollars

to the voice of the heavenly Father on the mountain of transfiguration, who proclaimed Jesus as his own Son, Jesus was recognized for who he was—God in the flesh!

As God incarnate, Jesus had every right to flaunt his deity. But he did not do that. Instead, he came as a servant, humbly born and quietly raised. Rather than heading up a powerful army, or taking over the world politically, he traveled the dusty back roads of Judea and Galilee meeting the needs of the common people, to whom he had his greatest appeal. When the daughter of an outcast woman needed healing, Jesus did not neglect her. Nor an unknown deaf-mute. When a blind man begged for Jesus' healing touch, he was not denied. And when still another swelling crowd was parched and hungry, Jesus fed them all, as he had done once before.

Yet Jesus often told those whom he had healed to tell no one about it. Nor was he selfish in the use of his gifts; he wanted to share his own power with us. Over and over he said that we too could do quite amazing things if we would believe on him. But he did insist on one thing that we learn from his example—the attributes of humility and service. For Jesus, recognition is born of responsibility. Honor and fame can be achieved easily enough if one is driven to find them, but it is the one who serves with quiet humility who receives God's approval. And there is this practical aspect to consider: If one is in the limelight, there is risk that the light will expose not only his finer side but his faults as well.

Are we willing to take a backseat and let others assume the spotlight? Are we willing to be as insignificant as a child in a crowd of dignitaries? Having an attitude of humility is not just some hypothetical moral attribute; it has practical spin-offs that we might never suspect. For example, if we could ever reach the point where our desire for recognition is brought under control, then perhaps we could more easily accept Jesus' answer to Peter about forgiveness. After all, the ability to forgive is directly tied to our pride. Once pride is sacrificed, there is nothing difficult about forgiving someone.

That's good to know, for if we are ever to be forgiven of our constant clamor for recognition, we can take comfort in knowing that Christ our Savior not only sacrificed his life but humbled himself daily.

QUESTIONING

In Jerusalem for the Feast of Tabernacles

IT HAS BEEN SIX MONTHS SINCE THE LAST PASSOVER, WHICH JESUS evidently did not attend because of threats on his life. However, as the time arrives for the annual Feast of Tabernacles, held for eight days in late September and early October, apparently Jesus feels that he can once again journey safely to Jerusalem. The Feast of Tabernacles, one of three national festivals (along with Passover and Pentecost) which all males are obliged to attend, is a commemoration of the ancient wilderness journey, during which the Israelites had lived in tents. Accordingly, during the festival the people live in improvised booths made of tree branches. For this reason the feast is also known as the Festival of Booths. More anciently, the feast was referred to as the Feast of the Harvest, or the Feast of the Ingathering, since it was celebrated after the vintage and harvest were gathered.

Though some of Jesus' brothers will later become leaders in the church, apparently at this point they cannot bring themselves to believe that their brother is the Messiah. Almost tauntingly, it seems, they urge him to go up to Jerusalem to celebrate the feast. Jesus puts them off, however, perhaps realizing that their intentions for him are not sincere. For his own reasons he prefers to go up quietly and therefore tells them that he is not yet ready to go. Jesus will follow them after they have gone, but only after some delay.

When Jesus finally arrives in Jerusalem he will spend his time teaching and confronting the religious leaders who have assembled. It is a time of mixed feelings among the Jews. Some are busy trying to have Jesus arrested, while others are convinced by his teaching and miraculous works that he is the Messiah.

Jn. 7:2-9
Capernaum
(Sept./
Oct.,
A.D. 29)

BROTHERS TAUNT JESUS. But when the Jewish Feast of Tabernacles was near, Jesus' brothers said to him, "You ought to leave here and go to Judea, so that your disciples may see the miracles you do. No one who wants to become a public figure acts in secret. Since you are doing these things, show yourself to the world." For even his own brothers did not believe in him.

Therefore Jesus told them, "The right time for me has not yet come; for you any time is right. The world cannot hate you, but it hates me because I testify that what it does is evil. You go to the Feast. I am not yet' going up to this Feast, because for me the right time has not yet come." Having said this, he stayed in Galilee.

Jn. 7:10-13 Jeru- salem (Oct., A.D. 29) | JESUS GOES PRIVATELY. However, after his brothers had left for the Feast, he went also, not publicly, but in secret. Now at the Feast the Jews were watching for him and asking, "Where is that man?"

Among the crowds there was widespread whispering about him. Some said, "He is a good man."

Others replied, "No, he deceives the people." But no one would say anything publicly about him for fear of the Jews.

Jn. 7:14-24 | JESUS TEACHES IN TEMPLE. Not until halfway through the Feast did Jesus go up to the temple courts and begin to teach. The Jews were amazed and asked, "How did this man get such learning without having studied?"

Jesus answered, "My teaching is not my own. It comes from him who sent me. If anyone chooses to do God's will, he will find out whether my teaching comes from God or whether I speak on my own. He who speaks on his own does so to gain honor for himself, but he who works for the honor of the one who sent him is a man of truth; there is nothing false about him. Has not Moses given you the law? Yet not one of you keeps the law. Why are you trying to kill me?"

"You are demon-possessed," the crowd answered. "Who is trying to kill you?"

Jesus said to them, "I did one miracle, and you are all astonished. Yet, because Moses gave you circumcision (though actually it did not come from Moses, but from the patriarchs), you circumcise a child on the Sabbath. Now if a child can be circumcised on the Sabbath so that the law of Moses may not be broken, why are you angry with me for healing the whole man

'Some early manuscripts do not have yet.

on the Sabbath? Stop judging by mere appearances, and make a right judgment."

Jn. 7:25-31 JEWS DISCUSS CHRIST. At that point some of the people of Jerusalem began to ask, "Isn't this the man they are trying to kill? Here he is, speaking publicly, and they are not saying a word to him. Have the authorities really concluded that he is the Christ[s]? But we know where this man is from; when the Christ comes, no one will know where he is from."

Then Jesus, still teaching in the temple courts, cried out, "Yes, you know me, and you know where I am from. I am not here on my own, but he who sent me is true. You do not know him, but I know him because I am from him and he sent me."

At this they tried to seize him, but no one laid a hand on him, because his time had not yet come. Still, many in the crowd put their faith in him. They said, "When the Christ comes, will he do more miraculous signs than this man?"

Jn. 7:32-36 GUARDS SENT TO ARREST. The Pharisees heard the crowd whispering such things about him. Then the chief priests and the Pharisees sent temple guards to arrest him.

Jesus said, "I am with you for only a short time, and then I go to the one who sent me. You will look for me, but you will not find me; and where I am, you cannot come."

The Jews said to one another, "Where does this man intend to go that we cannot find him? Will he go where our people live scattered among the Greeks, and teach the Greeks? What did he mean when he said, 'You will look for me, but you will not find me,' and 'Where I am, you cannot come'?"

Jn. 7:37-39 SPIRITUAL DRINK. On the last and greatest day of the Feast, Jesus stood and said in a loud voice, "If anyone is thirsty, let him come to me and drink. Whoever believes in me, as[t] the Scripture has said, streams of living water will flow from within him." By this he meant the Spirit, whom those who believed in him were later to receive. Up to that time the Spirit had not been given, since Jesus had not yet been glorified.

Jn. 7:40-44 MORE DIVISION AMONG JEWS. On hearing his words, some of the people said, "Surely this man is the Prophet."

---

[s]Or *Messiah* [t]Or / *If anyone is thirsty, let him come to me. / And let him drink,*
[38]*who believes in me. / As*

Others said, "He is the Christ."

Still others asked, "How can the Christ come from Galilee? Does not the Scripture say that the Christ will come from David's family[u] and from Bethlehem, the town where David lived?" Thus the people were divided because of Jesus. Some wanted to seize him, but no one laid a hand on him.

Jn.
7:45-52

NICODEMUS COUNSELS CAUTION. Finally the temple guards went back to the chief priests and Pharisees, who asked them, "Why didn't you bring him in?"

"No one ever spoke the way this man does," the guards declared.

"You mean he has deceived you also?" the Pharisees retorted. "Has any of the rulers or of the Pharisees believed in him? No! But this mob that knows nothing of the law—there is a curse on them."

Nicodemus, who had gone to Jesus earlier and who was one of their own number, asked, "Does our law condemn anyone without first hearing him to find out what he is doing?"

They replied, "Are you from Galilee, too? Look into it, and you will find that a prophet[v] does not come out of Galilee."

[The earliest and most reliable manuscripts and other ancient witnesses do not have John 7:53–8:11.]

Jn.
7:53–
8:11
In
temple

WOMAN CAUGHT IN ADULTERY. Then each went to his own home. But Jesus went to the Mount of Olives. At dawn he appeared again in the temple courts, where all the people gathered around him, and he sat down to teach them. The teachers of the law and the Pharisees brought in a woman caught in adultery. They made her stand before the group and said to Jesus, "Teacher, this woman was caught in the act of adultery. In the Law Moses commanded us to stone such women. Now what do you say?" They were using this question as a trap, in order to have a basis for accusing him.

But Jesus bent down and started to write on the ground with his finger. When they kept on questioning him, he straightened up and said to them, "If any one of you is without sin, let him be the first to throw a stone at her." Again he stooped down and wrote on the ground.

[u]Greek *seed*   [v]Two early manuscripts *the Prophet*

At this, those who heard began to go away one at a time, the older ones first, until only Jesus was left, with the woman still standing there. Jesus straightened up and asked her, "Woman, where are they? Has no one condemned you?"

"No one, sir," she said.

"Then neither do I condemn you," Jesus declared. "Go now and leave your life of sin."

Jn. 8:12-20 LIGHT OF THE WORLD. When Jesus spoke again to the people, he said, "I am the light of the world. Whoever follows me will never walk in darkness, but will have the light of life."

The Pharisees challenged him, "Here you are, appearing as your own witness; your testimony is not valid."

Jesus answered, "Even if I testify on my own behalf, my testimony is valid, for I know where I came from and where I am going. But you have no idea where I come from or where I am going. You judge by human standards; I pass judgment on no one. But if I do judge, my decisions are right, because I am not alone. I stand with the Father, who sent me. In your own Law it is written that the testimony of two men is valid. I am one who testifies for myself; my other witness is the Father, who sent me."

Then they asked him, "Where is your father?"

"You do not know me or my Father," Jesus replied. "If you knew me, you would know my Father also." He spoke these words while teaching in the temple area near the place where the offerings were put. Yet no one seized him, because his time had not yet come.

Jn. 8:21-30 WARNING AGAINST UNBELIEF. Once more Jesus said to them, "I am going away, and you will look for me, and you will die in your sin. Where I go, you cannot come."

This made the Jews ask, "Will he kill himself? Is that why he says, 'Where I go, you cannot come'?"

But he continued, "You are from below; I am from above. You are of this world; I am not of this world. I told you that you would die in your sins; if you do not believe that I am the one I claim to be,*w* you will indeed die in your sins."

*w*Or *I am he*

"Who are you?" they asked.

"Just what I have been claiming all along," Jesus replied, "I have much to say in judgment of you. But he who sent me is reliable, and what I have heard from him I tell the world."

They did not understand that he was telling them about his Father. So Jesus said, "When you have lifted up the Son of Man, then you will know that I am the one I claim to be and that I do nothing on my own but speak just what the Father has taught me. The one who sent me is with me; he has not left me alone, for I always do what pleases him." Even as he spoke, many put their faith in him.

Jn.
8:31-38

ON SPIRITUAL FREEDOM. To the Jews who had believed him, Jesus said, "If you hold to my teaching, you are really my disciples. Then you will know the truth, and the truth will set you free."

They answered him, "We are Abraham's descendants[x] and have never been slaves of anyone. How can you say that we shall be set free?"

Jesus replied, "I tell you the truth, everyone who sins is a slave to sin. Now a slave has no permanent place in the family, but a son belongs to it forever. So if the Son sets you free, you will be free indeed. I know you are Abraham's descendants. Yet you are ready to kill me, because you have no room for my word. I am telling you what I have seen in the Father's presence, and you do what you have heard from your father.[y]"

Jn.
8:39-47

TRUE CHILDREN OF ABRAHAM. "Abraham is our father," they answered.

"If you were Abraham's children," said Jesus, "then you would[z] do the things Abraham did. As it is, you are determined to kill me, a man who has told you the truth that I heard from God. Abraham did not do such things. You are doing the things your own father does."

"We are not illegitimate children," they protested. "The only Father we have is God himself."

Jesus said to them, "If God were your Father, you would love me, for I came from God and now am here. I have not come on my own; but he sent me. Why is my language not

[x]Greek *seed*; also in verse 37   [y]Or *presence. Therefore do what you have heard from the Father*.   [z]Some early manuscripts *"If you are Abraham's children," said Jesus, "then*

clear to you? Because you are unable to hear what I say. You belong to your father, the devil, and you want to carry out your father's desire. He was a murderer from the beginning, not holding to the truth, for there is no truth in him. When he lies, he speaks his native language, for he is a liar and the father of lies. Yet because I tell the truth, you do not believe me! Can any of you prove me guilty of sin? If I am telling the truth, why don't you believe me? He who belongs to God hears what God says. The reason you do not hear is that you do not belong to God."

Jn.
8:48-59

DECLARES ETERNAL EXISTENCE. The Jews answered him, "Aren't we right in saying that you are a Samaritan and demon-possessed?"

"I am not possessed by a demon," said Jesus, "but I honor my Father and you dishonor me. I am not seeking glory for myself; but there is one who seeks it, and he is the judge. I tell you the truth, if anyone keeps my word, he will never see death."

At this the Jews exclaimed, "Now we know that you are demon-possessed! Abraham died and so did the prophets, yet you say that if anyone keeps your word, he will never taste death. Are you greater than our father Abraham? He died, and so did the prophets. Who do you think you are?"

Jesus replied, "If I glorify myself, my glory means nothing. My Father, whom you claim as your God, is the one who glorifies me. Though you do not know him, I know him. If I said I did not, I would be a liar like you, but I do know him and keep his word. Your father Abraham rejoiced at the thought of seeing my day; he saw it and was glad."

"You are not yet fifty years old," the Jews said to him, "and you have seen Abraham!"

"I tell you the truth," Jesus answered, "before Abraham was born, I am!" At this, they picked up stones to stone him, but Jesus hid himself, slipping away from the temple grounds.

Jn.
9:1-12

HEALING OF MAN BORN BLIND. As he went along, he saw a man blind from birth. His disciples asked him, "Rabbi, who sinned, this man or his parents, that he was born blind?"

"Neither this man nor his parents sinned," said Jesus, "but this happened so that the work of God might be displayed in his life. As long as it is day, we must do the work of him who sent me. Night is coming, when no one can work. While I am in the world, I am the light of the world."

Having said this, he spit on the ground, made some mud with the saliva, and put it on the man's eyes. "Go," he told him, "wash in the Pool of Siloam" (this word means Sent). So the man went and washed, and came home seeing.

His neighbors and those who had formerly seen him begging asked, "Isn't this the same man who used to sit and beg?" Some claimed that he was.

Others said, "No, he only looks like him."

But he himself insisted, "I am the man."

"How then were your eyes opened?" they demanded.

He replied, "The man they call Jesus made some mud and put it on my eyes. He told me to go to Siloam and wash. So I went and washed, and then I could see."

"Where is this man?" they asked him.

"I don't know," he said.

Jn. 9:13-17

PHARISEES QUESTION MAN. They brought to the Pharisees the man who had been blind. Now the day on which Jesus had made the mud and opened the man's eyes was a Sabbath. Therefore the Pharisees also asked him how he had received his sight. "He put mud on my eyes," the man replied, "and I washed, and now I see."

Some of the Pharisees said, "This man is not from God, for he does not keep the Sabbath."

But others asked, "How can a sinner do such miraculous signs?" So they were divided.

Finally they turned again to the blind man, "What have you to say about him? It was your eyes he opened."

The man replied, "He is a prophet."

Jn. 9:18-23

PARENTS ARE QUESTIONED. The Jews still did not believe that he had been blind and had received his sight until they sent for the man's parents. "Is this your son?" they asked. "Is this the one you say was born blind? How is it that now he can see?"

"We know he is our son," the parents answered, "and we know he was born blind. But how he can see now, or who opened his eyes, we don't know. Ask him. He is of age; he will speak for himself." His parents said this because they were afraid of the Jews, for already the Jews had decided that anyone who acknowledged that Jesus was the Christ[a] would be put out of the synagogue. That was why his parents said, "He is of age; ask him."

Jn.
9:24-34

MAN QUESTIONED AGAIN. A second time they summoned the man who had been blind. "Give glory to God,[b]" they said. "We know this man is a sinner."

He replied, "Whether he is a sinner or not, I don't know. One thing I do know. I was blind but now I see!"

Then they asked him, "What did he do to you? How did he open your eyes?"

He answered, "I have told you already and you did not listen. Why do you want to hear it again? Do you want to become his disciples, too?"

Then they hurled insults at him and said, "You are this fellow's disciple! We are disciples of Moses! We know that God spoke to Moses, but as for this fellow, we don't even know where he comes from."

The man answered, "Now that is remarkable! You don't know where he comes from, yet he opened my eyes. We know that God does not listen to sinners. He listens to the godly man who does his will. Nobody has ever heard of opening the eyes of a man born blind. If this man were not from God, he could do nothing."

To this they replied, "You were steeped in sin at birth; how dare you lecture us!" And they threw him out.

Jn.
9:35-41

JESUS CONFRONTS HEALED MAN. Jesus heard that they had thrown him out, and when he found him, he said, "Do you believe in the Son of Man?"

"Who is he, sir?" the man asked. "Tell me so that I may believe in him."

Jesus said, "You have now seen him; in fact, he is the one speaking with you."

Then the man said, "Lord, I believe," and he worshiped him.

Jesus said, "For judgment I have come into this world, so that the blind will see and those who see will become blind."

Some Pharisees who were with him heard him say this and asked, "What? Are we blind too?"

---

[a]Or *Messiah*   [b]A solemn charge to tell the truth (see Joshua 7:19)

Jesus said, "If you were blind, you would not be guilty of sin; but now that you claim you can see, your guilt remains.

Jn.
10:1-6

SHEEP AND THEIR SHEPHERD. "I tell you the truth, the man who does not enter the sheep pen by the gate, but climbs in by some other way, is a thief and a robber. The man who enters by the gate is the shepherd of his sheep. The watchman opens the gate for him, and the sheep listen to his voice. He calls his own sheep by name and leads them out. When he has brought out all his own, he goes on ahead of them, and his sheep follow him because they know his voice. But they will never follow a stranger; in fact, they will run away from him because they do not recognize a stranger's voice." Jesus used this figure of speech, but they did not understand what he was telling them.

Jn.
10:7-10

THE GATE FOR THE SHEEP. Therefore Jesus said again, "I tell you the truth, I am the gate for the sheep. All who ever came before me were thieves and robbers, but the sheep did not listen to them. I am the gate; whoever enters through me will be saved.ᶜ He will come in and go out, and find pasture. The thief comes only to steal and kill and destroy; I have come that they may have life, and have it to the full.

Jn.
10:11-18

THE GOOD SHEPHERD. "I am the good shepherd. The good shepherd lays down his life for the sheep. The hired hand is not the shepherd who owns the sheep. So when he sees the wolf coming, he abandons the sheep and runs away. Then the wolf attacks the flock and scatters it. The man runs away because he is a hired hand and cares nothing for the sheep.

"I am the good shepherd; I know my sheep and my sheep know me—just as the Father knows me and I know the Father—and I lay down my life for the sheep. I have other sheep that are not of this sheep pen. I must bring them also. They too will listen to my voice, and there shall be one flock and one shepherd. The reason my Father loves me is that I lay down my life—only to take it up again. No one takes it from me, but I lay it down of my own accord. I have authority to lay it down and authority to take it up again. This command I received from my Father."

ᶜOr *kept safe*

| Jn. 10:19-21 | JEWS STILL DIVIDED. At these words the Jews were again divided. Many of them said, "He is demon-possessed and raving mad. Why listen to him?"
But others said, "These are not the sayings of a man possessed by a demon. <u>Can a demon open the eyes of the blind?</u>" |

TODAY'S INSIGHTS

Questioning

Are there times when doubts creep into your mind about Jesus? Or perhaps about God, or Christianity? Do you ever feel a twinge of guilt for questioning what you think you ought to believe without question? For the people who saw Jesus face-to-face, there seemed to be no end to questions. "How did this man get such learning without having studied?" "Have the authorities really concluded that he is the Christ?" "Where does this man intend to go that we cannot find him?" "Aren't we right in saying that you are a Samaritan and demon-possessed?" "How can a sinner do such miraculous signs?"

So many questions came to their minds. But they were all secondary to the most important question of all: "Who are you?" And that is the question which all of us are entitled to ask—indeed, *must* ask. Who was this man Jesus? If we take him seriously, he said he is the Gate through which we enter into salvation. He said he is the One who brings us eternal life. He said he is the Good Shepherd who lays down his life for us all. But can we believe his claims, or is Jesus to be dismissed as the world's greatest fraud?

The answer comes, as it has many times before, in the supernatural power which Jesus possessed. As some of those who saw his miracles observed, "These are not the sayings of a man possessed by a demon." A demon, or a fake, or a madman could never open the eyes of a person who has been blind from birth. Only someone with divine power could do such a thing. And if he has divine power, then he must be who he claims to be—God in the flesh!

So the question comes to us, as it did to the blind man whom Jesus healed: What are we to believe about Jesus? And Jesus leaves little room for us to fudge on the answer: "If you do not believe that

I am the one I claim to be, you will indeed die in your sins." By no means is that the threat of an egotistical maniac. Hell is the ever-present reality that mankind faces because of sin, and Jesus urgently wants to save us from ourselves.

If we believe in his teaching and submit our lives to his lordship, then his grace works unimpeded in our lives to save us from our condemnation. "If you hold to my teaching," he assures us, "then you will know the truth, and the truth will set you free."

So what do we say? Do we believe that Jesus is telling us the truth? That, indeed, he *is* the truth? Jesus appeals to us as none other through his superior teaching, which has opened the eyes of millions to love and goodness. Could a fraud give such insight? Could a madman give us such understanding? God permits our questioning as the exercise of the free will with which he has created us, but he compels our positive response through the incomparable character of Christ. Can we dare deny him?

DAY

17

WITH

JESUS

GIVING

Ministry from Galilee to Judea

AFTER THE FEAST OF DEDICATION, JESUS APPARENTLY RETURNS to Capernaum for the final two months of his Galilean ministry. He not only feels growing opposition from the people there who want a political leader, but also knows that it is nearing the time for him to be delivered up. From this time forward, Jesus resolutely faces his final suffering. As he sets out on his journey to Jerusalem, in Samaria he again encounters immediate rejection. Making what amounts to a final appeal to the northern region, Jesus sends out 72 of his disciples, to whom he gives the power to heal in his name, with the mission of proclaiming the coming of his kingdom.

As Jesus proceeds down through Judea, he is apparently near Jericho when he tells the parable of the Good Samaritan, an illustration all the more remarkable in view of Jesus' own rejection by the Samaritans just a short time before. Jesus will then travel on to Bethany, visiting in the home of Martha and Mary, and later proceed to Jerusalem for the Feast of Dedication.

This is a time of transition for the Master. Initial excitement among the masses is followed by doubt and even hostility as Jesus refuses to accept the role that most people want him to play. In a way it is characteristic of the turnabout which inevitably comes when people accept Jesus into their lives for any number of wrong reasons: The excitement can give way to disappointment.

Mt.
19:1,2
Mk.
10:1
Lk.
9:51-56
Samaria
to Judea

GALILEAN MINISTRY ENDS. As the time approached for him to be taken up to heaven, Jesus resolutely set out for Jerusalem. And he sent messengers on ahead, who went into a Samaritan village to get things ready for him; but the people there did not welcome him, because he was heading for Jerusalem. When the disciples James and John saw this, they asked, "Lord, do you want us to call fire down from heaven to destroy them[d]?" But Jesus turned and rebuked them, and[e] they went to another village.

Lk. 17:11-19

TEN LEPERS HEALED. Now on his way to Jerusalem, Jesus traveled along the border between Samaria and Galilee. As he was going into a village, ten men who had leprosy[f] met him. They stood at a distance and called out in a loud voice, "Jesus, Master, have pity on us!"

When he saw them, he said, "Go show yourselves to the priests." And as they went, they were cleansed.

One of them, when he saw he was healed, came back, praising God in a loud voice. He threw himself at Jesus' feet and thanked him—and he was a Samaritan.

Jesus asked, "Were not all ten cleansed? Where are the other nine? Was no one found to return and give praise to God except this foreigner?" Then he said to him, "Rise and go; your faith has made you well."

Mt. 11:20-24 Lk. 10:1-16

SEVENTY-TWO SENT OUT. After this the Lord appointed seventy-two[g] others and sent them two by two ahead of him to every town and place where he was about to go. He told them, "The harvest is plentiful, but the workers are few. Ask the Lord of the harvest, therefore, to send out workers into his harvest field. Go! I am sending you out like lambs among wolves. Do not take a purse or bag or sandals; and do not greet anyone on the road.

"When you enter a house, first say, 'Peace to this house.' If a man of peace is there, your peace will rest on him; if not, it will return to you. Stay in that house, eating and drinking whatever they give you, for the worker deserves his wages. Do not move around from house to house.

"When you enter a town and are welcomed, eat what is set before you. Heal the sick who are there and tell them, 'The kingdom of God is near you.' But when you enter a town and are not welcomed, go into its streets and say, 'Even the dust of your town that sticks to our feet we wipe off against you. Yet

---

[d]Some manuscripts *them, even as Elijah did*   [e]Some manuscripts *them. And he said, "You do not know what kind of spirit you are of, for the son of Man did not come to destroy men's lives, but to save them." [56]And*   [f]The Greek word was used for various diseases affecting the skin—not necessarily leprosy.   [g]Some manuscripts *seventy*

be sure of this: The kingdom of God is near.' I tell you, it will be more bearable on that day for Sodom than for that town.

"Woe to you, Korazin! Woe to you, Bethsaida! For if the miracles that were performed in you had been performed in Tyre and Sidon, they would have repented long ago, sitting in sackcloth and ashes. But it will be more bearable for Tyre and Sidon at the judgment than for you. And you, Capernaum, will you be lifted up to the skies? No, you will go down to the depths.[h]

"He who listens to you listens to me; he who rejects you rejects me; but he who rejects me rejects him who sent me."

Lk.
10:17-20

SEVENTY-TWO RETURN. The seventy-two returned with joy and said, "Lord, even the demons submit to us in your name."

He replied, "I saw Satan fall like lightning from heaven. I have given you authority to trample on snakes and scorpions and to overcome all the power of the enemy; nothing will harm you. However, do not rejoice that the spirits submit to you, but rejoice that your names are written in heaven."

Mt.
11:25-27
Lk.
10:21-24

THANKS GIVEN FOR REVELATION. At that time Jesus, full of joy through the Holy Spirit, said, "I praise you, Father, Lord of heaven and earth, because you have hidden these things from the wise and learned, and revealed them to little children. Yes, Father, for this was your good pleasure.

"All things have been committed to me by my Father. No one knows who the Son is except the Father, and no one knows who the Father is except the Son and those to whom the Son chooses to reveal him."

Then he turned to his disciples and said privately, "Blessed are the eyes that see what you see. For I tell you that many prophets and kings wanted to see what you see but did not see it, and to hear what you hear but did not hear it."

Mt.
11:28-30

REST FOR THE WEARY. "Come to me, all you who are weary and burdened, and I will give you rest. Take my yoke upon you and learn from me, for I am gentle and humble in heart, and you will find rest for your souls. For my yoke is easy and my burden is light."

[h]Greek *Hades*

Lk.
10:25-37
Jericho?

PARABLE OF GOOD SAMARITAN. On one occasion an expert in the law stood up to test Jesus. "Teacher," he asked, "what must I do to inherit eternal life?"

"What is written in the Law?" he replied. "How do you read it?"

He answered: "'Love the Lord your God with all your heart and with all your soul and with all your strength and with all your mind'[i]; and, 'Love your neighbor as yourself.'[j]"

"You have answered correctly," Jesus replied. "Do this and you will live."

But he wanted to justify himself, so he asked Jesus, "And who is my neighbor?"

In reply Jesus said: "A man was going down from Jerusalem to Jericho, when he fell into the hands of robbers. They stripped him of his clothes, beat him and went away, leaving him half dead. A priest happened to be going down the same road, and when he saw the man, he passed by on the other side. So too, a Levite, when he came to the place and saw him, passed by on the other side. But a Samaritan, as he traveled, came where the man was; and when he saw him, he took pity on him. He went to him and bandaged his wounds, pouring on oil and wine. Then he put the man on his own donkey, took him to an inn and took care of him. The next day he took out two silver coins[k] and gave them to the innkeeper. 'Look after him,' he said, 'and when I return, I will reimburse you for any extra expense you may have.'

"Which of these three do you think was a neighbor to the man who fell into the hands of robbers?"

The expert in the law replied, "The one who had mercy on him."

Jesus told him, "Go and do likewise."

Lk.
10:38-42
Bethany?

WITH MARTHA AND MARY. As Jesus and his disciples were on their way, he came to a village where a woman named Martha opened her home to him. She had a sister called Mary, who sat at the Lord's feet listening to what he said. But Martha was distracted by all the preparations that had to be made. She came to him and asked, "Lord, don't you care that my sister has left me to do the work by myself? Tell her to help me!"

[i]Deut, 6:5   [j]Lev. 19:18   [k]Greek *two denarii*

"Martha, Martha," the Lord answered, "you are worried and upset about many things, but only one thing is needed.[l] Mary has chosen what is better, and it will not be taken away from her."

Lk. 11:1-4 Mount of Olives? TEACHING HOW TO PRAY. One day Jesus was praying in a certain place. When he finished, one of his disciples said to him, "Lord, teach us to pray, just as John taught his disciples."

He said to them, "When you pray, say:

"'Father,[m]
hallowed be your name,
your kingdom come.[n]
Give us each day our daily bread.
Forgive us our sins,
    for we also forgive everyone who sins against us.[o]
And lead us not into temptation.[p]'"

Lk. 11:5-8 PARABLE OF PERSISTENCE. Then he said to them, "Suppose one of you has a friend, and he goes to him at midnight and says, 'Friend, lend me three loaves of bread, because a friend of mine on a journey has come to me, and I have nothing to set before him.'

"Then the one inside answers, 'Don't bother me. The door is already locked, and my children are with me in bed. I can't get up and give you anything.' I tell you, though he will not get up and give him the bread because he is his friend, yet because of the man's boldness[q] he will get up and give him as much as he needs.

Lk. 11:9-13 PRAYING WITH FAITH. "So I say to you: Ask and it will be given to you; seek and you will find; knock and the door will be opened to you. For everyone who asks receives; he who seeks finds; and to him who knocks, the door will be opened.

"Which of you fathers, if your son asks for[r] a fish, will give him a snake instead? Or if he asks for an egg, will give him a scorpion? If you then, though you are evil, know how to give good gifts to your children, how much more will your Father in heaven give the Holy Spirit to those who ask him!"

[l]Some manuscripts *but few things are needed—or only one*   [m]Some manuscripts *Our Father in heaven*   [n]Some manuscripts *come. May your will be done on earth as it is in heaven.*   [o]Greek *everyone who is indebted to us*   [p]Some manuscripts *temptation but deliver us from the evil one*   [q]Or *persistence*   [r]Some manuscripts *for bread, will give him a stone; or if he asks for*

In Jerusalem for Feast of Dedication

Whether intentionally present for the feast or there for other reasons, Jesus is in Jerusalem in December during the eight-day Feast of Dedication, known more modernly as Hanukkah. This feast was instituted as recently as 164 B.C. by Judas Maccabaeus in commemoration of the refurbishing of the temple after it had been profaned for idolatrous use in 168 B.C. by Antiochus Epiphanes. Faithful Jews are gathering in Jerusalem in order to celebrate the rededication of the temple, and Jesus takes this opportunity to reach out to the large number of people present.

When various Jewish leaders ask Jesus whether he is the Christ, he reminds them of his miraculous works as proof of his deity. He then says that he and the Father are one, thereby infuriating the Jews, who see this as rank blasphemy. They take up rocks to stone Jesus and try to have him arrested, but Jesus escapes.

Jn. 10:22-30 (Nov./ Dec., A.D. 29)	JESUS AFFIRMS OWN DEITY. Then came the Feast of Dedication[s] at Jerusalem. It was winter, and Jesus was in the temple area walking in Solomon's Colonnade. The Jews gathered around him, saying, "How long will you keep us in suspense? If you are the Christ,[t] tell us plainly." Jesus answered, "I did tell you, but you do not believe. The miracles I do in my Father's name speak for me, but you do not believe because you are not my sheep. My sheep listen to my voice; I know them, and they follow me. I give them eternal life, and they shall never perish; no one can snatch them out of my hand. My Father, who has given them to me, is greater than all[u]; no one can snatch them out of my Father's hand. I and the Father are one."
Jn. 10:31-39	ATTEMPT TO STONE JESUS. Again the Jews picked up stones to stone him, but Jesus said to them, "I have shown you many great miracles from the Father. For which of these do you stone me?"

[s]That is, Hanukkah   [t]Or *Messiah*   [u]Many early manuscripts *What my Father has given me is greater than all*

"We are not stoning you for any of these," replied the Jews, "but for blasphemy, because you, a mere man, claim to be God."

Jesus answered them, "Is it not written in your Law, 'I have said you are gods'[v]? If he called them 'gods,' to whom the word of God came—and the Scripture cannot be broken— what about the one whom the Father set apart as his very own and sent into the world? Why then do you accuse me of blasphemy because I said, 'I am God's Son'? Do not believe me unless I do what my Father does. But if I do it, even though you do not believe me, believe the miracles, that you may know and understand that the Father is in me, and I in the Father." Again they tried to seize him, but he escaped their grasp.

Jn.
10:40-42
Perea

TO PEREA. Then Jesus went back across the Jordan to the place where John had been baptizing in the early days. Here he stayed and many people came to him. They said, "Though John never performed a miraculous sign, all that John said about this man was true." And in that place many believed in Jesus.

TODAY'S INSIGHTS

Giving

If you were asked to name one quality which would best characterize Jesus, what would it be? Humility? Love? Compassion? Service? So many good qualities could well be nominated. But one character trait which is seen repeatedly throughout Jesus' ministry is his exemplary giving, both in attitude and in action. In each of his miracles there is a gift of health, or peace, or forgiveness, or even life itself. Sometimes the response was thankless, as in the case of the nine lepers who never bothered to express their gratitude to Jesus.

Jesus not only gave generously and unselfishly to others, but he also demonstrated an attitude of gratitude for the spiritual blessings which had come to himself and to his disciples. For example, we see here the Son of God taking time to thank the Father for

[v]Psalm 82:6

giving his divine wisdom to the common people who were so eager to accept it.

And what marvelous lessons Jesus taught us about giving! In the story of the Good Samaritan, we see that giving crosses all cultural and economic barriers. By using lepers as his example of giving to a person who is considered an outcast, Jesus drives home the point that our giving must bring us into contact with people in need, wherever and whoever they might be. In the incident with Martha and her sister Mary, we see that giving attention and love is more important than supplying everyday physical needs.

In Jesus' example of how we ought to pray, we see that giving may in some instances be less important than *for*giving. In the parable of the persistent friend, we learn the value of asking God not for just our daily bread but for wisdom and insight through the Holy Spirit that we might live our lives fully and productively in his service.

Of course the greatest of all God's gifts is the gracious gift of Jesus Christ, who is our divine role model. In view of that gift alone, the question must be asked: What have we given in return? Surely we would be supremely ungrateful to take such blessings for granted. Yet another question immediately presents itself: How may we give anything to God? Apart from our love and our faith and our obedience, how else can we give to God?

It has been suggested that we can never repay our parents, relatives, and friends for what they have given to us as we grew up over the years—that all we can do is to "pass it on." And perhaps that's part of the reason for the second-greatest commandment, which calls on us to love our neighbors as ourselves. The love and gratitude we have for God our Father may best be demonstrated by our gifts of love and service to his children, and to all whom we find to be our neighbors.

In what new ways can our giving better express our love to God? How best can we use the blessings which have come to us so abundantly? What gifts will we share with others even this day?

DAY
18
WITH
JESUS

WARNING

The Perean Ministry

WHEN JESUS GOES INTO THE AREA BEYOND THE JORDAN RIVER, he is entering the Perean province ruled by the tetrarch Herod Antipas, who also rules Galilee. It is this same Herod who had earlier beheaded John the Baptist, and he probably now fears a popular uprising of the people in response to Jesus' presence in that territory. Jesus does not fear Herod, however, because he knows that his end will come only in Jerusalem. It is unclear whether a warning about Herod comes from Pharisees who really believe in Jesus or whether they are simply trying to get Jesus to leave their area.

During this period of his ministry Jesus once again teaches through numerous parables. His parables cover a wide range of subjects, including the cost of discipleship, the value of lost souls, the rejection of his kingdom, the need for humility, and the unrighteousness of hypocritical religion.

Lk. 13:22-30 Perea	NUMBER TO BE SAVED. Then Jesus went through the towns and villages, teaching as he made his way to Jerusalem. Someone asked him, "Lord are only a few people going to be saved?"

He said to them, "Make every effort to enter through the narrow door, because many, I tell you, will try to enter and will not be able to. Once the owner of the house gets up and closes the door, you will stand outside knocking and pleading, 'Sir, open the door for us.'

"But he will answer, 'I don't know you or where you come from.'

"Then you will say, 'We ate and drank with you, and you taught in our streets.'

"But he will reply, 'I don't know you or where you come from. Away from me, all you evildoers!'

"There will be weeping there, and gnashing of teeth, when you see Abraham, Isaac and Jacob and all the prophets in the kingdom of God, but you yourselves thrown out. People will come from east and west and north and south, and will take their places at the feast in the kingdom of God. Indeed there are those who are last who will be first, and first who will be last."

Lk. 13:31-33 JESUS WARNED ABOUT HEROD. At that time some Pharisees came to Jesus and said to him, "Leave this place and go somewhere else. Herod wants to kill you."

He replied, "Go tell that fox, 'I will drive out demons and heal people today and tomorrow, and on the third day I will reach my goal.' In any case, I must keep going today and tomorrow and the next day—for surely no prophet can die outside Jerusalem!

Lk. 13:34,35 LAMENT OVER JERUSALEM. "O Jerusalem, Jerusalem, you who kill the prophets and stone those sent to you, how often I have longed to gather your children together, as a hen gathers her chicks under her wings, but you were not willing! Look, your house is left to you desolate. I tell you, you will not see me again until you say, 'Blessed is he who comes in the name of the Lord.'*w*"

Lk. 14:1-6 MAN HEALED OF DROPSY. One Sabbath, when Jesus went to eat in the house of a prominent Pharisee, he was being carefully watched. There in front of him was a man suffering from dropsy. Jesus asked the Pharisees and experts in the law, "Is it lawful to heal on the Sabbath or not?" But they remained silent. So taking hold of the man, he healed him and sent him away.

Then he asked them, "If one of you has a son*x* or an ox that falls into a well on the Sabbath day, will you not immediately pull him out?" And they had nothing to say.

Lk. 14:7-11 PARABLE OF PLACE OF HONOR. When he noticed how the guests picked the places of honor at the table, he told them this parable: "When someone invites you to a wedding feast, do not take the place of honor, for a person more distinguished than you may have been invited. If so, the host who invited both of you will come and say to you, 'Give this man your seat.' Then, humiliated, you will have to take the least important place. But when you are invited, take the lowest place, so that when your host comes, he will say to you, 'Friend, move up to a better place.' Then you will be honored in the presence

*w*Psalm 118:26   *x*Some manuscripts *donkey*

of all your fellow guests. For everyone who exalts himself will be humbled, and he who humbles himself will be exalted."

Lk.
14:12-14

URGING UNSELFISHNESS. Then Jesus said to his host, "When you give a luncheon or dinner, do not invite your friends, your brothers or relatives, or your rich neighbors; if you do, they may invite you back and so you will be repaid. But when you give a banquet, invite the poor, the crippled, the lame, the blind, and you will be blessed. Although they cannot repay you, you will be repaid at the resurrection of the righteous."

Lk.
14:15-24

PARABLE OF GREAT BANQUET. When one of those at the table with him heard this, he said to Jesus, "Blessed is the man who will eat at the feast in the kingdom of God."

Jesus replied: "A certain man was preparing a great banquet and invited many guests. At the time of the banquet he sent his servant to tell those who had been invited, 'Come, for everything is now ready.'

"But they all alike began to make excuses. The first said, 'I have just bought a field, and I must go and see it. Please excuse me.'

"Another said, 'I have just bought five yoke of oxen, and I'm on my way to try them out. Please excuse me.'

"Still another said, 'I just got married, so I can't come.'

"The servant came back and reported this to his master. Then the owner of the house became angry and ordered his servant, 'Go out quickly into the streets and alleys of the town and bring in the poor, the crippled, the blind and the lame.'

"'Sir,' the servant said, 'what you ordered has been done, but there is still room.'

"Then the master told his servant, 'Go out to the roads and country lanes and make them come in, so that my house will be full. I tell you, not one of those men who were invited will get a taste of my banquet.'"

Lk.
14:25-33

COST OF DISCIPLESHIP. Large crowds were traveling with Jesus, and turning to them he said: "If anyone comes to me and does not hate his father and mother, his wife and children, his brothers and sisters—yes, even his own life—he cannot be my disciple. And anyone who does not carry his cross and follow me cannot be my disciple.

"Suppose one of you wants to build a tower. Will he not first sit down and estimate the cost to see if he has enough money to complete it? For if he lays the foundation and is not able to finish it, everyone who sees it will ridicule him, saying, 'This fellow began to build and was not able to finish.'

"Or suppose a king is about to go to war against another king. Will he not first sit down and consider whether he is able with ten thousand men to oppose the one coming against him with twenty thousand? If he is not able, he will send a delegation while the other is still a long way off and will ask for terms of peace. In the same way, any of you who does not give up everything he has cannot be my disciple.

Lk. 14:34,35 PARABLE OF THE SALT. "Salt is good, but if it loses its saltiness, how can it be made salty again? It is fit neither for the soil nor for the manure pile; it is thrown out.

"He who has ears to hear, let him hear."

Lk. 15:1-7 PARABLE OF LOST SHEEP. Now the tax collectors and "sinners" were all gathering around to hear him. But the Pharisees and the teachers of the law muttered, "This man welcomes sinners and eats with them."

Then Jesus told them this parable: "Suppose one of you has a hundred sheep and loses one of them. Does he not leave the ninety-nine in the open country and go after the lost sheep until he finds it? And when he finds it, he joyfully puts it on his shoulders and goes home. Then he calls his friends and neighbors together and says, 'Rejoice with me; I have found my lost sheep.' I tell you that in the same way there will be more rejoicing in heaven over one sinner who repents than over ninety-nine righteous persons who do not need to repent.

Lk. 15:8-10 PARABLE OF LOST COIN. "Or suppose a woman has ten silver coins[y] and loses one. Does she not light a lamp, sweep the house and search carefully until she finds it? And when she finds it, she calls her friends and neighbors together and says, 'Rejoice with me; I have found my lost coin.' In the same way, I tell you, there is rejoicing in the presence of the angels of God over one sinner who repents."

[y]Greek *ten drachmas*, each worth about a day's wages

Lk.
15:11-32
PARABLE OF LOST SON. Jesus continued: "There was a man who had two sons. The younger one said to his father, 'Father, give me my share of the estate.' So he divided his property between them.

"Not long after that, the younger son got together all he had, set off for a distant country and there squandered his wealth in wild living. After he had spent everything, there was a severe famine in that whole country, and he began to be in need. So he went and hired himself out to a citizen of that country, who sent him to his fields to feed pigs. He longed to fill his stomach with the pods that the pigs were eating, but no one gave him anything.

"When he came to his senses, he said, 'How many of my father's hired men have food to spare, and here I am starving to death! I will set out and go back to my father and say to him: Father, I have sinned against heaven and against you. I am no longer worthy to be called your son; make me like one of your hired men.' So he got up and went to his father.

"But while he was still a long way off, his father saw him and was filled with compassion for him; he ran to his son, threw his arms around him and kissed him.

"The son said to him, 'Father, I have sinned against heaven and against you. I am no longer worthy to be called your son.ᶻ'

"But the father said to his servants, 'Quick! Bring the best robe and put it on him. Put a ring on his finger and sandals on his feet. Bring the fattened calf and kill it. Let's have a feast and celebrate. For this son of mine was dead and is alive again; he was lost and is found.' So they began to celebrate.

"Meanwhile, the older son was in the field. When he came near the house, he heard music and dancing. So he called one of the servants and asked him what was going on. 'Your brother has come,' he replied, 'and your father has killed the fattened calf because he has him back safe and sound.'

"The older brother became angry and refused to go in. So his father went out and pleaded with him. But he answered his father, 'Look! All these years I've been slaving for you and never disobeyed your orders. Yet you never gave me even a young goat so I could celebrate with my friends. But when this

ᶻSome early manuscripts son. Make me like one of your hired men.

son of yours who has squandered your property with prostitutes comes home, you kill the fattened calf for him!'

"'My son,' the father said, 'you are always with me, and everything I have is yours. But we had to celebrate and be glad, because this brother of yours was dead and is alive again; he was lost and is found.'"

Lk.
16:1-13

PARABLE OF DISHONEST MANAGER. Jesus told his disciples: "There was a rich man whose manager was accused of wasting his possessions. So he called him in and asked him, 'What is this I hear about you? Give an account of your management, because you cannot be manager any longer.'

"The manager said to himself, 'What shall I do now? My master is taking away my job. I'm not strong enough to dig, and I'm ashamed to beg—I know what I'll do so that, when I lose my job here, people will welcome me into their houses.'

"So he called in each one of his master's debtors. He asked the first, 'How much do you owe my master?'

"'Eight hundred gallons*a* of olive oil,' he replied.

"The manager told him, 'Take your bill, sit down quickly, and make it four hundred.'

"Then he asked the second, 'And how much do you owe?'

"'A thousand bushels*b* of wheat,' he replied.

"He told him, 'Take your bill and make it eight hundred.'

"The master commended the dishonest manager because he had acted shrewdly. For the people of this world are more shrewd in dealing with their own kind than are the people of the light. I tell you, use worldly wealth to gain friends for yourselves, so that when it is gone, you will be welcomed into eternal dwellings.

"Whoever can be trusted with very little can also be trusted with much, and whoever is dishonest with very little will also be dishonest with much. So if you have not been trustworthy in handling worldly wealth, who will trust you with true riches? And if you have not been trustworthy with someone else's property, who will give you property of your own?

"No servant can serve two masters. Either he will hate the one and love the other, or he will be devoted to the one and despise the other. You cannot serve both God and Money."

*a*Greek *one hundred batous* (probably about 3 kiloliters)   *b*Greek *one hundred korous* (probably about 35 kiloliters)

Lk. 16:14,15 PHARISEES SCOFF AT PARABLE. The Pharisees, who loved money, heard all this and were sneering at Jesus. He said to them, "You are the ones who justify yourselves in the eyes of men, but God knows your hearts. What is highly valued among men is detestable in God's sight.

Lk. 16:16-18 SUBSTANCE OF LAW. "The Law and the Prophets were proclaimed until John. Since that time, the good news of the kingdom of God is being preached, and everyone is forcing his way into it. It is easier for heaven and earth to disappear than for the least stroke of a pen to drop out of the Law.

"Anyone who divorces his wife and marries another woman commits adultery, and the man who marries a divorced woman commits adultery.

Lk. 16:19-31 RICH MAN AND LAZARUS. "There was a rich man who was dressed in purple and fine linen and lived in luxury every day. At his gate was laid a beggar named Lazarus, covered with sores and longing to eat what fell from the rich man's table. Even the dogs came and licked his sores.

"The time came when the beggar died and the angels carried him to Abraham's side. The rich man also died and was buried. In hell,[c] where he was in torment, he looked up and saw Abraham far away, with Lazarus by his side. So he called to him, 'Father Abraham, have pity on me and send Lazarus to dip the tip of his finger in water and cool my tongue, because I am in agony in this fire.'

"But Abraham replied, 'Son, remember that in your lifetime you received your good things, while Lazarus received bad things, but now he is comforted here and you are in agony. And besides all this, between us and you a great chasm has been fixed, so that those who want to go from here to you cannot, nor can anyone cross over from there to us.'

"He answered, 'Then I beg you, father, send Lazarus to my father's house, for I have five brothers. Let him warn them, so that they will not also come to this place of torment.'

"Abraham replied, 'They have Moses and the Prophets; let them listen to them.'

"'No, father Abraham,' he said, 'but if someone from the dead goes to them, they will repent.'

[c]Greek Hades

"He said to him, 'If they do not listen to Moses and the Prophets, they will not be convinced even if someone rises from the dead.'"

Lk. 17:20-35,37 COMING OF KINGDOM. Once, having been asked by the Pharisees when the kingdom of God would come, Jesus replied, "The kingdom of God does not come with your careful observation, nor will people say, 'Here it is,' or 'There it is,' because the kingdom of God is within[d] you."

Then he said to his disciples, "The time is coming when you will long to see one of the days of the Son of Man, but you will not see it. Men will tell you, 'There he is!' or 'Here he is!' Do not go running off after them. For the Son of Man in his day[e] will be like the lightning, which flashes and lights up the sky from one end to the other. But first he must suffer many things and be rejected by this generation.

"Just as it was in the days of Noah, so also will it be in the days of the Son of Man. People were eating, drinking, marrying and being given in marriage up to the day Noah entered the ark. Then the flood came and destroyed them all.

"It was the same in the days of Lot. People were eating and drinking, buying and selling, planting and building. But the day Lot left Sodom, fire and sulfur rained down from heaven and destroyed them all.

"It will be just like this on the day the Son of Man is revealed. On that day no one who is on the roof of his house, with his goods inside, should go down to get them. Likewise, no one in the field should go back for anything. Remember Lot's wife! Whoever tries to keep his life will lose it, and whoever loses his life will preserve it. I tell you, on that night two people will be in one bed; one will be taken and the other left. Two women will be grinding grain together; one will be taken and the other left.[f]"

"Where, Lord!" they asked.

He replied, "Where there is a dead body, there the vultures will gather."

Lk. 18:1-8 PERSISTENT WIDOW. Then Jesus told his disciples a parable to show them that they should always pray and not give up. He said: "In a certain town there was a judge who neither

---

[d]Or *among*   [e]Some manuscripts do not have *in his day*.   [f]Some manuscripts left. [36]*Two men will be in the field; one will be taken and the other left.*

feared God nor cared about men. And there was a widow in that town who kept coming to him with the plea, 'Grant me justice against my adversary.'

"For some time he refused. But finally he said to himself, 'Even though I don't fear God or care about men, yet because this widow keeps bothering me, I will see that she gets justice, so that she won't eventually wear me out with her coming!'"

And the Lord said, "Listen to what the unjust judge says. And will not God bring about justice for his chosen ones, who cry out to him day and night? Will he keep putting them off? I tell you, he will see that they get justice, and quickly. However, when the Son of Man comes, will he find faith on the earth?"

Lk.
18:9-14

PHARISEE AND TAX COLLECTOR. To some who were confident of their own righteousness and looked down on everybody else, Jesus told this parable: "Two men went up to the temple to pray, one a Pharisee and the other a tax collector. The Pharisee stood up and prayed about[8] himself: 'God, I thank you that I am not like other men—robbers, evildoers, adulterers—or even like this tax collector. I fast twice a week and give a tenth of all I get.'

"But the tax collector stood at a distance. He would not even look up to heaven, but beat his breast and said, 'God, have mercy on me, a sinner.'

"I tell you that this man, rather than the other, went home justified before God. For everyone who exalts himself will be humbled, and he who humbles himself will be exalted."

Mt.
20:1-16

VINEYARD WORKERS. "For the kingdom of heaven is like a landowner who went out early in the morning to hire men to work in his vineyard. He agreed to pay them a denarius for the day and sent them into his vineyard.

"About the third hour he went out and saw others standing in the marketplace doing nothing. He told them, 'You also go and work in my vineyard, and I will pay you whatever is right.' So they went.

"He went out again about the sixth hour and the ninth hour and did the same thing. About the eleventh hour he went out and found still others standing around. He asked them, 'Why have you been standing here all day long doing nothing?'

"'Because no one has hired us,' they answered.

8Or to

"He said to them, 'You also go and work in my vineyard.'

"When evening came, the owner of the vineyard said to his foreman, 'Call the workers and pay them their wages, beginning with the last ones hired and going on to the first.'

"The workers who were hired about the eleventh hour came and each received a denarius. So when those came who were hired first, they expected to receive more. But each one of them also received a denarius. When they received it, they began to grumble against the landowner. 'These men who were hired last worked only one hour,' they said, 'and you have made them equal to us who have borne the burden of the work and the heat of the day.'

"But he answered one of them, 'Friend, I am not being unfair to you. Didn't you agree to work for a denarius? Take your pay and go. I want to give the man who was hired last the same as I gave you. Don't I have the right to do what I want with my own money? Or are you envious because I am generous?'

"So the last will be first, and the first will be last."

TODAY'S INSIGHTS

Warning

Do you sometimes find it difficult to see Jesus as anyone other than a gentle, quiet teacher, with a kind face and with arms that are spread open to embrace the whole world in love and forgiveness? Isn't that the usual picture which has been painted for us? But again and again in the Gospels we see Jesus in the midst of conflict and controversy, and he more than holds his own during those heated debates. Our Lord was no wimpy, weak, or wobbly-kneed man of God!

However mild his manners, Jesus was intent on warning us about our spiritual destiny beyond this life. And surely his intense concern was not misplaced. How often do we *really* stop and think about life after death and about the possibility of hell and punishment? Those aren't subjects we want to dwell on while we eat our breakfast and read the morning paper. But if we listen carefully to Jesus, he is saying that many people are standing in spiritual jeopardy at this very moment. "Many are trying to enter through the narrow door of heaven," says Jesus, "but not all will succeed."

WARNING

Let's be honest—don't we sometimes have real difficulty believing that there is a place of eternal destruction called hell? Isn't that why we make jokes about it? Isn't that why we hear the word tossed around like any other expletive and reduced to some bad experience we might have in *this* life? But the same Jesus who tells us there is a heaven also tells us in no uncertain terms that there is a hell. Can we accept one and ignore the other? Hell is God's love expressed as a warning.

As Christians, we take confidence in God's saving grace, as well we should. We have eternal life as a promise of God! But Jesus warns that we should not take his mercy for granted and turn our backs on his forgiveness. There are going to be more than a few surprises in heaven and hell. In view of our eternal destiny, there are more than a few questions we need to ask.

Who are we *really* serving in our lives: God or Money? Have we *really* given up our lives for Christ, or are we just toying around with the idea of self-sacrifice? Have we *really* humbled our hearts before God to do his will, or is our humility just a photo opportunity for those around us? Is the kingdom of God *really* within us, or have we substituted a bustle of "church activities" in its place? Are we *really* taking up Jesus' cross, or are we just wearing it around our necks for decoration? We need to take a hard, honest look at ourselves as we come ever closer to eternity!

But if our answers are not always the most encouraging, there is yet hope. Jesus' warnings are invariably accompanied by precious promises. You can almost imagine the picture he paints, of angels in heaven looking down in anticipation of the unnamed, unknown, insignificant sinner who is about to repent. Will ours be the name which initiates their celebration today?

4Witness.org

DAY
19
WITH
JESUS

FRIENDSHIP

Return to Judea to Raise Lazarus

JOHN RECORDS ONE OF THE MOST POIGNANT EVENTS FOUND IN ALL of the Gospel accounts. While Jesus is in Perea he learns that his friend Lazarus is seriously ill in Bethany, near Jerusalem. Jesus, of course, wants to be with Lazarus, despite his fearful disciples' counsel against returning that close to Jerusalem. Knowing that Lazarus has died, Jesus immediately sets out for Bethany.

What follows is a touching account of Jesus meeting Lazarus' sisters, Martha and Mary, and being moved to tears. Then, although it has been four days since Lazarus died, Jesus goes to the tomb and raises Lazarus from the dead. This, of course, is such a dramatic and conclusive demonstration of Jesus' power that his opponents call a hasty conference and immediately plot to kill him. Aware of the danger, Jesus withdraws northward to the town of Ephraim, near the wilderness.

| Jn. 11:1-4 Perea | LAZARUS' ILLNESS TOLD. Now a man named Lazarus was sick. He was from Bethany, the village of Mary and her sister Martha. This Mary, whose brother Lazarus now lay sick, was the same one who poured perfume on the Lord and wiped his feet with her hair. So the sisters sent word to Jesus, "Lord, the one you love is sick." |

When he heard this, Jesus said, "This sickness will not end in death. No, it is for God's glory so that God's Son may be glorified through it."

| Jn. 11:5-16 | DISCIPLES FEAR RETURN. Jesus loved Martha and her sister and Lazarus. Yet when he heard that Lazarus was sick, he stayed where he was two more days. |

Then he said to his disciples, "Let us go back to Judea."

"But Rabbi," they said, "a short while ago the Jews tried to stone you, and yet you are going back there?"

Jesus answered, "Are there not twelve hours of daylight? A man who walks by day will not stumble, for he sees by this world's light. It is when he walks by night that he stumbles, for he has no light."

After he had said this, he went on to tell them, "Our friend Lazarus has fallen asleep; but I am going there to wake him up."

His disciples replied, "Lord, if he sleeps, he will get better." Jesus had been speaking of his death, but his disciples thought he meant natural sleep.

So then he told them plainly, "Lazarus is dead, and for your sake I am glad I was not there, so that you may believe. But let us go to him."

Then Thomas (called Didymus) said to the rest of the disciples, "Let us also go, that we may die with him."

Jn.
11:17-27
Near
Bethany

JESUS TALKS WITH MARTHA. On his arrival, Jesus found that Lazarus had already been in the tomb for four days. Bethany was less than two miles[h] from Jerusalem, and many Jews had come to Martha and Mary to comfort them in the loss of their brother. When Martha heard that Jesus was coming, she went out to meet him, but Mary stayed at home.

"Lord," Martha said to Jesus, "if you had been here, my brother would not have died. But I know that even now God will give you whatever you ask."

Jesus said to her, "Your brother will rise again."

Martha answered, "I know he will rise again in the resurrection at the last day."

Jesus said to her, "I am the resurrection and the life. He who believes in me will live, even though he dies; and whoever lives and believes in me will never die. Do you believe this?"

"Yes, Lord," she told him, "I believe that you are the Christ,[i] the Son of God, who was to come into the world."

Jn.
11:28-37

JESUS TALKS WITH MARY. And after she had said this, she went back and called her sister Mary aside. "The Teacher is here," she said, "and is asking for you." When Mary heard this, she got up quickly and went to him. Now Jesus had not yet entered the village, but was still at the place where Martha had met him. When the Jews who had been with Mary in the house, comforting her, noticed how quickly she got up and went out, they followed her, supposing she was going to the tomb to mourn there.

[h]Greek *fifteen stadia* (about 3 kilometers)   [i]Or *Messiah*

When Mary reached the place where Jesus was and saw him, she fell at his feet and said, "Lord, if you had been here, my brother would not have died."

When Jesus saw her weeping, and the Jews who had come along with her also weeping, he was deeply moved in spirit and troubled. "Where have you laid him?" he asked.

"Come and see, Lord," they replied.

Jesus wept.

Then the Jews said, "See how he loved him!"

But some of them said, "Could not he who opened the eyes of the blind man have kept this man from dying?"

Jn.
11:38-44

LAZARUS RAISED. Jesus, once more deeply moved, came to the tomb. It was a cave with a stone laid across the entrance. "Take away the stone," he said.

"But, Lord," said Martha, the sister of the dead man, "by this time there is a bad odor, for he has been there four days."

Then Jesus said, "Did I not tell you that if you believed, you would see the glory of God?"

So they took away the stone. Then Jesus looked up and said, "Father, I thank you that you have heard me. I knew that you always hear me, but I said this for the benefit of the people standing here, that they may believe that you sent me."

When he had said this, Jesus called in a loud voice, "Lazarus, come out!" The dead man came out, his hands and feet wrapped with strips of linen, and a cloth around his face.

Jesus said to them, "Take off the grave clothes and let him go."

Jn.
11:45-53

COUNCIL PLOTS TO KILL JESUS. Therefore many of the Jews who had come to visit Mary, and had seen what Jesus did, put their faith in him. But some of them went to the Pharisees and told them what Jesus had done. Then the chief priests and the Pharisees called a meeting of the Sanhedrin.

"What are we accomplishing?" they asked. "Here is this man performing many miraculous signs. If we let him go on like this, everyone will believe in him, and then the Romans will come and take away both our place[j] and our nation."

Then one of them, named Caiaphas, who was high priest that year, spoke up, "You know nothing at all! You do not

[j]Or temple

realize that it is better for you that one man die for the people than that the whole nation perish."

He did not say this on his own, but as high priest that year he prophesied that Jesus would die for the Jewish nation, and not only for that nation but also for the scattered children of God, to bring them together and make them one. So from that day on they plotted to take his life.

Jn. 11:54
Ephraim

JESUS GOES TO EPHRAIM. Therefore Jesus no longer moved about publicly among the Jews. Instead he withdrew to a region near the desert, to a village called Ephraim, where he stayed with his disciples.

Today's Insights

Friendship

When you look around you at all the religions in the world, what stands out about Christianity? Is it Christianity's system of worship, or its high standards of morality? Or its call for love and goodness? Is it perhaps its explanation of life and afterlife? Other major religions could claim some honors in these categories. But what they cannot claim is the *friendship* with God which is found in Jesus Christ.

In many belief systems, God is not a person at all but only an impersonal "it"—an illusive "god force," or a ball of energy pulsating in the cosmos. For some people God is in fact a person—*just* a person and no more—who has been artificially elevated to the status of deity. And sadly, for an increasing number of people today there is no god beyond one's own self.

The idea of a caring, feeling God of free will who has chosen to clothe himself with human flesh in order to serve those whom he has created is the astounding affirmation which sets Christianity apart from all the rest. That God should honor us with his presence on earth approaches the unthinkable. But that God, in the Person of Jesus Christ, should call us his friends—what greater honor could there possibly be!

In the brief story of Jesus' friendship with Lazarus is a profound message for us all. Though we are dead in our sins, Jesus Christ still loves us. He truly cares that we hurt from life's conflicts and that we feel the pain of broken relationships. He knows that we are debilitated by our sins and weakened by the material world in which we too often indulge ourselves. When we cry, Jesus cries with us. But Jesus also knows that our spiritual death can be overcome through his power.

When Martha suggested that Lazarus would rise again at the resurrection, Jesus responded quite remarkably: "I am the resurrection and the life." What could Jesus possibly have meant but that through him we can have new life, right now, in this world, before we die! Yes, we will be raised from the dead to live an eternal life with God, but *even now*, says Jesus, we can live like we have never lived before. Believing in Jesus as Martha and Mary did—despite how little they really understood about God's power—can bring us life-changing results as dramatic as Lazarus coming forth from the tomb after four days. Oh, if we could only grasp the possibilities!

Have you ever felt as if you were spiritually dead? Are you even now entombed in self-pity or doubt, or perhaps surrounded on every side by guilt? You have a friend who has come to give you new life. Even now he calls for you to hear his voice of loving acceptance and to "come out"—out to the light of his truth and the freedom of his forgiveness.

What other religion or belief system could bring us a personal Savior who loves us? The words of the hymn are true: Indeed, what a friend we have in Jesus!

DAY
20
WITH
JESUS

VALUE

The Final Journey

FROM EPHRAIM, THE FINAL DAYS OF JESUS' LIFE AND MINISTRY begin to count down. What occurs during this period, probably between January and the end of March, is a microcosm of his entire ministry. There is more teaching to be done and, as always, the need for dialogue and confrontation with the Pharisees. Jesus once again blesses little children and once again reminds those who would follow him of the burdens they must bear. As he has done twice before, Jesus again tells of his impending death. And there are more parables to be taught and still more people to be healed.

Surely it is a constant source of discouragement to Jesus—even in these last days, and after repeated lessons on humility—that his disciples are still seeking personal glory in the kingdom. Even now the apostles continue to think only in terms of an earthly kingdom. James and John, prompted by their mother, ask that they be given special positions. Jesus admonishes them once again, pointing to the spiritual nature of his kingdom and to the need for humility and service. Yet the time is short now, and Jesus knows that they will soon understand.

There is at least one person who already seems to understand about Jesus' mission and his call for humility. That person is Mary, the sister of Lazarus. As Jesus' journey to Jerusalem comes to an end, the Gospel accounts tell the beautiful story of Mary anointing Jesus with precious ointments. It will be a touching prelude to the brutal events of the final week.

Mt. 19:3-9 Mk. 10:2-9	PHARISEES QUESTION DIVORCE. Some Pharisees came to him to test him. They asked, "Is it lawful for a man to divorce his wife for any and every reason?"

"Haven't you read," he replied, "that at the beginning the Creator 'made them male and female,'*k* and said, 'For this reason a man will leave his father and mother and be united to his wife, and the two will become one flesh'*l*? So they are no

*k*Gen. 1:27   *l*Gen. 2:24

longer two, but one. Therefore what God has joined together, let man not separate."

"Why then," they asked, "did Moses command that a man give his wife a certificate of divorce and send her away?"

Jesus replied, "Moses permitted you to divorce your wives because your hearts were hard. But it was not this way from the beginning. I tell you that anyone who divorces his wife, except for marital unfaithfulness, and marries another woman commits adultery."

Mt.
19:10-12
Mk.
10:10-12

DISCIPLES QUESTION JESUS. MkWhen they were in the house again, the disciples asked Jesus about this. He answered, "Anyone who divorces his wife and marries another woman commits adultery against her. And if she divorces her husband and marries another man, she commits adultery." MtThe disciples said to him, "If this is the situation between a husband and wife, it is better not to marry."

Jesus replied, "Not everyone can accept this word, but only those to whom it has been given. For some are eunuchs because they were born that way; others were made that way by men; and others have renounced marriage[m] because of the kingdom of heaven. The one who can accept this should accept it."

Mt.
19:13-15
Mk.
10:13-16
Lk.
18:15-17

JESUS BLESSES CHILDREN. People were bringing little children to Jesus to have him touch them, but the disciples rebuked them. When Jesus saw this, he was indignant. He said to them, "Let the little children come to me, and do not hinder them, for the kingdom of God belongs to such as these. I tell you the truth, anyone who will not receive the kingdom of God like a little child will never enter it." And he took the children in his arms, put his hands on them and blessed them.

Mt.
19:16-22
Mk.
10:17-22
Lk.
18:18-23

RICH YOUNG MAN. As Jesus started on his way, a man ran up to him and fell on his knees before him. "Good teacher," he asked, "what must I do to inherit eternal life?"

"Why do you call me good?" Jesus answered. "No one is good—except God alone. You know the commandments: 'Do not murder, do not commit adultery, do not steal, do not give false testimony, do not defraud, honor your father and mother.'[n]"

---

[m]Or *have made themselves eunuchs*   [n]Exodus 20:12-16; Deut. 5:16-20

"Teacher," he declared, "all these I have kept since I was a boy."

Jesus looked at him and loved him. "One thing you lack," he said. "Go, sell everything you have and give to the poor, and you will have treasure in heaven. Then come, follow me."

At this the man's face fell. He went away sad, because he had great wealth.

Mt.
19:23-26
Mk.
10:23-27
Lk.
18:24-27

LOVE OF POSSESSIONS. Jesus looked around and said to his disciples, "How hard it is for the rich to enter the kingdom of God!"

The disciples were amazed at his words. But Jesus said again, "Children, how hard it is° to enter the kingdom of God! It is easier for a camel to go through the eye of a needle than for a rich man to enter the kingdom of God."

The disciples were even more amazed, and said to each other, "Who then can be saved?"

Jesus looked at them and said, "With man this is impossible, but not with God; all things are possible with God."

Mt.
19:27-30
Mk.
10:28-31
Lk.
18:28-30

FORSAKING EARTHLY ATTACHMENTS. Peter answered him, "We have left everything to follow you! What then will there be for us?" Jesus said to them, "I tell you the truth, at the renewal of all things, when the Son of Man sits on his glorious throne, you who have followed me will also sit on twelve thrones, judging the twelve tribes of Israel. And everyone who has left houses or brothers or sisters or father or mother^p or children or fields for my sake will receive a hundred times as much and will inherit eternal life. But many who are first will be last, and many who are last will be first."

Mt.
20:17-19
Mk.
10:32-34
Lk.
18:31-34
On road
to Jeru-
salem

DEATH FORETOLD THIRD TIME. ^MkThey were on their way up to Jerusalem, with Jesus leading the way, and the disciples were astonished, while those who followed were afraid. Again he took the Twelve aside and told them what was going to happen to him. "We are going up to Jerusalem," he said, "and the Son of Man will be betrayed to the chief priests and teachers of the law. They will condemn him to death and will hand him over to the Gentiles, who will mock him and spit on him, flog him and kill him. Three days later he will rise." ^LkThe

---

°Some manuscripts *is for those who trust in riches*   ^pSome manuscripts *mother or wife*

disciples did not understand any of this. Its meaning was hidden from them, and they did not know what he was talking about.

Mt.
20:20-23
Mk.
10:35-40

REQUEST BY JAMES AND JOHN. ᴹᵗThen the mother of Zebedee's sons came to Jesus with her sons and, kneeling down, asked a favor of him.

"What is it you want?" he asked.

She said, "Grant that one of these two sons of mine may sit at your right and the other at your left in your kingdom." ᴹᵏThen James and John, the sons of Zebedee, came to him. "Teacher," they said, "we want you to do for us whatever we ask."

"What do you want me to do for you?" he asked.

They replied, "Let one of us sit at your right and the other at your left in your glory."

"You don't know what you are asking," Jesus said. "Can you drink the cup I drink or be baptized with the baptism I am baptized with?"

"We can," they answered.

Jesus said to them, "You will drink the cup I drink and be baptized with the baptism I am baptized with, but to sit at my right or left is not for me to grant. These places belong to those for whom they have been prepared."

Think of others 1st

Mt.
20:24-28
Mk.
10:41-45

JESUS TEACHES HUMILITY. When the ten heard about this, they became indignant with James and John. Jesus called them together and said, "You know that those who are regarded as rulers of the Gentiles lord it over them, and their high officials exercise authority over them. Not so with you. Instead, whoever wants to become great among you must be your servant, and whoever wants to be first must be slave of all. For even the Son of Man did not come to be served, but to serve, and to give his life as a ransom for many."

Lk.
19:1-10
In
Jericho

ZACCHAEUS RECEIVES JESUS. Jesus entered Jericho and was passing through. A man was there by the name of Zacchaeus; he was a chief tax collector and was wealthy. He wanted to see who Jesus was, but being a short man he could not, because of the crowd. So he ran ahead and climbed a sycamore-fig tree to see him, since Jesus was coming that way.

When Jesus reached the spot, he looked up and said to him, "Zacchaeus, come down immediately. I must stay at your house today." So he came down at once and welcomed him gladly.

All the people saw this and began to mutter, "He has gone to be the guest of a 'sinner.'"

But Zacchaeus stood up and said to the Lord, "Look, Lord! Here and now I give half of my possessions to the poor, and if I have cheated anybody out of anything, I will pay back four times the amount."

Jesus said to him, "Today salvation has come to this house, because this man, too, is a son of Abraham. For the Son of Man came to seek and to save what was lost."

Mt. 20:29-34 Mk. 10:46-52 Lk. 18:35-43	BLIND BARTIMAEUS HEALED. ^{Mk}As Jesus and his disciples, together with a large crowd, were leaving the city, a blind man, Bartimaeus (that is, the Son of Timaeus), was sitting by the roadside begging. When he heard that it was Jesus of Nazareth, he began to shout, "Jesus, Son of David, have mercy on me!"

Many rebuked him and told him to be quiet, but he shouted all the more, "Son of David, have mercy on me!"

Jesus stopped and said, "Call him."

So they called to the blind man, "Cheer up! On your feet! He's calling you." Throwing his cloak aside, he jumped to his feet and came to Jesus.

"What do you want me to do for you?" Jesus asked him.

The blind man said, "Rabbi, I want to see."

"Go," said Jesus, "your faith has healed you." ^{Lk}Immediately he received his sight and followed Jesus, praising God. When all the people saw it, they also praised God.

Lk. 19:11-27	PARABLE OF THE TEN MINAS. While they were listening to this, he went on to tell them a parable, because he was near Jerusalem and the people thought that the kingdom of God was going to appear at once. He said: "A man of noble birth went to a distant country to have himself appointed king and then to return. So he called ten of his servants and gave them ten minas.^q 'Put this money to work,' he said, 'until I come back.'

---

^qA mina was about three months' wages

"But his subjects hated him and sent a delegation after him to say, 'We don't want this man to be our king.'

"He was made king, however, and returned home. Then he sent for the servants to whom he had given the money, in order to find out what they had gained with it.

"The first one came and said, 'Sir, your mina has earned ten more.'

"'Well done, my good servant!' his master replied. 'Because you have been trustworthy in a very small matter, take charge of ten cities.'

"The second came and said, 'Sir, your mina has earned five more.'

"His master answered, 'You take charge of five cities.'

"Then another servant came and said, 'Sir, here is your mina; I have kept it laid away in a piece of cloth. I was afraid of you, because you are a hard man. You take out what you did not put in and reap what you did not sow.'

"His master replied, 'I will judge you by your own words, you wicked servant! You knew, did you, that I am a hard man, taking out what I did not put in, and reaping what I did not sow? Why then didn't you put my money on deposit, so that when I came back, I could have collected it with interest?'

"Then he said to those standing by, 'Take his mina away from him and give it to the one who has ten minas.'

"'Sir,' they replied, 'he already has ten!'

"He replied, 'I tell you that to everyone who has, more will be given, but as for the one who has nothing, even what he has will be taken away. But those enemies of mine who did not want me to be king over them—bring them here and kill them in front of me.'"

Lk.
19:28

TRAVELING TOWARD JERUSALEM. After Jesus had said this, he went on ahead, going up to Jerusalem.

Jn.
11:55-57

ARREST PLANNED FOR PASSOVER. When it was almost time for the Jewish Passover, many went up from the country to Jerusalem for their ceremonial cleansing before the Passover. They kept looking for Jesus, and as they stood in the temple area they asked one another, "What do you think? Isn't he coming to the Feast at all?" But the chief priests and Pharisees had given orders that if anyone found out where Jesus was, he should report it so that they might arrest him.

Mt. 26:6-13 Mk. 14:3-9 Jn. 12:1-8	MARY ANOINTS JESUS. JnSix days before the Passover, Jesus arrived at Bethany, where Lazarus lived, whom Jesus had raised from the dead. Here [Mtin the home of a man known as Simon the Leper] a dinner was given in Jesus' honor. Martha served, while Lazarus was among those reclining at the table with him. Then Mary took about a pint[r] of pure nard, an expensive perfume; she poured it on Jesus' feet and wiped his feet with her hair. And the house was filled with the fragrance of the perfume.

But one of his disciples, Judas Iscariot, who was later to betray him, objected, "Why wasn't this perfume sold and the money given to the poor? It was worth a year's wages.[s]" He did not say this because he cared about the poor but because he was a thief; as keeper of the money bag, he used to help himself to what was put into it.

"Leave her alone," Jesus replied. "It was intended that she should save this perfume for the day of my burial. You will always have the poor among you, but you will not always have me." Mk"I tell you the truth, wherever the gospel is preached throughout the world, what she has done will also be told, in memory of her."

Jn. 12:9-11 (Satur- day?)	PLOT TO KILL LAZARUS. Meanwhile a large crowd of Jews found out that Jesus was there and came, not only because of him but also to see Lazarus, whom he had raised from the dead. So the chief priests made plans to kill Lazarus as well, for on account of him many of the Jews were going over to Jesus and putting their faith in him.

TODAY'S INSIGHTS

Value

What is the most valuable thing you possess? Your house? Jewelry? An insurance policy? Stocks and bonds? If perhaps you are thinking of nonmaterial things, what do you consider most valuable? Your health? Love of family? Your relationship with Christ?

If Jesus were asked what is most valuable in this world, high on the list would be such things as faithfulness in marriage, the

---

[r]Greek *a litra* (probably about 0.5 liter)   [s]Greek *three hundred denarii*

trustfulness of children, and the joy of friendship. Assuredly missing from his list would be the material things which we spend much of our time chasing after. Indeed, Jesus uses some of his strongest language to denounce the love of possessions. The rich, says Jesus, can hardly make it to heaven because of the risk that their values have been misplaced. The rich young man who was unwilling to give up what he had (even to inherit eternal life!) is Jesus' graphic object lesson.

Ironically, that young man might have been surprised how his fortune could have been restored had he given up everything to follow Christ. The parable of the ten minas suggests that abundantly more will be given to those who wisely use that with which they have been blessed. And it may well be that such a reward is possible because one has already demonstrated correctly prioritized values.

But the issue of values does not apply merely to the decision as to whether we will work overtime toward the accumulation of wealth. There is a hierarchy of values to be considered in choosing how we *spend* whatever amount of money we may have, no matter how embarrassingly low our bank account may be. It is not to be supposed that Mary had great wealth, yet she chose to spend what she had on the seemingly wasteful exercise of anointing Jesus with expensive perfume.

The very thought of all that money being put to such a use while there were people starving makes one wonder if Mary's values were right after all. But the important question may be: What would Mary have done with the money if she had *not* spent it on the perfume for Jesus? Would the money have gone to feed the poor? Certainly, if left for Judas to decide, the money would have gone into his own pocket for his own selfish reasons. Can't that also happen to what little money we possess?

While Jesus was in her presence, Mary did the right thing by washing Jesus' feet with expensive perfume. Honoring Jesus Christ reflects the highest values possible. But in what way can we best honor Christ today? Perhaps we need to take seriously what Judas suggested only out of greed—that we honor Christ by sharing to the point of sacrifice with those who are economic outcasts. Better yet would be the sharing of our faith with those who don't know Jesus, the Holy One whose own highest value was placed on saving the lost. There must be infinite ways to serve. With what fragrance will we honor Christ today?

DAY
21
WITH
JESUS

TRIUMPH

The Triumphant Entry—Sunday

IT IS LATE MARCH AND THE FEAST OF THE PASSOVER IS NEAR. THE time has come for Jesus to be delivered up. No Jewish feast is more important to the people, and no feast could be more appropriate for the culmination of Jesus' life and ministry. Passover comes at the beginning of the Feast of Unleavened Bread, which lasts for seven days. It commemorates the Exodus of the people of ancient Israel from their captivity in Egypt. On the Passover, the paschal lamb is slain, just as it was at the beginning of the Exodus, at which time its blood was sprinkled over the doors of the Israelites' homes. When death passed over Egypt and the firstborn of each household was killed, God spared only those households whose doors were covered by the blood. As the perfect Lamb of God, Jesus himself is about to be slain for the salvation of all who would recognize and accept the power in his blood.

Even as Jesus approaches Jerusalem, his enemies are plotting his death. But the suffering will not come until Jesus has entered the city in triumph. Riding on a lowly colt, Jesus is met by multitudes who shout praise to God for having sent this "great prophet" in whom they now believe. Jesus knows, however, that most of them still do not understand the true nature of his messiahship and deity, and that there are many more who still do not believe in him at all. As Jesus is now given the greatest welcome of his ministry, his enemies fear his popularity and let him have his day of glory.

| Jn. 12:12,13 (Sunday) | CROWD GOES TO MEET JESUS. The next day the great crowd that had come for the Feast heard that Jesus was on his way to Jerusalem. They took palm branches and went out to meet him, shouting,
    "Hosanna!¹" |

¹A Hebrew expression meaning "Save!" which became an exclamation of praise

"Blessed is he who comes in the name of the Lord!"[u]
"Blessed is the King of Israel!"

Mt.
21:1-7
Mk.
11:1-7
Lk.
19:29-35
Jn.
12:14-16

JESUS SENDS FOR COLT. [Lk]As he approached Bethphage and Bethany at the hill called the Mount of Olives, he sent two of his disciples, saying to them, "Go to the village ahead of you, and as you enter it, you will find a colt tied there, which no one has ever ridden. Untie it and bring it here. If anyone asks you, 'Why are you untying it?' tell him, 'The Lord needs it.'" [Mt]This took place to fulfill what was spoken through the prophet:

"Say to the Daughter of Zion,
 'See, your king comes to you,
gentle and riding on a donkey,
 on a colt, the foal of a donkey.'"[v]

[Jn]At first his disciples did not understand all this. Only after Jesus was glorified did they realize that these things had been written about him and that they had done these things to him. [Mk]They went and found a colt outside in the street, tied at a doorway. As they untied it, some people standing there asked, "What are you doing, untying that colt?" They answered as Jesus had told them to, and the people let them go. When they brought the colt to Jesus and threw their cloaks over it, he sat on it.

Mt.
21:8,9
Mk.
11:8-10
Lk.
19:36-40
Jeru-
salem
(Sunday)

JESUS ENTERS JERUSALEM. [Lk]When he came near the place where the road goes down the Mount of Olives, the whole crowd of disciples began joyfully to praise God in loud voices for all the miracles they had seen:

"Blessed is the king who comes in the name of the
 Lord!"[w]
"Peace in heaven and glory in the highest!"

Some of the Pharisees in the crowd said to Jesus, "Teacher, rebuke your disciples!"

"I tell you," he replied, "if they keep quiet, the stones will cry out." [Mk]Many people spread their cloaks on the road, while others spread branches they had cut in the fields.

Lk.
19:41-44

JESUS FORESEES DESTRUCTION. As he approached Jerusalem and saw the city, he wept over it and said, "If you, even

[u]Psalm 118:25,26   [v]Zech. 9:9   [w]Psalm 118:26

you, had only known on this day what would bring you peace—but now it is hidden from your eyes. The days will come upon you when your enemies will build an embankment against you and encircle you and hem you in on every side. They will dash you to the ground, you and the children within your walls. They will not leave one stone on another, because you did not recognize the time of God's coming to you."

Mt. 21:10,11 Jn. 12:17-19	**JESUS' POPULARITY RECOGNIZED.** ^{Mt}When Jesus entered Jerusalem, the whole city was stirred and asked, "Who is this?"

The crowds answered, "This is Jesus, the prophet from Nazareth in Galilee." ^{Jn}Now the crowd that was with him when he called Lazarus from the tomb and raised him from the dead continued to spread the word. Many people, because they had heard that he had given this miraculous sign, went out to meet him. So the Pharisees said to one another, "See, this is getting us nowhere. Look how the whole world has gone after him!"

Mt. 21:17 Mk. 11:11 Bethany	**RETURN TO BETHANY.** Jesus entered Jerusalem and went to the temple. He looked around at everything, but since it was already late, he went out to Bethany with the Twelve.

Final Week—Monday

On the next day Jesus' popularity is still at a high peak, and children sing his praises as if to thank him for his continual remembrance of them. In a contrasting mood of the day, Matthew, Mark, and Luke each record an incident almost identical to one recorded by John at the beginning of Jesus' ministry—that is, the throwing out of the temple merchants. If this is in fact a separate incident, it just may be that Jesus is taking this last opportunity to purify the temple. Enraged as they must be, the merchants and the money changers, like the religious leaders, fear the people and will bide their time.

Jesus now speaks freely of his pending crucifixion and makes a special effort to explain its purpose. There are many who still disbelieve, but, as John observes, even their disbelief is the fulfillment of prophecy.

Now Jesus leaves Bethany and places a curse on an unfruitful fig tree, an incident which he will later use to illustrate a lesson on the power of faith.

Mt.
21:18,19
Mk.
11:12-14

UNFRUITFUL FIG TREE. The next day as they were leaving Bethany, Jesus was hungry. Seeing in the distance a fig tree in leaf, he went to find out if it had any fruit. When he reached it, he found nothing but leaves, because it was not the season for figs. Then he said to the tree, "May no one ever eat fruit from you again." And his disciples heard him say it.

Mt.
21:12,13
Mk.
11:15-17
Lk.
19:45,46
At temple

JESUS CLEANSES TEMPLE. On reaching Jerusalem, Jesus entered the temple area and began driving out those who were buying and selling there. He overturned the tables of the money changers and the benches of those selling doves, and would not allow anyone to carry merchandise through the temple courts. And as he taught them, he said, "Is it not written:

"'My house will be called
    a house of prayer for all nations'x?

But you have made it 'a den of robbers.'y"

Mk. 11:18
Lk.
19:47,48

PLOT DELAYED. MkThe chief priests and the teachers of the law heard this and began looking for a way to kill him, for they feared him, because the whole crowd was amazed at his teaching. LkYet they could not find any way to do it, because all the people hung on his words.

Mt.
21:14-16

CHILDREN PRAISE JESUS. The blind and the lame came to him at the temple, and he healed them. But when the chief priests and the teachers of the law saw the wonderful things he did and the children shouting in the temple area, "Hosanna to the Son of David," they were indignant.

"Do you hear what these children are saying?" they asked him.

"Yes," replied Jesus, "have you never read,

"'From the lips of children and infants
    you have ordained praise'z?"

xIsaiah 56:7   yJer. 7:11   zPsalm 8:2

Jn.
12:20-26

PURPOSE OF CHRIST'S DEATH. Now there were some Greeks among those who went up to worship at the Feast. They came to Philip, who was from Bethsaida in Galilee, with a request. "Sir," they said, "we would like to see Jesus." Philip went to tell Andrew; Andrew and Philip in turn told Jesus.

Jesus replied, "The hour has come for the Son of Man to be glorified. I tell you the truth, unless a kernel of wheat falls to the ground and dies, it remains only a single seed. But if it dies, it produces many seeds. The man who loves his life will lose it, while the man who hates his life in this world will keep it for eternal life. Whoever serves me must follow me; and where I am, my servant also will be. My Father will honor the one who serves me.

Jn.
12:27-33

FORETELLING CRUCIFIXION. "Now my heart is troubled, and what shall I say? 'Father, save me from this hour'? No, it was for this very reason I came to this hour. Father, glorify your name!"

Then a voice came from heaven, "I have glorified it, and will glorify it again." The crowd that was there and heard it said it had thundered; others said an angel had spoken to him.

Jesus said, "This voice was for your benefit, not mine. Now is the time for judgment on this world; now the prince of this world will be driven out. But I, when I am lifted up from the earth, will draw all men to myself." He said this to show the kind of death he was going to die.

Jn.
12:34-36

CALL FOR WALKING IN LIGHT. The crowd spoke up, "We have heard from the Law that the Christ[a] will remain forever, so how can you say, 'The Son of Man must be lifted up'? Who is this 'Son of Man'?"

Then Jesus told them, "You are going to have the light just a little while longer. Walk while you have the light, before darkness overtakes you. The man who walks in the dark does not know where he is going. Put your trust in the light while you have it, so that you may become sons of light." When he had finished speaking, Jesus left and hid himself from them.

Mk.
11:19
Bethany

RETURN TO BETHANY. When evening came, they[b] went out of the city.

---

[a]Or Messiah   [b]Some early manuscripts he

Today's Insights

Triumph

Does your life seem like one struggle after another? Does it seem like you survive one battle only to be assaulted on another front? A child is sick; a husband is laid off. Someone you've been particularly close to betrays your friendship; a loved one dies. Or perhaps, just when you're over the pain of a broken relationship, the doctor brings you a spine-chilling report from your latest checkup. The troubles which plague us seem always on the attack.

Jesus also knew the grief of loss and the pain of suffering. He already knew that one of his own disciples was soon to betray him. Ahead would lie more ridicule, suffering, and finally death. Yet as a prelude to what would follow, Jesus experienced a wonderful day of triumph. If there are times when a prophet is not given the honor due him, nevertheless the day of honor cannot be denied. It will come.

For Jesus, the overdue honor comes from the ordinary people of the world—the ones who know real suffering. The ones who see in Jesus a champion of the rejected. The ones who identify with his striking commonness. It's not that they take him for common, like themselves. Quite to the contrary, you can almost hear the roar of the crowds as Jesus proceeds slowly into Jerusalem, like a triumphant general returning from a great victory. Their cry? "Blessed is the King!" Even if their understanding about his kingdom is still imperfect, what they do understand is that Jesus is like no other prophet they have ever known or heard about.

From the dusty roads of this earth, where the lips of little children sang his praises, to the very throne of heaven where surely angel anthems rolled, this was Jesus' moment. Try to even remotely imagine the indescribable feeling all around when Jesus shouted, "Father, glorify your name!" and the voice of God pealed down like thunder, "I have glorified it, and will glorify it again." Can we even begin to comprehend such a divine conversation?

Not only on this day of days, but down through the centuries, Jesus has reigned in triumph in the hearts of men and women who have accepted his glorious life and teaching. The Pharisees could hardly have realized how prophetic their words would be: "Look how the whole world has gone after him!"

And why *wouldn't* we follow Jesus? He leads us in triumph! Just when we think we have had all the trouble we can handle, Jesus reaches down and lifts us gently onto the colt he is riding into Jerusalem. Just when we think nobody cares, he opens our ears and we can hear the crowds shout, "Look who's riding with the King!" And just when we think there is no reward for being righteous, Jesus smiles and quietly reassures us, "My Father will honor the one who serves me."

Not all of our hurt will go away, and our problems won't magically disappear. But through faith we can be a child of the King—a king of triumph!

DAY 22 WITH JESUS

REBUKE

Final Week—Tuesday Morning

TUESDAY COMES AS A DAY OF GREAT CONFRONTATION with the religious leaders assembled in Jerusalem. By way of parables, Jesus points out that the leaders' predecessors have always rejected God's messengers and that now they themselves are rejecting even the Son of God. This obviously angers the Pharisees, and they attempt to trap Jesus into making some statement by which they can have him arrested. His answer takes them by surprise, and they are left with no basis for a charge.

The Pharisees are then joined in their questioning by the Sadducees. Although the Sadducees often clash politically and religiously with the Pharisees, the Sadducees are equally threatened by Jesus' teaching. So they are willing to join with the Pharisees to rid themselves of this Galilean troublemaker. Since the Sadducees deny any resurrection from the dead, it is only natural that they try to catch Jesus by posing a potentially embarrassing hypothetical situation concerning any supposed life after death. To their dismay Jesus, as the Son of God, once again responds with superior spiritual insight.

When a Pharisee questions Jesus concerning the greatest commandment, he delivers a response that goes to the heart of his message and ministry. He then sharply chastises both sects for having failed to grasp the true meaning of worship and service before God. Observing a widow contributing all that she has—although it was only two small coins—Jesus points to her as an example of true spirituality.

Mt. 21:20-22 Mk. 11:20-25 From Bethany to Jerusalem	**LESSONS FROM FIG TREE.** ^{Mk}In the morning, as they went along, they saw the fig tree withered from the roots. Peter remembered and said to Jesus, "Rabbi, look! The fig tree you cursed has withered!" ^{Mt}When the disciples saw this, they were amazed. "How did the fig tree wither so quickly?" they asked.

Jesus replied, "I tell you the truth, if you have faith and do not doubt, not only can you do what was done to the fig tree, but also you can say to this mountain, 'Go, throw yourself into the sea,' and it will be done. If you believe, you will receive whatever you ask for in prayer. ^{Mk}And when you stand praying, if you hold anything against anyone, forgive him, so that your Father in heaven may forgive you your sins.^c"

Mt.
21:23-27
Mk.
11:27-33
Lk. 20:1-8

JESUS' AUTHORITY QUESTIONED. They arrived again in Jerusalem, and while Jesus was walking in the temple courts, the chief priests, the teachers of the law and the elders came to him. "By what authority are you doing these things?" they asked. "And who gave you authority to do this?"

Jesus replied, "I will ask you one question. Answer me, and I will tell you by what authority I am doing these things. John's baptism—was it from heaven, or from men? Tell me!"

They discussed it among themselves and said, "If we say, 'From heaven,' he will ask, 'Then why didn't you believe him?' But if we say, 'From men'...." (They feared the people, for everyone held that John really was a prophet.)

So they answered Jesus, "We don't know."

Jesus said, "Neither will I tell you by what authority I am doing these things."

Mt.
21:28-32

PARABLE OF TWO SONS. "What do you think? There was a man who had two sons. He went to the first and said, 'Son, go and work today in the vineyard.'

"'I will not,' he answered, but later he changed his mind and went.

"Then the father went to the other son and said the same thing. He answered, 'I will, sir,' but he did not go.

"Which of the two did what his father wanted?"

"The first," they answered.

Jesus said to them, "I tell you the truth, the tax collectors and the prostitutes are entering the kingdom of God ahead of you. For John came to you to show you the way of righteousness, and you did not believe him, but the tax collectors and the prostitutes did. And even after you saw this, you did not repent and believe him."

---

^cSome manuscripts sins. ²⁶But if you do not forgive, neither will your Father who is in heaven forgive your sins.

PARABLE OF MURDEROUS TENANTS. MkHe then began to speak to them in parables: "A man planted a vineyard. He put a wall around it, dug a pit for the winepress and built a watchtower. Then he rented the vineyard to some farmers and went away on a journey. At harvest time he sent a servant to the tenants to collect from them some of the fruit of the vineyard. But they seized him, beat him and sent him away empty-handed. Then he sent another servant to them; they struck this man on the head and treated him shamefully. He sent still another, and that one they killed. He sent many others; some of them they beat, others they killed.

"He had one left to send, a son, whom he loved. He sent him last of all, saying, 'They will respect my son.'

"But the tenants said to one another, 'This is the heir. Come, let's kill him, and the inheritance will be ours.' So they took him and killed him, and threw him out of the vineyard.

"What then will the owner of the vineyard do? He will come and kill those tenants and give the vineyard to others."

LkWhen the people heard this, they said, "May this never be!"

Mt.
21:33-41
Mk.
12:1-9
Lk.
20:9-16

THE REJECTED STONE. Jesus said to them, "Have you never read in the Scriptures:

"'The stone the builders rejected
     has become the capstone[d];
 the Lord has done this,
     and it is marvelous in our eyes'[e]?

"Therefore I tell you that the kingdom of God will be taken away from you and given to a people who will produce its fruit. He who falls on this stone will be broken to pieces, but he on whom it falls will be crushed."[f]

Mt.
21:42-44
Mk.
12:10,11
Lk.
20:17,18

RELIGIOUS LEADERS ANGERED. When the chief priests and the Pharisees heard Jesus' parables, they knew he was talking about them. They looked for a way to arrest him, but they were afraid of the crowd because the people held that he was a prophet.

Mt.
21:45,46
Mk.
12:12
Lk.
20:19

[d]Or *cornerstone*   [e]Psalm 118:22,23   [f]Some manuscripts do not have verse 44.

Mt.
22:1-14

PARABLE OF WEDDING BANQUET. Jesus spoke to them again in parables, saying: "The kingdom of heaven is like a king who prepared a wedding banquet for his son. He sent his servants to those who had been invited to the banquet to tell them to come, but they refused to come.

"Then he sent some more servants and said, 'Tell those who have been invited that I have prepared my dinner: My oxen and fattened cattle have been butchered, and everything is ready. Come to the wedding banquet.'

But they paid no attention and went off—one to his field, another to his business. The rest seized his servants, mistreated them and killed them. The king was enraged. He sent his army and destroyed those murderers and burned their city.

"Then he said to his servants, 'The wedding banquet is ready, but those I invited did not deserve to come. Go to the street corners and invite to the banquet anyone you find.' So the servants went out into the streets and gathered all the people they could find, both good and bad, and the wedding hall was filled with guests.

"But when the king came in to see the guests, he noticed a man there who was not wearing wedding clothes. 'Friend,' he asked, 'how did you get in here without wedding clothes?' The man was speechless.

"Then the king told the attendants, 'Tie him hand and foot, and throw him outside, into the darkness, where there will be weeping and gnashing of teeth.'

"For many are invited, but few are chosen."

Mt.
22:15-22
Mk.
12:13-17
Lk.
20:20-26

LEADERS ASK ABOUT TAXES. MtThen the Pharisees went out and laid plans to trap him in his words. They sent their disciples to him along with the Herodians...Lkspies, who pretended to be honest. They hoped to catch Jesus in something he said so that they might hand him over to the power and authority of the governor. So the spies questioned him: "Teacher, we know that you speak and teach what is right, and that you do not show partiality but teach the way of God in accordance with the truth. Is it right for us to pay taxes to Caesar or not?"

He saw through their duplicity and said to them, "Show me a denarius. Whose portrait and inscription are on it?"

"Caesar's," they replied.

He said to them, "Then give to Caesar what is Caesar's, and to God what is God's."

They were unable to trap him in what he had said there in public. And astonished by his answer, they became silent.

Mt.
22:23-33
Mk.
12:18-27
Lk.
20:27-38

RESURRECTION QUESTIONED. That same day the Sadducees, who say there is no resurrection, came to him with a question. "Teacher," they said, "Moses told us that if a man dies without having children, his brother must marry the widow and have children for him. Now there were seven brothers among us. The first one married and died, and since he had no children, he left his wife to his brother. The same thing happened to the second and third brother, right on down to the seventh. Finally, the woman died. Now then, at the resurrection, whose wife will she be of the seven, since all of them were married to her?"

Jesus replied, "You are in error because you do not know the Scriptures or the power of God. At the resurrection people will neither marry nor be given in marriage; they will be like the angels in heaven. But about the resurrection of the dead—have you not read what God said to you, 'I am the God of Abraham, the God of Isaac, and the God of Jacob'[g]? He is not the God of the dead but of the living."

When the crowds heard this, they were astonished at his teaching.

Mt.
22:34-40
Mk.
12:28-34
Lk.
20:39,40

THE GREATEST COMMANDMENT. One of the teachers of the law came and heard them debating. Noticing that Jesus had given them a good answer, he asked him, "Of all the commandments, which is the most important?"

"The most important one," answered Jesus, "is this: 'Hear, O Israel, the Lord our God, the Lord is one.[h] Love the Lord your God with all your heart and with all your soul and with all your mind and with all your strength.'[i] The second is this: 'Love your neighbor as yourself.'[j] There is no commandment greater than these."

"Well said, teacher," the man replied. "You are right in saying that God is one and there is no other but him. To love him with all your heart, with all your understanding and with

[g]Exodus 3:6   [h]Or *the Lord our God is one Lord*   [i]Deut. 6:4,5   [j]Lev. 19:18

all your strength, and to love your neighbor as yourself is more important than all burnt offerings and sacrifices."

When Jesus saw that he had answered wisely, he said to him, "You are not far from the kingdom of God."

Mt. 22:41-46
Mk. 12:35-37
Lk. 20:41-44

JESUS ASKS ABOUT ANCESTRY. [Mt]While the Pharisees were gathered together, Jesus asked them, "What do you think about the Christ[k]? Whose son is he?"

"The son of David," they replied.

He said to them, "How is it then that David, speaking by the Spirit, calls him 'Lord'? For he says,

"'The Lord said to my Lord:
"Sit at my right hand
until I put your enemies
under your feet."'[l]

If then David calls him 'Lord,' how can he be his son?"

[Mk]The large crowd listened to him with delight. [Mt]No one could say a word in reply, and from that day on no one dared to ask him any more questions.

Mt. 23:1-12
Mk. 12:38-40
Lk. 20:45-47

SELF-RIGHTEOUSNESS CONDEMNED. Then Jesus said to the crowds and to his disciples: "The teachers of the law and the Pharisees sit in Moses' seat. So you must obey them and do everything they tell you. But do not do what they do, for they do not practice what they preach. They tie up heavy loads and put them on men's shoulders, but they themselves are not willing to lift a finger to move them.

"Everything they do is done for men to see: They make their phylacteries[m] wide and the tassels on their garments long; they love the place of honor at banquets and the most important seats in the synagogues; they love to be greeted in the marketplaces and to have men call them 'Rabbi.'

"But you are not to be called 'Rabbi,' for you have only one Master and you are all brothers. And do not call anyone on earth 'father,' for you have one Father, and he is in heaven. Nor are you to be called 'teacher,' for you have one Teacher, the Christ. The greatest among you will be your servant. For whoever exalts himself will be humbled, and whoever humbles himself will be exalted.

[k]Or *Messiah*   [l]Psalm 110:1   [m]That is, boxes containing Scripture verses, worn on the forehead and arm

Mt.
23:13-15

FALSE RELIGION CONDEMNED. "Woe to you, teachers of the law and Pharisees, you hypocrites! You shut the kingdom of heaven in men's faces. You yourselves do not enter, nor will you let those enter who are trying to."

"Woe to you, teachers of the law and Pharisees, you hypocrites! You travel over land and sea to win a single convert, and when he becomes one, you make him twice as much a son of hell as you are.

Mt.
23:16-22

LEGALISM CONDEMNED. "Woe to you, blind guides! You say, 'If anyone swears by the temple, it means nothing; but if anyone swears by the gold of the temple, he is bound by his oath.' You blind fools! Which is greater: the gold, or the temple that makes the gold sacred? You also say, 'If anyone swears by the altar, it means nothing; but if anyone swears by the gift on it, he is bound by his oath.' You blind men! Which is greater: the gift, or the altar that makes the gift sacred? Therefore, he who swears by the altar swears by it and by everything on it. And he who swears by the temple swears by it and by the one who dwells in it. And he who swears by heaven swears by God's throne and by the one who sits on it.

Mt.
23:23,24

INJUSTICE CONDEMNED. "Woe to you, teachers of the law and Pharisees, you hypocrites! You give a tenth of your spices—mint, dill and cummin. But you have neglected the more important matters of the law—justice, mercy and faithfulness. You should have practiced the latter, without neglecting the former. You blind guides! You strain out a gnat but swallow a camel.

Mt.
23:25-28

HYPOCRISY CONDEMNED. "Woe to you, teachers of the law and Pharisees, you hypocrites! You clean the outside of the cup and dish, but inside they are full of greed and self-indulgence. Blind Pharisee! First clean the inside of the cup and dish, and then the outside also will be clean.

"Woe to you, teachers of the law and Pharisees, you hypocrites! You are like whitewashed tombs, which look beautiful on the outside but on the inside are full of dead men's bones

---

"Some manuscripts *to.* [14]*Woe to you, teachers of the law and Pharisees, you hypocrites! You devour widows' houses and for a show make lengthy prayers. Therefore you will be punished more severely.*

and everything unclean. In the same way, on the outside you appear to people as righteous but on the inside you are full of hypocrisy and wickedness.

Mt. 23:29-36 PERSECUTION CONDEMNED. "Woe to you, teachers of the law and Pharisees, you hypocrites! You build tombs for the prophets and decorate the graves of the righteous. And you say, 'If we had lived in the days of our forefathers, we would not have taken part with them in shedding the blood of the prophets.' So you testify against yourselves that you are the descendants of those who murdered the prophets. Fill up, then, the measure of the sin of your forefathers!

"You snakes! You brood of vipers! How will you escape being condemned to hell? Therefore I am sending you prophets and wise men and teachers. Some of them you will kill and crucify; others you will flog in your synagogues and pursue from town to town. And so upon you will come all the righteous blood that has been shed on earth, from the blood of righteous Abel to the blood of Zechariah son of Berekiah, whom you murdered between the temple and the altar. I tell you the truth, all this will come upon this generation.

Mt. 23:37-39 LAMENT OVER JERUSALEM. "O Jerusalem, Jerusalem, you who kill the prophets and stone those sent to you, how often I have longed to gather your children together, as a hen gathers her chicks under her wings, but you were not willing. Look, your house is left to you desolate. For I tell you, you will not see me again until you say, 'Blessed is he who comes in the name of the Lord.'[o]"

Mk. 12:41-44 Lk. 21:1-4 WIDOW AN EXAMPLE. Jesus sat down opposite the place where the offerings were put and watched the crowd putting their money into the temple treasury. Many rich people threw in large amounts. But a poor widow came and put in two very small copper coins,[p] worth only a fraction of a penny.[q]

Calling his disciples to him, Jesus said, "I tell you the truth, this poor widow has put more into the treasury than all the others. They all gave out of their wealth; but she, out of her poverty, put in everything—all she had to live on."

[o]Psalm 118:26 [p]Greek *two lepta* [q]Greek *kodrantes*

TODAY'S INSIGHTS

Rebuke

As you think back over Jesus' ministry, who are those on the receiving end of Jesus' rebuke? The religious or the irreligious? The leaders or the followers? The rich or the poor? The known or the unknown? The powerful or the weak? Can there be any doubt but that in each case it is the former?

And who was it that always reacted in anger to Jesus' teaching? The same group of people. Why did Jesus consistently single out the religious leaders, and the rich and powerful, for his stinging rebuke?

Several reasons might suggest themselves. First, it was these people who spent their time reading the law and the prophets, debating their meaning. Surely they should have been the first to recognize Jesus as the fulfillment of all they knew about the Messiah. They were in positions of influence over the multitudes of the uneducated, and therefore their rejection of Jesus would multiply many times over among those less informed.

But perhaps more important were their motives for rejecting Jesus. Because they were envious of Jesus' popularity and power, they didn't *want* to acknowledge him. Because they feared losing the respect of their peers in the upper circle of society, they refused to let potential belief develop within themselves. Because they were so caught up in their own arrogance, they simply couldn't believe that someone who didn't talk like them or follow their traditions could possibly be what they had always expected the Messiah to be.

At the center of the problem, of course, was the misdirection of their hearts. They were religious people, but they had no clue about true spirituality. For them, form had won out over substance. Going through the motions was the height of their spiritual capacity. So when Jesus called them beyond their familiar and comfortable religious exercises, they feared being set adrift from solid moorings.

Are they somehow different from us, or do we too hang on with all our might to what we have always known and done religiously?

For example, how do we receive those who may understand the Scriptures differently? Do we listen carefully and study to see if perhaps they might be right? Or do we reject them out of hand? Do we reject others simply because they are more "successful" in evangelizing than we are? Do we look down our noses at fellowships whose members are typically less well-educated, or perhaps in a lower economic bracket? Would we be willing to worship with certain people if only they were "more like us"?

How easy it is to read Jesus' rebuke of others and fail to see that he may be looking into our eyes when he says it. Jesus wants us, like those in his own day, to reach new heights of spiritual understanding. There is much for us to consider. In what way is Jesus calling us to a higher plane today?

DAY
23
WITH
JESUS

PREDICTION

Discourse on Future Events

JESUS AND HIS DISCIPLES NOW MAKE THEIR WAY out of the temple. When one of the disciples comments on the beauty of the temple and its stones, Jesus makes the cryptic observation that there will come a time when the temple will be destroyed. Jesus and his disciples then go to the Mount of Olives, just outside the city. Peter, Andrew, James, and John come to Jesus privately, wanting to know more about the temple's destruction, the signs of his coming, and the end of the age. From their Jewish apocalyptic perspective, they apparently anticipate that the end of the age will coincide with Jesus' imminent political ascendancy. Even now, they misunderstand the nature of his kingdom. Like many of the ancient prophecies, Jesus' answer has been the source of much discussion.

There is general agreement regarding Jesus' reference to the destruction of the temple. In retrospect, it is known that only 40 years later, in A.D. 70, the Roman legions laid siege to Jerusalem, thoroughly sacking it and completely destroying the temple. Most would agree that Jesus describes events which precede that destruction. Some feel that Jesus' entire discourse is made with reference to Jerusalem's destruction by the Romans, while others see in it additional apocalyptic prophecy concerning future events. Still others view it as one prophecy having a dual significance.

In order to underscore the need for watchfulness, faithfulness, and spiritual readiness, Jesus will conclude his prophecies by telling two parables and describing the final judgment.

Mt. 24:1,2 Mk. 13:1,2 Lk. 21:5,6 Leaving temple (Tuesday)	TEMPLE TO BE DESTROYED. As he was leaving the temple, one of his disciples said to him, "Look, Teacher! What massive stones! What magnificent buildings!" "Do you see all these great buildings?" replied Jesus. "Not one stone here will be left on another; every one will be thrown down."

Mt. 24:3
Mk.
13:3,4
Lk. 21:7
Mount of
Olives
(Tuesday)

DISCIPLES ASK QUESTIONS. MkAs Jesus was sitting on the Mount of Olives opposite the temple, Peter, James, John and Andrew asked him privately, Mt"Tell us," they said, "when will this happen, and what will be the sign of your coming and of the end of the age?"

Mt.
24:4-35
Mk.
13:5-31
Lk.
21:8-33

JESUS TELLS OF SIGNS. MtJesus answered: "Watch out that no one deceives you. For many will come in my name, claiming, 'I am the Christ,r' and will deceive many. You will hear of wars and rumors of wars, but see to it that you are not alarmed. Such things must happen, but the end is still to come. Nation will rise against nation, and kingdom against kingdom. There will be famines and earthquakes in various places. All these are the beginning of birth pains." MkYou must be on your guard. You will be handed over to the local councils and flogged in the synagogues. On account of me you will stand before governors and kings as witnesses to them. And the gospel must first be preached to all nations. Whenever you are arrested and brought to trial, do not worry beforehand about what to say. Just say whatever is given you at the time, for it is not you speaking, but the Holy Spirit.

"Brother will betray brother to death, and a father his child. Children will rebel against their parents and have them put to death. MtBecause of the increase of wickedness, the love of most will grow cold....MkAll men will hate you because of me, but he who stands firm to the end will be saved. MtAnd this gospel of the kingdom will be preached in the whole world as a testimony to all nations, and then the end will come.

"So when you see standing in the holy place 'the abomination that causes desolation,'s spoken of through the prophet Daniel—let the reader understand—then let those who are in Judea flee to the mountains. Let no one on the roof of his house go down to take anything out of the house. Let no one in the field go back to get his cloak.

Lk"When you see Jerusalem being surrounded by armies, you will know that its desolation is near. Then let those who are in Judea flee to the mountains, let those in the city get out, and let those in the country not enter the city. For this is the time of punishment in fulfillment of all that has been written.

rOr Messiah   sDaniel 9:27; 11:31; 12:11

^{Mt}How dreadful it will be in those days for pregnant women and nursing mothers! Pray that your flight will not take place in winter or on the Sabbath. For then there will be great distress, unequaled from the beginning of the world until now—and never to be equaled again. ^{Lk}There will be great distress in the land and wrath against this people. They will fall by the sword and will be taken as prisoners to all the nations. Jerusalem will be trampled on by the Gentiles until the times of the Gentiles are fulfilled. ^{Mt}If those days had not been cut short, no one would survive, but for the sake of the elect those days will be shortened. At that time if anyone says to you, 'Look, here is the Christ!' or, 'There he is!' do not believe it. For false Christs and false prophets will appear and perform great signs and miracles to deceive even the elect—if that were possible. See, I have told you ahead of time.

"So if anyone tells you, 'There he is, out in the desert,' do not go out; or, 'Here he is, in the inner rooms,' do not believe it. For as lightning that comes from the east is visible even in the west, so will be the coming of the Son of Man. Wherever there is a carcass, there the vultures will gather.

"Immediately after the distress of those days

"'the sun will be darkened,
   and the moon will not give its light;
the stars will fall from the sky,
   and the heavenly bodies will be shaken.'^t

"At that time the sign of the Son of Man will appear in the sky, and all the nations of the earth will mourn. They will see the Son of Man coming on the clouds of the sky, with power and great glory. And he will send his angels with a loud trumpet call, and they will gather his elect from the four winds, from one end of the heavens to the other." ^{Lk}"There will be signs in the sun, moon and stars. On the earth, nations will be in anguish and perplexity at the roaring and tossing of the sea. Men will faint from terror, apprehensive of what is coming on the world, for the heavenly bodies will be shaken. At that time they will see the Son of Man coming in a cloud with power and great glory. When these things begin to take place, stand up and lift up your heads, because your redemption is

^tIsaiah 13:10; 34:4

drawing near." ᴹᵗ"Now learn this lesson from the fig tree: As soon as its twigs get tender and its leaves come out, you know that summer is near. Even so, when you see all these things, you know that it*ᵘ* is near, right at the door. I tell you the truth, this generation*ᵛ* will certainly not pass away until all these things have happened. Heaven and earth will pass away, but my words will never pass away.

Mt.
24:36-44
Mk.
13:32,33

EXACT TIMES UNKNOWN. "No one knows about that day or hour, not even the angels in heaven, nor the Son,*ʷ* but only the Father. As it was in the days of Noah, so it will be at the coming of the Son of Man. For in the days before the flood, people were eating and drinking, marrying and giving in marriage, up to the day Noah entered the ark; and they knew nothing about what would happen until the flood came and took them all away. That is how it will be at the coming of the Son of Man. Two men will be in the field; one will be taken and the other left. Two women will be grinding with a hand mill; one will be taken and the other left.

"Therefore keep watch, because you do not know on what day your Lord will come. But understand this: If the owner of the house had known at what time of night the thief was coming, he would have kept watch and would not have let his house be broken into. So you also must be ready, because the Son of Man will come at an hour when you do not expect him."

Mt.
24:45-51
Mk.
13:34-37
Lk.
21:34-36

JESUS URGES WATCHFULNESS. ᴸᵏ"Be careful, or your hearts will be weighed down with dissipation, drunkenness and the anxieties of life, and that day will close on you unexpectedly like a trap. For it will come upon all those who live on the face of the whole earth. Be always on the watch, and pray that you may be able to escape all that is about to happen, and that you may be able to stand before the Son of Man. ᴹᵏIt's like a man going away: He leaves his house and puts his servants in charge, each with his assigned task, and tells the one at the door to keep watch.

ᴹᵗ"Who then is the faithful and wise servant, whom the master has put in charge of the servants in his household to give them their food at the proper time? It will be good for that servant whose master finds him doing so when he returns. I

ᵘOr he   ᵛOr race   ʷSome manuscripts do not have nor the Son.

tell you the truth, he will put him in charge of all his possessions. But suppose that servant is wicked and says to himself, 'My master is staying away a long time,' and he then begins to beat his fellow servants and to eat and drink with drunkards. The master of that servant will come on a day when he does not expect him and at an hour he is not aware of. He will cut him to pieces and assign him a place with the hypocrites, where there will be weeping and gnashing of teeth.

Mk"Therefore keep watch because you do not know when the owner of the house will come back—whether in the evening, or at midnight, or when the rooster crows, or at dawn. If he comes suddenly, do not let him find you sleeping. What I say to you, I say to everyone: 'Watch!'"

Mt. 25:1-13

WISE AND FOOLISH VIRGINS. "At that time the kingdom of heaven will be like ten virgins who took their lamps and went out to meet the bridegroom. Five of them were foolish and five were wise. The foolish ones took their lamps but did not take any oil with them. The wise, however, took oil in jars along with their lamps. The bridegroom was a long time in coming, and they all became drowsy and fell asleep.

"At midnight the cry rang out: 'Here's the bridegroom! Come out to meet him!'

"Then all the virgins woke up and trimmed their lamps. The foolish ones said to the wise, 'Give us some of your oil; our lamps are going out.'

"'No,' they replied, 'there may not be enough for both us and you. Instead go to those who sell oil and buy some for yourselves.'

"But while they were on their way to buy the oil, the bridegroom arrived. The virgins who were ready went in with him to the wedding banquet. And the door was shut.

"Later the others also came. 'Sir! Sir!' they said. 'Open the door for us!'

"But he replied, 'I tell you the truth, I don't know you.'

"Therefore keep watch, because you do not know the day or the hour.

Mt. 25:14-30

PARABLE OF TALENTS. "Again, it will be like a man going on a journey, who called his servants and entrusted his property to them. To one he gave five talents[x] of money, to another two talents, and to another one talent, each according to his ability. Then he went on his journey. The man who had received the five talents went at once and put his money to work and gained five more. So also, the one with the two talents gained two more. But the man who had received the one talent went off, dug a hole in the ground and hid his master's money.

"After a long time the master of those servants returned and settled accounts with them. The man who had received the five talents brought the other five. 'Master,' he said, 'you entrusted me with five talents. See, I have gained five more.'

"His master replied, 'Well done, good and faithful servant! You have been faithful with a few things; I will put you in charge of many things. Come and share your master's happiness!'

"The man with the two talents also came. 'Master,' he said, 'you entrusted me with two talents; see, I have gained two more.'

"His master replied, 'Well done, good and faithful servant! You have been faithful with a few things; I will put you in charge of many things. Come and share your master's happiness!'

"Then the man who had received the one talent came. 'Master,' he said, 'I knew that you are a hard man, harvesting where you have not sown and gathering where you have not scattered seed. So I was afraid and went out and hid your talent in the ground. See, here is what belongs to you.'

"His master replied, 'You wicked, lazy servant! So you knew that I harvest where I have not sown and gather where I have not scattered seed? Well then, you should have put my money on deposit with the bankers, so that when I returned I would have received it back with interest.

"'Take the talent from him and give it to the one who has the ten talents. For everyone who has will be given more, and he will have an abundance. Whoever does not have, even what he has will be taken from him. And throw that worthless servant outside, into the darkness, where there will be weeping and gnashing of teeth.'

Mt.
25:31-46 | CONCERNING LAST JUDGMENT. "When the Son of Man comes in his glory, and all the angels with him, he will sit on

[x]A talent was worth more than a thousand dollars.

his throne in heavenly glory. All the nations will be gathered before him, and he will separate the people one from another as a shepherd separates the sheep from the goats. He will put the sheep on his right and the goats on his left.

"Then the King will say to those on his right, 'Come, you who are blessed by my Father; take your inheritance, the kingdom prepared for you since the creation of the world. For I was hungry and you gave me something to eat, I was thirsty and you gave me something to drink, I was a stranger and you invited me in, I needed clothes and you clothed me, I was sick and you looked after me, I was in prison and you came to visit me.'

"Then the righteous will answer him, 'Lord, when did we see you hungry and feed you, or thirsty and give you something to drink? When did we see you a stranger and invite you in, or needing clothes and clothe you? When did we see you sick or in prison and go to visit you?'

"The King will reply, 'I tell you the truth, whatever you did for one of the least of these brothers of mine, you did for me.'

"Then he will say to those on his left, 'Depart from me, you who are cursed, into the eternal fire prepared for the devil and his angels. For I was hungry and you gave me nothing to eat, I was thirsty and you gave me nothing to drink, I was a stranger and you did not invite me in, I needed clothes and you did not clothe me, I was sick and in prison and you did not look after me.'

"They also will answer, 'Lord, when did we see you hungry or thirsty or a stranger or needing clothes or sick or in prison, and did not help you?'

"He will reply, 'I tell you the truth, whatever you did not do for one of the least of these, you did not do for me.'

"Then they will go away to eternal punishment, but the righteous to eternal life."

TODAY'S INSIGHTS

Prediction

Why are we so fascinated with the future and with predictions about the future? Are we dissatisfied with the present, or perhaps afraid of what might be coming? Or is it just our curiosity? Whatever it is, people are inexorably drawn to fortune cookies, horoscopes, and crystal balls of all types, including psychic mediums, palmists, and trance channelers. Unfortunately, none of these can really tell us about the future. If they could, horse races and stock market fluctuations would be easy for them to predict.

As Christians, however, we have some definite assurances about the future. That is why we proclaim Christ's second coming and sing about the world to come. We have the promised hope of God's ultimate victory over evil. For us, the future is not to be feared. We know that God is in control.

But even we Christians are curious about the details. Like generations before us, we too ask when Christ will come again, and what events will precede his appearance. We want to know what will happen at the end of time.

Will there be a battle between God and Satan? Will our bodies be changed, and if so, how? Will we recognize each other? Will we actually talk to Abraham and Moses and all the great people of faith about whom we have read in the Bible? For centuries, the answers to these questions have been the subject of speculation and discussion by the followers of Christ.

What, indeed, *can* we know? For starters, we know that God has a timetable for the world and a purpose to be completed before its end. That God will triumph over Satan and the evil of his kingdom. That before Christ's return there will be many who desire to turn us away from God by proclaiming substitute "Christs"—whether counterfeit religions, self-appointed gurus, or even the notion that each one of us is our own Savior!

What we can also know, from Jesus' own lips, is that no one can predict when the end of time will be. Such speculation is futile. If we really want to profit from what Jesus taught about the future, we must listen carefully to his words: "Keep watch, because you do not know on what day your Lord will come." Ours is not the responsibility of the forecaster, but of the worker. Can anyone miss the point of the parable of the talents, or of the wise and foolish virgins?

Be ready at all times

Judgment will not be based upon who has correctly predicted the coming of Christ, or the end of the world, or the events which might precede the end of time. Jesus said that judgment will be based upon how we have served the hungry, the sick, the needy, and strangers.

If Christ should come today, what would he find us doing?

BETRAYAL

Final Week—Tuesday Afternoon

As THE LONG DAY OF CONFRONTATION AND TEACHING comes to an end, Jesus tells his disciples that his death is only two days away. Already the chief priests and elders are conspiring against him in the palace of the high priest. Aware that the feast is almost upon them, the conspirators are anxious to have Jesus killed before that time. Even as they plot how to snare Jesus, they are approached by Judas Iscariot, one of Christ's chosen disciples.

For his own reasons, Judas has decided to betray Jesus and has therefore come to bargain with the members of the council. Of course they are delighted at this unexpected assistance. The amount agreed to is 30 pieces of silver (which at this time is the approximate price of a slave). It is not clear whether Judas knows fully the serious consequences of the betrayal. Later evidence indicates that he may not have anticipated that Jesus would actually die as a result. Be that as it may, Judas is apparently both covetous and dishonest—this despite the fact that he has been acting as a kind of treasurer for the disciples.

Mt. 26:1,2	JESUS FORESEES CRUCIFIXION. When Jesus had finished saying all these things, he said to his disciples, "As you know, the Passover is two days away—and the Son of Man will be handed over to be crucified."
Mt. 26:3-5 Mk. 14:1,2 Lk. 22:1,2	PRIESTS AND ELDERS CONSPIRE. Then the chief priests and the elders of the people assembled in the palace of the high priest, whose name was Caiaphas, and they plotted to arrest Jesus in some sly way and kill him. "But not during the Feast," they said, "or there may be a riot among the people."
Mt. 26:14-16 Mk. 14:10,11 Lk. 22:3-6	JUDAS BARGAINS TO BETRAY. LkThen Satan entered Judas, called Iscariot, one of the Twelve. And Judas went to the chief priests and the officers of the temple guard and discussed with them how he might betray Jesus Mtand asked, "What are you willing to give me if I hand him over to you?" So they counted

out for him thirty silver coins. LkHe consented, and watched for an opportunity to hand Jesus over to them when no crowd was present.

Final Week—Wednesday

The preceding events of this final week appear to be accounted for by the Gospel writers within the clear context of either Sunday, Monday, or Tuesday, just as they have been presented. The exact timing of what happens after those events, however, appears less certain. John in particular, touches only lightly upon the events between Jesus' triumphant entry and the so-called "last supper" which Jesus shares with his disciples. Referring to various public reactions during that time, John notes that, despite Jesus' teaching and miraculous works, there are still many people who either disbelieve or are afraid to acknowledge their belief. Then John records what is apparently Jesus' last public appeal before his subsequent arrest. As there is no evidence that these events occurred on any of the prior three days, they are set forth here as occurring on Wednesday, though that time frame is only speculative.

Of far greater significance at this point is the chronology related to the last supper, Jesus' crucifixion, and his subsequent resurrection. Traditionally the last supper is believed to have occurred on Thursday evening, followed by the crucifixion on Friday afternoon and the resurrection on Sunday morning. However, such reckoning raises at least two questions. First, in an action-packed final week, what reason is there to believe that there would be a whole day of either actual inactivity or activity which is left unrecorded? Second, and far more important—if Jesus is crucified on Friday afternoon and thereafter hurriedly put into the tomb, how can there be sufficient time to match Jesus' own prediction that he would remain in the tomb for three days and three nights before being resurrected? Even if one stretches imagination within the traditional time frame in order to find parts of three days, it is not possible to find three nights.

The resolution of both questions appears to be found in recognizing that the last supper took place on Wednesday evening, followed by the crucifixion and burial on Thursday. Acceptance of that assumption requires an understanding of the Passover, the Feast of Unleavened Bread, and the way in which the Jews reckon time. As for the reckoning of time, the Jewish day begins at sunset on the previous evening. This means, for example, that our Wednesday night is actually Thursday, and our Thursday night is actually Friday.

Passover is observed on the 14th day of the month of Nisan, corresponding to March-April. Passover is observed in commemoration of the deliverance of the ancient Israelites from their Egyptian bondage. The name derives from the "passing over" of the Israelites when death came to the firstborn of each Egyptian family. As part of that same commemoration, Passover is followed by the seven-day Feast of Unleavened Bread, which reminds the Jews of their forefathers' flight from Egypt, during which time the Israelites ate unleavened bread only. (It is common among Jews of Jesus' day to refer to both celebrations by only one name, either as "Passover" or as the "Feast of Unleavened Bread.") By God's direction (Leviticus 23), a lamb is to be slaughtered late on the 14th day (Passover) and the Passover meal eaten that evening, which would be the beginning of the 15th day, the first day of the Feast of Unleavened Bread. The entire 15th day is then to be observed as a special Sabbath, or high holy day, regardless of the day of the week on which it might fall in any given year. (If the 15th day is a Friday, then both that Friday and the next day, Saturday, are observed as Sabbaths.)

With that background the picture begins to come clear. Matthew, Mark, and Luke record the disciples' preparation for the Passover on the first day of the Feast of Unleavened Bread on which the Passover lamb had to be sacrificed. That would place their preparations, then, at the beginning of the 14th day, which, of course, begins on the evening of the 13th day. (Among the preparations common on the evening of the 13th day is the removal of all leaven from the house.) Therefore it appears that the disciples assume they are preparing the upper room primarily for the special paschal meal which they expect to share with Jesus the following evening, and they apparently do not contemplate that the regular meal on the first night will in fact be their "last supper" with Jesus.

Although generally referring to the occasion as a part of the Passover celebration, Jesus seems to explain why it is important for him to eat with them on the night before the actual Passover meal. As will be seen, Jesus' words are: "I have eagerly desired to eat this Passover with you before I suffer. For I tell you, I will not eat it again until it finds fulfillment in the kingdom of God." In referring to his suffering, Jesus is obviously anticipating that his own sacrificial death will take place later that day, preventing him from participating in the actual Passover supper.

John's account eliminates any doubt that this supper occurred prior to the actual Passover meal. When Jesus tells Judas during the supper to do what he is about to do, some of the other disciples "thought Jesus was telling him to buy what was needed for the Feast." Furthermore, the Jews who have obtained Jesus' arrest will not enter Caiaphas' palace for fear that they will be ceremonially unclean, and therefore unable to eat the Passover. Most convincing is the fact that the day of Jesus' crucifixion is plainly stated to be "the day of Preparation of Passover Week"—the day on which the paschal lamb is slain for the Passover meal taken during the evening of that day.

The most meaningful result of moving away from the traditional time frame is seeing how Jesus' crucifixion becomes the perfect "type" of the Passover Lamb. Under Hebrew law, the paschal lamb is chosen on the tenth day and then "kept up" until the 14th day, when it is sacrificed for the sins of the people. If Jesus' triumphant entry into Jerusalem is counted as the tenth day, Thursday would be the 14th day, and thus the day on which Jesus is crucified. Far more important than this possible parallel is the fact that Jesus, as the perfect Lamb of God, does not celebrate the Passover with some other ordinary sacrificial lamb, but rather becomes himself the Lamb who is slain—precisely at the appropriate hour!

There is therefore strong evidence that the last supper takes place on the evening prior to the Day of Preparation, which by modern reckoning would be Wednesday night. Proceeding upon that assumption, the events associated with this final Wednesday include not only Jesus' last public teaching, but also the account of Peter and John finding the upper room and making preparations for the Passover celebration.

Lk.
21:37,38
At
temple
(Wed.
morning)

JESUS TEACHES AT TEMPLE. Each day Jesus was teaching at the temple, and each evening he went out to spend the night on the hill called the Mount of Olives, and all the people came early in the morning to hear him at the temple.

Jn.
12:37

MANY STILL DISBELIEVE. Even after Jesus had done all these miraculous signs in their presence, they still would not believe in him.

Jn.
12:38-41

DISBELIEF FULFILLS PROPHECY. This was to fulfill the word of Isaiah the prophet:

> "Lord, who has believed our message
>> and to whom has the arm of the Lord been revealed?"[y]

For this reason they could not believe, because, as Isaiah says elsewhere:

> "He has blinded their eyes
>> and deadened their hearts,
> so they can neither see with their eyes,
>> nor understand with their hearts,
>> nor turn—and I would heal them."[z]

Isaiah said this because he saw Jesus' glory and spoke about him.

Jn.
12:42,43

SOME ARE AFRAID. Yet at the same time many even among the leaders believed in him. But because of the Pharisees they would not confess their faith for fear they would be put out of the synagogue; for they loved praise from men more than praise from God.

Jn.
12:44-50

FINAL PUBLIC APPEAL. Then Jesus cried out, "When a man believes in me, he does not believe in me only, but in the one who sent me. When he looks at me, he sees the one who sent me. I have come into the world as a light, so that no one who believes in me should stay in darkness.

"As for the person who hears my words but does not keep them, I do not judge him. For I did not come to judge the world, but to save it. There is a judge for the one who rejects me and does not accept my words; that very word which I spoke will condemn him at the last day. For I did not speak of

[y]Isaiah 53:1   [z]Isaiah 6:10

my own accord, but the Father who sent me commanded me what to say and how to say it. I know that his command leads to eternal life. So whatever I say is just what the Father has told me to say."

Mt.
26:17-19
Mk.
14:12-16
Lk.
22:7-13
Upper
room
(Wednesday
afternoon)

DISCIPLES MAKE PREPARATIONS. Then came the day of Unleavened Bread on which the Passover lamb had to be sacrificed. Jesus sent Peter and John, saying, "Go and make preparations for us to eat the Passover."

"Where do you want us to prepare for it?" they asked.

He replied, "As you enter the city, a man carrying a jar of water will meet you. Follow him to the house that he enters, and say to the owner of the house, 'The Teacher asks: Where is the guest room, where I may eat the Passover with my disciples?' He will show you a large upper room, all furnished. Make preparations there."

They left and found things just as Jesus had told them. So they prepared the Passover.

TODAY'S INSIGHTS

Betrayal

Have you ever been betrayed by a friend? If so, you know the pain of separation which resembles the grief of death. When Judas agreed to betray Jesus, he might just as well have hammered the spikes that would later be driven through Jesus' hands.

Have you ever wondered how it was possible for one of the apostles (who had witnessed Jesus' power, teaching, and love) to turn him over to his enemies for *any* amount of money? This, of course, was not Judas' first act of betrayal. As treasurer for the disciples, Judas had been dipping into the till all along. He was a dishonest and greedy man. Even so, the mind races: How in the world could he have betrayed Jesus?

And isn't it intriguing that Jesus would have chosen Judas in the first place? Surely Jesus must have known Judas' character from the beginning. Was Judas no more than an unwitting puppet predestined to fulfill prophecy? That such is *not* the case is seen in what the Scripture says: "Then Satan entered Judas...." Judas was

Satan's agent, not God's. Nevertheless, the question still haunts us: How could Judas do such a thing?

Perhaps we have a clue when we are told about others who also refused to accept Jesus as the Christ: "Even after Jesus had done all these miraculous signs in their presence, they still would not believe in him." Judas was not the only one to betray Jesus. All those who refused to believe on him despite the overwhelming evidence of his deity might as well have picked up their own 30 silver coins when Judas did.

Even today there are those who, despite the evidence, continue to betray Jesus through disbelief. How is it possible? Why do they choose to ignore him?

Are we to understand Isaiah's prophecy as saying that God himself is the cause of their disbelief? Surely not, "for God so loved the world that he gave his one and only Son, that whoever believes in him shall not perish but have eternal life." In what way, then, did God blind their eyes and deaden their hearts? In the same way that he sometimes blinds our own eyes and deadens our own hearts— by refusing to *force* us to believe. In allowing us the free choice about what we will do with Jesus, God permits us to close our eyes and hearts to Christ if we so choose.

We are no more puppets than was Judas. We can choose Christ, or we can choose the world with its false allure. Yet it is not a choice that we make just once in a lifetime. Each day that Judas robbed Jesus was a day of betrayal. And for those who heard Jesus teach, and watched his miracles, yet refused to believe—for them, every day was a day of betrayal.

Do we believe in Jesus, yet live our lives as if we didn't? If so, we too betray Jesus. Will today be a day of faith or a day of betrayal?

LOVE

The Upper Room

WITH THE PLOT TO KILL JESUS TAKING ITS FINAL FORM, AND WITH the clamor for his life reaching a crescendo, an upper room in Jerusalem becomes the calm at the center of the storm. Here Jesus and his chosen disciples withdraw to themselves to await participation in the Passover Feast. Undoubtedly because Jesus has indicated that the coming of his kingdom is imminent, the apostles begin to discuss who among themselves is the greatest. Is it conceivable that, after having been with Jesus throughout his ministry, and having listened to all his teaching about the nature of the kingdom, his chosen 12 still have political aspirations for power and rank within an earthly kingdom? What must Jesus do to convince them otherwise? Taking on the role of a servant, Jesus begins to wash the feet of his disciples in order to teach them the need, not for power and position, but for humility and service to others.

As the supper progresses, Jesus takes the bread and wine and tells his disciples to partake of them as symbols of his body and blood, thereby instituting his special memorial and covenant with all his disciples. Then, as if to prepare for the sealing of that covenant, Jesus reveals Judas as his betrayer and sends him out to complete the betrayal, now near at hand.

What follows is a call for mutual love, not only because of the petty rivalries which continue to divide the disciples, but also because Jesus knows they will need each other's support in order to endure the challenges soon to come their way.

When Jesus tells them that he is going away, Peter replies that he wants to follow. And when Jesus responds that Peter cannot go with him at this time, Peter insists that, if necessary, he is willing to die for Jesus. Luke and John record the first of two warnings to Peter that he will deny Jesus before the coming of daylight. Matthew and Mark show that Jesus repeats the warning a little later in a different setting as the disciples make their way toward the Mount of Olives.

The events in the upper room begin now with Jesus expressing his love for his disciples.

Lk.
22:14-16
Upper
room

IMPORTANCE OF OCCASION. When the hour came, Jesus and his apostles reclined at the table. And he said to them, "I have eagerly desired to eat this Passover with you before I suffer. For I tell you, I will not eat it again until it finds fulfillment in the kingdom of God."

Mt.
26:26-29
Mk.
14:22-25
Lk.
22:17-20

INSTITUTION OF MEMORIAL. After taking the cup, he gave thanks and said, "Take this and divide it among you. For I tell you I will not drink again of the fruit of the vine until the kingdom of God comes."

And he took bread, gave thanks and broke it, and gave it to them, saying, "This is my body given for you; do this in remembrance of me."

In the same way, after the supper he took the cup, saying, "This cup is the new covenant in my blood, which is poured out for you.

Lk.
22:21,23

JESUS HINTS OF BETRAYER. But the hand of him who is going to betray me is with mine on the table." They began to question among themselves which of them it might be who would do this.

Lk.
22:24-30

APOSTLES DISPUTE. Also a dispute arose among them as to which of them was considered to be greatest. Jesus said to them, "The kings of the Gentiles lord it over them; and those who exercise authority over them call themselves Benefactors. But you are not to be like that. Instead, the greatest among you should be like the youngest, and the one who rules like the one who serves. For who is greater, the one who is at the table or the one who serves? Is it not the one who is at the table? But I am among you as one who serves. You are those who have stood by me in my trials. And I confer on you a kingdom, just as my Father conferred one on me, so that you may eat and drink at my table in my kingdom and sit on thrones, judging the twelve tribes of Israel."

Jn.
13:1-5

JESUS WASHES APOSTLES' FEET. Jesus knew that the time had come for him to leave this world and go to the Father.

Having loved his own who were in the world, he now showed them the full extent of his love.[a]

The evening meal was being served, and the devil had already prompted Judas Iscariot, son of Simon, to betray Jesus. Jesus knew that the Father had put all things under his power, and that he had come from God and was returning to God; so he got up from the meal, took off his outer clothing, and wrapped a towel around his waist. After that, he poured water into a basin and began to wash his disciples' feet, drying them with the towel that was wrapped around him.

Jn.
13:6-11

PETER IS HESITANT. He came to Simon Peter, who said to him, "Lord, are you going to wash my feet?"

Jesus replied, "You do not realize now what I am doing, but later you will understand."

"No," said Peter, "you shall never wash my feet."

Jesus answered, "Unless I wash you, you have no part with me."

"Then, Lord," Simon Peter replied, "not just my feet but my hands and my head as well!"

Jesus answered, "A person who has had a bath needs only to wash his feet; his whole body is clean. And you are clean, though not every one of you." For he knew who was going to betray him, and that was why he said not every one was clean.

Jn.
13:12-17

JESUS EXPLAINS WASHING. When he had finished washing their feet, he put on his clothes and returned to his place. "Do you understand what I have done for you?" he asked them. "You call me 'Teacher' and 'Lord,' and rightly so, for that is what I am. Now that I, your Lord and Teacher, have washed your feet, you also should wash one another's feet. I have set you an example that you should do as I have done for you. I tell you the truth, no servant is greater than his master, nor is a messenger greater than the one who sent him. Now that you know these things, you will be blessed if you do them.

Mt.
26:20,21
Mk.
14:17,18
Jn.
13:18-21

JESUS PREDICTS BETRAYAL. "I am not referring to all of you; I know those I have chosen. But this is to fulfill the scripture: 'He who shares my bread has lifted up his heel against me.'[b]

"I am telling you now before it happens, so that when it does happen you will believe that I am He. I tell you the truth,

[a]Or *he loved them to the last*   [b]Psalm 41:9

whoever accepts anyone I send accepts me; and whoever accepts me accepts the one who sent me."

After he had said this, Jesus was troubled in spirit and testified, "I tell you the truth, one of you is going to betray me."

Mt.
26:22-25
Mk.
14:19-21
Lk.
22:22
Jn.
13:22-27a

BETRAYER IDENTIFIED. ^{Mt}They were very sad and began to say to him one after the other, "Surely not I, Lord?"

Jesus replied, "The one who has dipped his hand into the bowl with me will betray me. The Son of Man will go just as it is written about him. But woe to that man who betrays the Son of Man! It would be better for him if he had not been born."

^{Jn}His disciples stared at one another, at a loss to know which of them he meant. One of them, the disciple whom Jesus loved, was reclining next to him. Simon Peter motioned to this disciple and said, "Ask him which one he means."

Leaning back against Jesus, he asked him, "Lord, who is it?"

Jesus answered, "It is the one to whom I will give this piece of bread when I have dipped it in the dish." Then, dipping the piece of bread, he gave it to Judas Iscariot, son of Simon. As soon as Judas took the bread, Satan entered into him. ^{Mt}Then Judas, the one who would betray him, said, "Surely not I, Rabbi?"

Jesus answered, "Yes, it is you."[c]

Jn.
13:27b-30

JESUS SENDS JUDAS OUT. "What you are about to do, do quickly," Jesus told him, but no one at the meal understood why Jesus said this to him. Since Judas had charge of the money, some thought Jesus was telling him to buy what was needed for the Feast, or to give something to the poor. As soon as Judas had taken the bread, he went out. And it was night.

Jn.
13:31-35

JESUS CALLS FOR LOVE. When he was gone, Jesus said, "Now is the Son of Man glorified and God is glorified in him. If God is glorified in him,[d] God will glorify the Son in himself, and will glorify him at once.

"My children, I will be with you only a little longer. You will look for me, and just as I told the Jews, so I tell you now: Where I am going, you cannot come.

"A new command I give you: Love one another. As I have loved you, so you must love one another. By this all men will know that you are my disciples, if you love one another."

[c]Or *"You yourself have said it"*   [d]Many early manuscripts do not have *If God is glorified in him.*

Lk.
22:31-34
Jn.
13:36-38

PETER MAKES REQUEST. JnSimon Peter asked him, "Lord, where are you going?"

Jesus replied, "Where I am going, you cannot follow now, but you will follow later."

Peter asked, "Lord, why can't I follow you now? I will lay down my life for you."

Lk"Simon, Simon, Satan has asked to sift youe as wheat. But I have prayed for you, Simon, that your faith may not fail. And when you have turned back, strengthen your brothers."

But he replied, "Lord, I am ready to go with you to prison and to death."

Jesus answered, "I tell you, Peter, before the rooster crows today, you will deny three times that you know me."

Jn.
14:1-4

JESUS TO PREPARE PLACE. "Do not let your hearts be troubled. Trust in Godf; trust also in me. In my Father's house are many rooms; if it were not so, I would have told you. I am going there to prepare a place for you. And if I go and prepare a place for you, I will come back and take you to be with me that you also may be where I am. You know the way to the place where I am going."

Jn.
14:5-7

THOMAS WANTS TO KNOW WAY. Thomas said to him, "Lord, we don't know where you are going, so how can we know the way?"

Jesus answered, "I am the way and the truth and the life. No one comes to the Father except through me. If you really knew me, you would knowg my Father as well. From now on, you do know him and have seen him."

Jn.
14:8-15

PHILIP WANTS TO SEE FATHER. Philip said, "Lord, show us the Father and that will be enough for us."

Jesus answered: "Don't you know me, Philip, even after I have been among you such a long time? Anyone who has seen me has seen the Father. How can you say, 'Show us the Father'? Don't you believe that I am in the Father, and that the Father is in me? The words I say to you are not just my own. Rather, it is the Father, living in me, who is doing his work. Believe me when I say that I am in the Father and the Father is in me; or at least believe on the evidence of the miracles themselves. I tell

eThe Greek is plural.   fOr You trust in God   gSome early manuscripts If you really have known me, you will know you the truth, anyone who has faith in me will do what I have been doing. He will do even greater things than these, because I am going to the Father. And I will do whatever you ask in my name, so that the Son may bring glory to the Father. You may ask me for anything in my name, and I will do it.

"If you love me, you will obey what I command.

Jn. 14:16-21

JESUS PROMISES HOLY SPIRIT. "And I will ask the Father, and he will give you another Counselor to be with you forever—the Spirit of truth. The world cannot accept him, because it neither sees him nor knows him. But you know him, for he lives with you and will be[h] in you. I will not leave you as orphans; I will come to you. Before long, the world will not see me anymore, but you will see me. Because I live, you also will live. On that day you will realize that I am in my Father, and you are in me, and I am in you. Whoever has my commands and obeys them, he is the one who loves me. He who loves me will be loved by my Father, and I too will love him and show myself to him."

Jn. 14:22-24

JUDAS IS PUZZLED. Then Judas (not Judas Iscariot) said, "But, Lord, why do you intend to show yourself to us and not to the world?"

Jesus replied, "If anyone loves me, he will obey my teaching. My Father will love him, and we will come to him and make our home with him. He who does not love me will not obey my teaching. These words you hear are not my own; they belong to the Father who sent me.

Jn. 14:25-31a

JESUS PREDICTS RETURN. "All this I have spoken while still with you. But the Counselor, the Holy Spirit, whom the Father will send in my name, will teach you all things and will remind you of everything I have said to you. Peace I leave with you; my peace I give you. I do not give to you as the world gives. Do not let your hearts be troubled and do not be afraid.

"You heard me say, 'I am going away and I am coming back to you.' If you loved me, you would be glad that I am going to the Father, for the Father is greater than I. I have told you now before it happens, so that when it does happen you will believe. I will not speak with you much longer, for the prince of this world is coming. He has no hold on me, but the world

[h]Some early manuscripts *and is*

must learn that I love the Father and that I do exactly what my Father has commanded me."

Lk. 22:35-38

FULFILLMENT OF PROPHECY. Then Jesus asked them, "When I sent you without purse, bag or sandals, did you lack anything?"

"Nothing," they answered.

He said to them, "But now if you have a purse, take it, and also a bag; and if you don't have a sword, sell your cloak and buy one. It is written: 'And he was numbered with the transgressors'[i]; and I tell you that this must be fulfilled in me. Yes, what is written about me is reaching its fulfillment."

The disciples said, "See, Lord, here are two swords."

"That is enough," he replied.

**Mt. 26:30
Mk. 14:26
Lk. 22:39
Jn. 14:31b**

TO MOUNT OF OLIVES. [Jn]"Come now; let us leave."

[Mt]When they had sung a hymn, they went out to the Mount of Olives.

**Mt. 26:31,32
Mk. 14:27,28**

WARNING ABOUT FORSAKING. Then Jesus told them, "This very night you will all fall away on account of me, for it is written:

"'I will strike the shepherd,
     and the sheep of the flock will be scattered.'[j]

But after I have risen, I will go ahead of you into Galilee."

**Mt. 26:33-35
Mk. 14:29-31**

PETER BOASTS LOYALTY. Peter replied, "Even if all fall away on account of you, I never will."

"I tell you the truth," Jesus answered, "this very night, before the rooster crows, you will disown me three times."

But Peter declared, "Even if I have to die with you, I will never disown you." And all the other disciples said the same.

TODAY'S INSIGHTS

Love

Is there a more abused word in the English language than the word "love"? What does "love" mean to us if it can refer to people, pets, paintings, and pickles—all with seemingly equal vigor! Even if we restricted its use to people, "love" can mean parental love,

[i]Isaiah 53:12   [j]Zech. 13:7

romantic love, sexual love, or just a special friendship. "Love" has meaning only in its context.

"Christian love" provides a meaningful context, as does "godly love." But even "God is love" can be used in such a sugary, exploitive way that it can rationalize anything the speaker might have in mind.

For Jesus, "love" was concern and compassion for those in need. "Love" was a spiritual relationship with the people in his life. "Love" was the motivation for emptying himself of the glory of heaven to become a broken sacrifice on our behalf. Yet virtually always for Jesus, "love" was not a noun but a verb. It was compassion in action. It was relationship with interaction. For Jesus, "love" was not merely a lofty ideal but a lifestyle.

That Christ would humble himself to come to this earth and take on our struggling humanity is amazing enough. But for Jesus Christ to have washed the feet of his disciples—an act normally performed by household servants—makes such a dramatic point about love. Through this simple act Jesus Christ, the Creator of the universe and the Son of God on high, totally redefined "love" as "servanthood."

If we say we love God, we must express it in the context of Jesus' own definition of love, which is *servanthood*. Are we committed to servanthood? Servanthood means doing whatever has to be done in the furtherance of Christ's kingdom—even washing feet if necessary. It means not worrying about what position we may occupy. In fact, it means actively seeking the backseat when others can do a better job, and volunteering to do the grub work behind the scenes where little credit is ever given. It means loving each other even when we don't want to. No, it's more than that. It means actually *serving* others, even if we don't love them!

But can we really do that? It's easy to say that we ought to serve the unlovable while they are doing their best to ridicule us, or even to hurt us, but few of us have the natural will power to do that. And Jesus knew that. That's why he gave us this promise: I am sending you the Spirit, who "lives with you and will be in you." We don't have to struggle alone. When loving becomes the most difficult, we can still hear Jesus say, "And we will come to you and make our home with you!"

Is there someone you are having difficulty loving? Has resentment burdened you with guilt? Do you sometimes feel that God's love is missing in your life? Invite him in—through servanthood love. Let him wash your feet…then pass it on.

DAY
26
WITH
JESUS

UNITY

Final Discourse

JOHN ALONE RECORDS THE FINAL DISCOURSE OF JESUS with his chosen disciples. It comes as Jesus and his disciples continue toward the Mount of Olives, just before they cross the Kidron Valley, which forms the eastern border of Jerusalem. Each word Jesus speaks reflects the burden which he feels in leaving these men to finish the work which he has begun. Jesus encourages them in their faith and promises that in his name they will perform great works. Again he calls them to mutual love in order to withstand the inevitable persecution which awaits them. Explaining the necessity of his going away, Jesus promises that they will not be left wholly on their own. Jesus reassures them that the Holy Spirit will be with them and will guide them in their mission.

After reminding them that joy will come from the sorrow they are about to bear, Jesus offers up a prayer. In that prayer Jesus asks first for glorification that God himself might be glorified, then prays for the 11 disciples, and finally for all his disciples, that they might love one another and thereby be a continuing witness to the world.

The final discourse begins with an allegory about the vine and its branches as a lesson in fruitfulness through Christ.

Jn.
15:1-8

VINE AND BRANCHES. "I am the true vine, and my Father is the gardener. He cuts off every branch in me that bears no fruit, while every branch that does bear fruit he prunes[k] so that it will be even more fruitful. You are already clean because of the word I have spoken to you. Remain in me, and I will remain in you. No branch can bear fruit by itself; it must remain in the vine. Neither can you bear fruit unless you remain in me.

"I am the vine; you are the branches. If a man remains in me and I in him, he will bear much fruit; apart from me you can do nothing. If anyone does not remain in me, he is like a

[k]The Greek form *prunes* also means *cleans*.

branch that is thrown away and withers; such branches are picked up, thrown into the fire and burned. If you remain in me and my words remain in you, ask whatever you wish, and it will be given you. This is to my Father's glory, that you bear much fruit, showing yourselves to be my disciples.

Jn.
15:9-17

TO LOVE ONE ANOTHER. "As the Father has loved me, so have I loved you. Now remain in my love. If you obey my commands, you will remain in my love, just as I have obeyed my Father's commands and remain in his love. I have told you this so that my joy may be in you and that your joy may be complete. My command is this: Love each other as I have loved you. Greater love has no one than this, that he lay down his life for his friends. You are my friends if you do what I command. I no longer call you servants, because a servant does not know his master's business. Instead, I have called you friends, for everything that I learned from my Father I have made known to you. You did not choose me, but I chose you and appointed you to go and bear fruit—fruit that will last. Then the Father will give you whatever you ask in my name. This is my command: Love each other.

Jn.
15:18–16:4

PREPARATION FOR PERSECUTION. "If the world hates you, keep in mind that it hated me first. If you belonged to the world, it would love you as its own. As it is, you do not belong to the world, but I have chosen you out of the world. That is why the world hates you. Remember the words I spoke to you: 'No servant is greater than his master.'[l] If they persecuted me, they will persecute you also. If they obeyed my teaching, they will obey yours also. They will treat you this way because of my name, for they do not know the One who sent me. If I had not come and spoken to them, they would not be guilty of sin. Now, however, they have no excuse for their sin. He who hates me hates my Father as well. If I had not done among them what no one else did, they would not be guilty of sin. But now they have seen these miracles, and yet they have hated both me and my Father. But this is to fulfill what is written in their Law: 'They hated me without reason.'[m]

"When the Counselor comes, whom I will send to you from the Father, the Spirit of truth who goes out from the Father, he

[l]John 13:16   [m]Psalms 35:19; 69:4

will testify about me. And you also must testify, for you have been with me from the beginning.

"All this I have told you so that you will not go astray. They will put you out of the synagogue; in fact, a time is coming when anyone who kills you will think he is offering a service to God. They will do such things because they have not known the Father or me. I have told you this, so that when the time comes you will remember that I warned you. I did not tell you this at first because I was with you.

Jn. 16:5-11
NECESSITY OF GOING AWAY. "Now I am going to him who sent me, yet none of you asks me, 'Where are you going?' Because I have said these things, you are filled with grief. But I tell you the truth: It is for your good that I am going away. Unless I go away, the Counselor will not come to you; but if I go, I will send him to you. When he comes, he will convict the world of guilt[n] in regard to sin and righteousness and judgment: in regard to sin, because men do not believe in me; in regard to righteousness, because I am going to the Father, where you can see me no longer; and in regard to judgment, because the prince of this world now stands condemned.

Jn. 16:12-15
HOLY SPIRIT'S GUIDANCE. "I have much more to say to you, more than you can now bear. But when he, the Spirit of truth, comes, he will guide you into all truth. He will not speak on his own; he will speak only what he hears, and he will tell you what is yet to come. He will bring glory to me by taking from what is mine and making it known to you. All that belongs to the Father is mine. That is why I said the Spirit will take from what is mine and make it known to you.

Jn. 16:16-18
DISCIPLES PERPLEXED. "In a little while you will see me no more, and then after a little while you will see me."

Some of his disciples said to one another, "What does he mean by saying, 'In a little while you will see me no more, and then after a little while you will see me,' and 'Because I am going to the Father'?" They kept asking, "What does he mean by 'a little while'? We don't understand what he is saying."

Jn. 16:19-24
JOY OUT OF SORROW. Jesus saw that they wanted to ask him about this, so he said to them, "Are you asking one another

[n]Or *will expose the guilt of the world*

what I meant when I said, 'In a little while you will see me no more, and then after a little while you will see me'? I tell you the truth, you will weep and mourn while the world rejoices. You will grieve, but your grief will turn to joy. A woman giving birth to a child has pain because her time has come; but when her baby is born she forgets the anguish because of her joy that a child is born into the world. So with you: Now is your time of grief, but I will see you again and you will rejoice, and no one will take away your joy. In that day you will no longer ask me anything. I tell you the truth, my Father will give you whatever you ask in my name. Until now you have not asked for anything in my name. Ask and you will receive, and your joy will be complete.

Jn.
16:25-28

SPEECH WILL BE MADE CLEAR. "Though I have been speaking figuratively, a time is coming when I will no longer use this kind of language but will tell you plainly about my Father. In that day you will ask in my name. I am not saying that I will ask the Father on your behalf. No, the Father himself loves you because you have loved me and have believed that I came from God. I came from the Father and entered the world; now I am leaving the world and going back to the Father."

Jn.
16:29-33

DISCIPLES EXPRESS BELIEF. Then Jesus' disciples said, "Now you are speaking clearly and without figures of speech. Now we can see that you know all things and that you do not even need to have anyone ask you questions. This makes us believe that you came from God."

"You believe at last!"[o] Jesus answered. "But a time is coming, and has come, when you will be scattered, each to his own home. You will leave me all alone. Yet I am not alone, for my Father is with me.

"I have told you these things, so that in me you may have peace. In this world you will have trouble. But take heart! I have overcome the world."

Jn.
17:1-5

JESUS PRAYS FOR HIMSELF. After Jesus said this, he looked toward heaven and prayed:

[o]Or "Do you now believe?"

"Father, the time has come. Glorify your Son, that your Son may glorify you. For you granted him authority over all people that he might give eternal life to all those you have given him. Now this is eternal life: that they may know you, the only true God, and Jesus Christ, whom you have sent. I have brought you glory on earth by completing the work you gave me to do. And now, Father, glorify me in your presence with the glory I had with you before the world began.

Jn.
17:6-19
JESUS PRAYS FOR DISCIPLES. "I have revealed you[p] to those whom you gave me out of the world. They were yours; you gave them to me and they have obeyed your word. Now they know that everything you have given me comes from you. For I gave them the words you gave me and they accepted them. They knew with certainty that I came from you, and they believed that you sent me. I pray for them. I am not praying for the world, but for those you have given me, for they are yours. All I have is yours, and all you have is mine. And glory has come to me through them. I will remain in the world no longer, but they are still in the world, and I am coming to you. Holy Father, protect them by the power of your name—the name you gave me—so that they may be one as we are one. While I was with them, I protected them and kept them safe by that name you gave me. None has been lost except the one doomed to destruction so that Scripture would be fulfilled.

"I am coming to you now, but I say these things while I am still in the world, so that they may have the full measure of my joy within them. I have given them your word and the world has hated them, for they are not of the world any more than I am of the world. My prayer is not that you take them out of the world but that you protect them from the evil one. They are not of the world, even as I am not of it. Sanctify[q] them by the truth; your word is truth. As you sent me into the world, I have sent them into the world. For them I sanctify myself, that they too may be truly sanctified.

Jn.
17:20-26
JESUS PRAYS FOR BELIEVERS. "My prayer is not for them alone. I pray also for those who will believe in me through their message, that all of them may be one, Father, just as you are in me and I am in you. May they also be in us so that the

---

[p]Greek *your name*   [q]Greek *hagiazo (set apart for sacred use* or *make holy)*

world may believe that you have sent me. I have given them the glory that you gave me, that they may be one as we are one: I in them and you in me. May they be brought to complete unity to let the world know that you sent me and have loved them even as you have loved me.

"Father, I want those you have given me to be with me where I am, and to see my glory, the glory you have given me because you loved me before the creation of the world.

"Righteous Father, though the world does not know you, I know you, and they know that you have sent me. I have made you known to them, and will continue to make you known in order that the love you have for me may be in them and that I myself may be in them."

TODAY'S INSIGHTS
Unity

Are you sometimes perplexed about the Trinity? Many Christians are. By faith, of course, we accept that God is Father, Son, and Holy Spirit. But have you ever wondered exactly how it happened, for example, that when Jesus was baptized there was a voice heard from heaven saying, "This is my Son, whom I love," and the Holy Spirit descended like a dove upon Jesus? On that occasion, all three Persons of the Godhead were manifested at one time!

And now, as Jesus brings his ministry on earth to a close, we see him praying to the Father. But if Jesus really is "one" with the Father, as he says he is, then doesn't that mean he is praying to himself? Why does Christ the Son ask God the Father to glorify him (and to protect his disciples, and to sanctify them) if all along the Father and the Son are one? The easiest answer, of course, is to say that it is a mystery which will be revealed at the end of time. And that is true. But praise God that we are not left in a state of doubt and bewilderment.

God has given us insight into this divine mystery through the words of the apostle Paul, who will later write that we Christians become "one" with Christ, like the bride becomes "one" with her husband. Mystical though it may be, the union of two souls in marriage is a reality to which multitudes of married couples will testify.

If someone were to protest that in marriage we can actually see two distinct and separate individuals, perhaps this is the very key that unlocks the mystery.

Our problem may be that we are looking too closely at a material world where natural logic is never permitted to fail us. A man and a woman united as one? Impossible! But in the spiritual realm, all things are possible with God. Whether it be the unity of commitment and purpose that is found in marriage (despite differences between the man and the woman in form and function), or whether it is the unity of Father, Son, and Holy Spirit (despite their different personhood and functional roles)—the reality itself cannot be denied.

And what a benefit this is for us! For Jesus has invited us to be "one" with him, as branches in a vine. And if we are "one" with Christ, then we have eternal life as only God can have. And glory. And honor. And truth. And joy. And fellowship with all those who have loved his appearing.

Yet if we cherish our oneness with Jesus, he leaves us with this sobering thought: Just as many people in his day persecuted Jesus, it is altogether likely that we too will be persecuted. Are we willing to accept that kind of unity with Christ?

What an awesome responsibility he has given us! Jesus said that unity among his believers is his witness to the world of his own unity with God the Father. Can God ever forgive us for our division and strife? Lord, help us to be truly one!

DAY
27
WITH
JESUS

DENIAL

Betrayal and Arrest

AT THE END OF THIS PARTING DISCOURSE, THERE IS LITTLE TIME remaining for solitude or reflection. The time of betrayal is near. Very soon now Judas will lead the officers of the chief priests to Jesus and betray him in the presence of the other apostles. So the stage is now set, and the arrest is soon to take place. As the hour of betrayal fast approaches, the record begins now with Jesus leading his disciples to an olive grove known as Gethsemane, on the Mount of Olives, just east of Jerusalem. As they arrive in the quiet garden, Jesus' heart is clearly heavy with the prospect of the events soon to take place. Taking Peter, James, and John beyond the others, Jesus goes still further to a quiet place alone, where he agonizes in prayer with the Father. And his aloneness during this critical time is all the more reinforced when three times Jesus returns to the disciples only to find them asleep.

Mt.
26:36-38
Mk.
14:32-34
Lk.
22:40
Jn 18:1
(Wednes-
day
night)

TO GETHSEMANE. JnWhen he had finished praying, Jesus left with his disciples and crossed the Kidron Valley. On the other side there was an olive grove, and he and his disciples went into it. MkThey went to a place called Gethsemane, and Jesus said to his disciples, "Sit here while I pray." He took Peter, James and John along with him, and he began to be deeply distressed and troubled. "My soul is overwhelmed with sorrow to the point of death," he said to them. "Stay here and keep watch."

Mt.
26:39
Mk.
14:35,36
Lk.
22:41-45

JESUS PRAYS IN AGONY. He withdrew about a stone's throw beyond them, knelt down and prayed, "Father, if you are willing, take this cup from me; yet not my will, but yours be done." An angel from heaven appeared to him and strengthened him. And being in anguish, he prayed more earnestly, and his sweat was like drops of blood falling to the ground.[r]

When he rose from prayer and went back to the disciples, he found them asleep, exhausted from sorrow.

[r] Some early manuscripts do not have verses 43 and 44.

Mt.
26:40-42
Mk.
14:37-39
Lk. 22:46

JESUS PRAYS A SECOND TIME. "Could you men not keep watch with me for one hour?" he asked Peter. "Watch and pray so that you will not fall into temptation. The spirit is willing, but the body is weak."

He went away a second time and prayed, "My Father, if it is not possible for this cup to be taken away unless I drink it, may your will be done."

Mt.
26:43-46
Mk.
14:40-42

JESUS PRAYS A THIRD TIME. When he came back, he again found them sleeping, because their eyes were heavy. So he left them and went away once more and prayed the third time, saying the same thing.

Then he returned to the disciples and said to them, "Are you still sleeping and resting? Look, the hour is near, and the Son of Man is betrayed into the hands of sinners. Rise, let us go! Here comes my betrayer!"

Mt.
26:47-50a
Mk.
14:43-45
Lk.
22:47,48
Jn. 18:2,3

JUDAS BETRAYS JESUS. JnNow Judas, who betrayed him, knew the place, because Jesus had often met there with his disciples. So Judas came to the grove, guiding a detachment of soldiers and some officials from the chief priests and Pharisees. They were carrying torches, lanterns and weapons. MkNow the betrayer had arranged a signal with them: "The one I kiss is the man; arrest him and lead him away under guard." LkHe approached Jesus to kiss him, but Jesus asked him, "Judas, are you betraying the Son of Man with a kiss?" MkGoing at once to Jesus, Judas said, "Rabbi!" and kissed him.

Jn. 18:4-9

DISCIPLES' SAFETY INSURED. Jesus, knowing all that was going to happen to him, went out and asked them, "Who is it you want?"

"Jesus of Nazareth," they replied.

"I am he," Jesus said. (And Judas the traitor was standing there with them.) When Jesus said, "I am he," they drew back and fell to the ground.

Again he asked them, "Who is it you want?"

And they said, "Jesus of Nazareth."

"I told you that I am he," Jesus answered. "If you are looking for me, then let these men go." This happened so that the words he had spoken would be fulfilled: "I have not lost one of those you gave me."[s]

sJohn 6:39

Mt. 5:50b-54 Mk. 14:46,47 Lk. 22:49-51 Jn. 18:10,11	**PETER CUTS OFF EAR.** MkThe men seized Jesus and arrested him. LkWhen Jesus' followers saw what was going to happen, they said, "Lord, should we strike with our swords?" JnThen Simon Peter, who had a sword, drew it and struck the high priest's servant, cutting off his right ear. (The servant's name was Malchus.) Mt"Put your sword back in its place," Jesus said to him, "for all who draw the sword will die by the sword. Do you think I cannot call on my Father, and he will at once put at my disposal more than twelve legions of angels? But how then would the Scriptures be fulfilled that say it must happen in this way?" LkBut Jesus answered, "No more of this!" And he touched the man's ear and healed him.
Mt. 6:55,56a Mk. 14:48,49 Lk. 22:52,53	**JESUS CHIDES ARREST.** Then Jesus said to the chief priests, the officers of the temple guard, and the elders, who had come for him, "Am I leading a rebellion, that you have come with swords and clubs? Every day I was with you in the temple courts, and you did not lay a hand on me. But this is your hour—when darkness reigns."
Mt. 26:56b Mk. 14:50-52 Jn. 18:12a	**JESUS ARRESTED.** JnThen the detachment of soldiers with its commander and the Jewish officials arrested Jesus. MtThen all the disciples deserted him and fled. MkA young man, wearing nothing but a linen garment, was following Jesus. When they seized him, he fled naked, leaving his garment behind.

Trial Before Sanhedrin

Following Jesus' arrest, John records that Jesus is first taken before Annas, who had been high priest from A.D. 6-15, before being deposed by the Roman procurator Valerius Gratus. It appears that Annas continued to exercise great influence among the Jews, and so it is no surprise that Jesus is brought before him for questioning. Jesus is sent next to Annas' son-in-law, Caiaphas, who has served as high priest since A.D. 18. Caiaphas presides over the Sanhedrin (also known as the Council), which is the Jewish Supreme Court, composed of 71 elders drawn from among the chief priests and scribes. Some of the members of the Sanhedrin apparently join Caiaphas at his house in the late hours of the night in order to interrogate Jesus regarding his claims of messiahship.

Then, as day breaks on Thursday morning, the entire Council is called together in order to vote official condemnation.

Laced throughout the record of Jesus' trial before the Jewish leaders is a moving account of Peter's personal struggle with loyalty to Jesus. In the garden Peter had been characteristically impulsive in rushing to Jesus' defense. But now, as he comes to understand the seriousness of Jesus' arrest, Peter realizes his own potential jeopardy. When confronted with charges that he is one of Jesus' disciples, Peter weakens and denies any such association. On three separate occasions throughout this long night, and to a number of different accusers, Peter will make vehement and even profane denials in order to shield himself. His later feelings of remorse and his subsequent leadership in the establishment of the church will stand in clear contrast to Judas, who on this same day will be consumed by his guilt and take his own life.

Jn.
18:12b-14
Jerusalem

JESUS LED TO ANNAS. They bound him and brought him first to Annas, who was the father-in-law of Caiaphas, the high priest that year. Caiaphas was the one who had advised the Jews that it would be good if one man died for the people.

Jn.
18:15-17

PETER'S FIRST DENIAL. Simon Peter and another disciple were following Jesus. Because this disciple was known to the high priest, he went with Jesus into the high priest's courtyard, but Peter had to wait outside at the door. The other disciple, who was known to the high priest, came back, spoke to the girl on duty there and brought Peter in.

"You are not one of this man's disciples, are you?" the girl at the door asked Peter.

He replied, "I am not."

Jn.
18:19-23

JESUS BEFORE ANNAS. Meanwhile, the high priest questioned Jesus about his disciples and his teaching.

"I have spoken openly to the world," Jesus replied. "I always taught in synagogues or at the temple, where all the Jews come together. I said nothing in secret. Why question me? Ask those who heard me. Surely they know what I said."

When Jesus said this, one of the officials nearby struck him in the face. "Is this the way you answer the high priest?" he demanded.

"If I said something wrong," Jesus replied, "testify as to what is wrong. But if I spoke the truth, why did you strike me?"

Mt.
26:57,58
Mk.
14:53,54
Lk. 22:54
Jn.
18:18,24

TO CAIAPHAS, HIGH PRIEST. JnThen Annas sent him, still bound, to Caiaphas the high priest.ᵗ LkThen seizing him, they led him away and took him into the house of the high priest. Peter followed at a distance.

Mt.
26:69-72
Mk.
14:66-70a
Lk.
22:55-58
Jn.
18:25

PETER AGAIN DENIES. LkBut when they had kindled a fire in the middle of the courtyard and had sat down together, Peter sat down with them. A servant girl saw him seated there in the firelight. She looked closely at him and said, "This man was with him."

But he denied it. "Woman, I don't know him," he said. MtThen he went out to the gateway, where another girl saw him and said to the people there, "This fellow was with Jesus of Nazareth."

He denied it again, with an oath: "I don't know the man!" LkA little later someone else saw him and said, "You also are one of them."

"Man, I am not!" Peter replied.

Mt.
26:59-66
Mk.
14:55-64

BEFORE CAIAPHAS AND COUNCIL. The chief priests and the whole Sanhedrin were looking for evidence against Jesus so that they could put him to death, but they did not find any. Many testified falsely against him, but their statements did not agree.

Then some stood up and gave this false testimony against him: "We heard him say, 'I will destroy this man-made temple and in three days will build another, not made by man.'" Yet even then their testimony did not agree.

Then the high priest stood up before them and asked Jesus, "Are you not going to answer? What is this testimony that these men are bringing against you?" But Jesus remained silent and gave no answer.

Again the high priest asked him, "Are you the Christ,ᵘ the Son of the Blessed One?"

"I am," said Jesus. "And you will see the Son of Man sitting at the right hand of the Mighty One and coming on the clouds of heaven."

ᵗOr (Now Annas had sent him, still bound, to Caiaphas the high priest.)
ᵘOr Messiah

The high priest tore his clothes. "Why do we need any more witnesses?" he asked. "You have heard the blasphemy. What do you think?"

They all condemned him as worthy of death.

Mt.
26:67,68
Mk.
14:65
Lk.
22:63-65

JESUS IS ABUSED. The men who were guarding Jesus began mocking and beating him. They blindfolded him and demanded, "Prophesy! Who hit you?" And they said many other insulting things to him.

Mt.
26:73,74a
Mk.
14:70b,71
Lk.
22:59,60a
Jn.
18:26,27

PETER DENIES STILL AGAIN. MtAfter a little while [Lkabout an hour later], those standing there went up to Peter and said, "Surely you are one of them, for your accent gives you away."

Then he began to call down curses on himself and he swore to them, "I don't know the man!" JnOne of the high priest's servants, a relative of the man whose ear Peter had cut off, challenged him, "Didn't I see you with him in the olive grove?"

LkPeter replied, "Man, I don't know what you're talking about!"

Mt.
26:74b,75
Mk.
14:72
Lk.
22:60b-62

PETER WEEPS. Just as he was speaking, the rooster crowed. The Lord turned and looked straight at Peter. Then Peter remembered the word the Lord had spoken to him: "Before the rooster crows today, you will disown me three times." And he went outside and wept bitterly.

Mt. 27:1
Mk.
15:1a
Lk.
22:66-71
(Early
Thursday
morning)

COUNCIL CONDEMNS JESUS. LkAt daybreak the council of the elders of the people, both the chief priests and teachers of the law, met together, and Jesus was led before them. "If you are the Christ,v" they said, "tell us."

Jesus answered, "If I tell you, you will not believe me, and if I asked you, you would not answer. But from now on, the Son of Man will be seated at the right hand of the mighty God."

They all asked, "Are you then the Son of God?"

He replied, "You are right in saying I am."

Then they said, "Why do we need any more testimony? We have heard it from his own lips." MtEarly in the morning, all the chief priests and the elders of the people came to the decision to put Jesus to death.

Mt.
27:3-10

JUDAS COMMITS SUICIDE. When Judas, who had betrayed him, saw that Jesus was condemned, he was seized with

vOr *Messiah*

remorse and returned the thirty silver coins to the chief priests and the elders. "I have sinned," he said, "for I have betrayed innocent blood."

"What is that to us?" they replied. "That's your responsibility."

So Judas threw the money into the temple and left. Then he went away and hanged himself.

The chief priests picked up the coins and said, "It is against the law to put this into the treasury, since it is blood money." So they decided to use the money to buy the potter's field as a burial place for foreigners. That is why it has been called the Field of Blood to this day. Then what was spoken by Jeremiah the prophet was fulfilled: "They took the thirty silver coins, the price set on him by the people of Israel, and they used them to buy the potter's field, as the Lord commanded me."*w*

TODAY'S INSIGHTS

Denial

Have you ever taken a stand for something you strongly believed to be right, only to be deserted by someone you expected to support you? Have you yourself ever hesitated to back someone up because you were afraid of the consequences if you did? Have you ever been surprised to hear yourself downplaying the fact you are a Christian because you were embarrassed to be recognized as a religious person? More than a few of us will have to admit that we have looked defeat in the eye.

Displays of weakness in character among God's children are a continual source of amazement, aren't they? Imagine Abraham lying about his own wife! David ordering Uriah's death to cover up his adultery with Bathsheba! And now Peter denying even knowing Jesus! Nor was Peter the only one who let him down. In the garden, *all* the disciples deserted Jesus and fled.

The sad thing is that we too can find ourselves denying Jesus. Sometimes our denial of Jesus comes as we "sleep through the sermon," as it were. Exhausted by worldly pursuits, we sometimes

*w*See Zech. 11:12,13; Jer. 19:1-13; 32:6-9.

run out of strength to do the Lord's work. As with Peter, James, and John, our spirits are willing but the flesh is weak.

When was the last time we committed ourselves to reading the Bible through in a year? Or to having a quiet time each morning? Or to giving more for the Lord's work? Or to spending more time with our families? Have we remained faithful to our commitments, or have we let them slide?

Sometimes we deny Jesus by fleeing as fast as we can when trouble comes our way—particularly in the church. Let's face it—not many of us are good at handling conflict. If we could solve the problem by some dramatic impulsive act, then we, like Peter, might be willing to draw our swords and fight it out in anger. But to deal with problems quietly, lovingly, and patiently sometimes requires more spiritual stamina than we can muster.

Like Peter, sometimes we deny Jesus by simply *denying* him! For whatever reasons we may have, there are times when we do whatever we can to put distance between ourselves and Christ. Maybe it's because we want to do things we know he wouldn't approve of. Maybe it's because we want to keep friends who wouldn't appreciate our relationship with Christ. Maybe we just get tired of taking abuse for being a Christian. At one time or another, some of us have decided that faith in Christ is too simplistic for the level of sophistication we have recently achieved.

If these reminders leave us with little comfort about ourselves, we must look ahead to the end of the story with Peter. As we know, Peter later rebounded with irrepressible strength and power when he was filled with the Holy Spirit. And so can we. It comes to us as a promise! As Christians we will never be perfect. But as God's children we will never be denied.

DAY
28
WITH
JESUS

COURAGE

Trial Before Pilate

THE SIGNIFICANCE OF WHAT IS ABOUT TO HAPPEN CAN ONLY BE understood in the context of the political relationship between the Jews and their Roman rulers. The Jews have condemned Jesus to death on the basis of their own religious laws against blasphemy, in response to Jesus' claim to be the Son of God. But the Sanhedrin has no power to execute condemned prisoners without approval of the Roman government. Yet clearly such a pagan government will not regard a charge of blasphemy with the same degree of seriousness as do the Jews. Therefore more appropriate charges will have to be laid before the governor. Being politically astute, the Jewish leaders will accuse Jesus of sedition in allegedly urging refusal to pay taxes and in claiming to be the King of the Jews.

The man to hear these charges is the Roman procurator and governor, Pontius Pilate, who rules over Judea, Idumea, and Samaria. Pilate began his rule about the time John the Baptist began his ministry. Although his primary responsibility is that of financial administration and collection of taxes for the Roman Empire, Pilate is also burdened with the responsibility of approving and carrying out the execution of anyone sentenced to death by the people's own government—in this case the Sanhedrin. Pilate has a reputation for unprincipled capriciousness, and the manner in which he handles Jesus' case gives no reason to doubt the truth of that reputation. Apparently convinced of Jesus' innocence, Pilate initially takes every available step to avoid personal responsibility. He sends Jesus to Herod Antipas (beheader of John the Baptist), but Herod wants no part of it either. Pilate then tries to release Jesus, but the mob insists that a notorious insurrectionist by the name of Barabbas be released instead. When even a scourging of Jesus fails to placate the crowd, Pilate finally washes his hands of the matter and orders that Jesus be put to death.

Matthew's account begins the record of these tense hours as Jesus is first led to Pilate.

[Fourth
Passover
April,
A.D. 30]
Mt. 27:2
Mk.
15:1b
Lk.
23:1,2
Jn.
18:28-32
Prae-
torium
(Thurs-
day
morning)
JESUS TAKEN TO PILATE. MtThey bound him, led him away and handed him over to Pilate, the governor. JnBy now it was early morning, and to avoid ceremonial uncleanness the Jews did not enter the palace; they wanted to be able to eat the Passover. So Pilate came out to them and asked, "What charges are you bringing against this man?"

"If he were not a criminal," they replied, "we would not have handed him over to you." LkAnd they began to accuse him, saying, "We have found this man subverting our nation. He opposes payment of taxes to Caesar and claims to be Christ,x a king." JnPilate said, "Take him yourselves and judge him by your own law."

"But we have no right to execute anyone," the Jews objected. This happened so that the words Jesus had spoken indicating the kind of death he was going to die would be fulfilled.

Mt.
27:11-14
Mk.
15:2-5
Lk.
23:3,4
Jn.
18:33-38
PILATE QUESTIONS JESUS. JnPilate then went back inside the palace, summoned Jesus and asked him, "Are you the king of the Jews?"

"Is that your own idea," Jesus asked, "or did others talk to you about me?"

"Am I a Jew?" Pilate replied. "It was your people and your chief priests who handed you over to me. What is it you have done?"

Jesus said, "My kingdom is not of this world. If it were, my servants would fight to prevent my arrest by the Jews. But now my kingdom is from another place."

"You are a king, then?" said Pilate.

Jesus answered, "You are right in saying I am a king. In fact, for this reason I was born, and for this I came into the world, to testify to the truth. Everyone on the side of truth listens to me."

"What is truth?" Pilate asked. With this he went out again to the Jews and said, "I find no basis for a charge against him." MtWhen he was accused by the chief priests and the elders, he gave no answer. Then Pilate asked him, "Don't you hear the testimony they are bringing against you?" But Jesus made no reply, not even to a single charge—to the great amazement of the governor.

xOr Messiah

Lk.
23:5-7

PILATE SENDS JESUS TO HEROD. But they insisted, "He stirs up the people all over Judea[y] by his teaching. He started in Galilee and has come all the way here."

On hearing this, Pilate asked if the man was a Galilean. When he learned that Jesus was under Herod's jurisdiction, he sent him to Herod, who was also in Jerusalem at that time.

Lk.
23:8-12
Palace of
Herod
(Thurs-
day
morn-
ing)

JESUS BEFORE HEROD ANTIPAS. When Herod saw Jesus, he was greatly pleased, because for a long time he had been wanting to see him. From what he had heard about him, he hoped to see him perform some miracle. He plied him with many questions, but Jesus gave him no answer. The chief priests and the teachers of the law were standing there, vehemently accusing him. Then Herod and his soldiers ridiculed and mocked him. Dressing him in an elegant robe, they sent him back to Pilate. That day Herod and Pilate became friends—before this they had been enemies.

Mt.
27:19

PILATE'S WIFE SENDS WARNING. While Pilate was sitting on the judge's seat, his wife sent him this message: "Don't have anything to do with that innocent man, for I have suffered a great deal today in a dream because of him."

Lk.
23:13-16
Prae-
torium
(Thurs-
day
morn-
ing)

PILATE SEEKS TO RELEASE. Pilate called together the chief priests, the rulers and the people, and said to them, "You brought me this man as one who was inciting the people to rebellion. I have examined him in your presence and have found no basis for your charges against him. Neither has Herod, for he sent him back to us; as you can see, he has done nothing to deserve death. Therefore, I will punish him and then release him.[z]"

Mt.
27:15-18
Mk.
15:6-10
Jn.
18:39

JESUS OR BARABBAS. Now it was the custom at the Feast to release a prisoner whom the people requested. A man called Barabbas was in prison with the insurrectionists who had committed murder in the uprising. The crowd came up and asked Pilate to do for them what he usually did.

"Do you want me to release to you the king of the Jews?" asked Pilate, knowing that it was out of envy that the chief priests had handed Jesus over to him.

[y]Or *over the land of the Jews*   [z]Some manuscripts *him."* [17]*Now he was obliged to release one man to them at the Feast.*

CROWD DEMANDS BARABBAS. ᴹᵏBut the chief priests stirred up the crowd to have Pilate release Barabbas instead. ᴶⁿThey shouted back, "No, not him! Give us Barabbas!" ᴸᵏWith one voice they cried out, "Away with this man! Release Barabbas to us!"

Mt.
27:20,21
Mk.
15:11
Lk.
23:18,19
Jn. 18:40

ᴹᵗ"Which of the two do you want me to release to you?" asked the governor.

"Barabbas," they answered.

JESUS' CRUCIFIXION DEMANDED. ᴹᵗ"What shall I do, then, with Jesus who is called Christ?" Pilate asked.

Mt.
27:22,23
Mk.
15:12-14
Lk.
23:20-23

They all answered, "Crucify him!"

"Why? What crime has he committed?" asked Pilate.

But they shouted all the louder, "Crucify him!" ᴸᵏWanting to release Jesus, Pilate appealed to them again. But they kept shouting, "Crucify him! Crucify him!"

For the third time he spoke to them: "Why? What crime has this man committed? I have found in him no grounds for the death penalty. Therefore I will have him punished and then release him."

But with loud shouts they insistently demanded that he be crucified, and their shouts prevailed.

CROWN OF THORNS. ᴶⁿThen Pilate took Jesus and had him flogged. ᴹᵗThen the governor's soldiers took Jesus into the Praetorium and gathered the whole company of soldiers around him. They stripped him and put a scarlet robe on him, and then twisted together a crown of thorns and set it on his head. They put a staff in his right hand and knelt in front of him and mocked him. "Hail, king of the Jews!" they said. They spit on him, and took the staff and struck him on the head again and again.

Mt.
27:27-30
Mk.
15:16-19
Jn.
19:1-3

PILATE PRESENTS JESUS. Once more Pilate came out and said to the Jews, "Look, I am bringing him out to you to let you know that I find no basis for a charge against him." When Jesus came out wearing the crown of thorns and the purple robe, Pilate said to them, "Here is the man!"

Jn.
19:4-6

As soon as the chief priests and their officials saw him, they shouted, "Crucify! Crucify!"

But Pilate answered, "You take him and crucify him. As for me, I find no basis for a charge against him."

Jn.
19:7-11

JESUS QUESTIONED AGAIN. The Jews insisted, "We have a law, and according to that law he must die, because he claimed to be the Son of God."

When Pilate heard this, he was even more afraid, and he went back inside the palace. "Where do you come from?" he asked Jesus, but Jesus gave him no answer. "Do you refuse to speak to me?" Pilate said. "Don't you realize I have power either to free you or to crucify you?"

Jesus answered, "You would have no power over me if it were not given to you from above. Therefore the one who handed me over to you is guilty of a greater sin."

Jn.
19:12-15

PLAY ON PILATE'S LOYALTY. From then on, Pilate tried to set Jesus free, but the Jews kept shouting, "If you let this man go, you are no friend of Caesar. Anyone who claims to be a king opposes Caesar."

When Pilate heard this, he brought Jesus out and sat down on the judge's seat at a place known as the Stone Pavement (which in Aramaic is Gabbatha). It was the day of Preparation of Passover Week, about the sixth hour.

"Here is your king," Pilate said to the Jews.

But they shouted, "Take him away! Take him away! Crucify him!"

"Shall I crucify your king?" Pilate asked.

"We have no king but Caesar," the chief priests answered.

Mt.
27:24,25

PILATE WASHES HANDS. When Pilate saw that he was getting nowhere, but that instead an uproar was starting, he took water and washed his hands in front of the crowd. "I am innocent of this man's blood," he said. "It is your responsibility!"

All the people answered, "Let his blood be on us and on our children!"

Mt. 27:26
Mk. 15:15
Lk.
23:24,25
Jn. 19:16

BARABBAS IS RELEASED. So Pilate decided to grant their demand. He released the man who had been thrown into prison for insurrection and murder, the one they asked for, and surrendered Jesus to their will.

Mt.
27:31
Mk.
15:20
Jn.
19:17

JESUS IS LED OUT. MkAnd when they had mocked him, they took off the purple robe and put his own clothes on him. Then they led him out to crucify him. JnCarrying his own cross, he went out...

Mt.
27:32
Mk.
15:21,22
Lk.
23:26

SIMON OF CYRENE. A certain man from Cyrene, Simon, the father of Alexander and Rufus, was passing by on his way in from the country, and they forced him to carry the cross. They brought Jesus to the place called Golgotha (which means the Place of the Skull).

Lk.
23:27-31

WOMEN WEEP FOR JESUS. A large number of people followed him, including women who mourned and wailed for him. Jesus turned and said to them, "Daughters of Jerusalem, do not weep for me; weep for yourselves and for your children. For the time will come when you will say, 'Blessed are the barren women, the wombs that never bore and the breasts that never nursed!' Then

"'they will say to the mountains, "Fall on us!"
and to the hills, "Cover us!"'*

For if men do these things when the tree is green, what will happen when it is dry?"

TODAY'S INSIGHTS

Courage

Have you ever known such a contrast in courage as seen in the actions of Pilate and Jesus? His life at stake, his character impeached, his body abused, and his kingship ridiculed, Jesus exhibits a degree of courage rarely seen. Instead of weakening and begging for release, or fighting back to save himself, Jesus hardly utters a word in his own defense.

And we shouldn't be fooled into thinking that Jesus can shrug it all off because he knows he will triumph over his death. Jesus is a real person of flesh and blood, with real feelings. He feels the agony of the beating, just as you and I would. And he feels the pain of the thorns. Yet he bravely faces the inevitable, with its prospect of an even crueler death.

By contrast, there is Pilate—that weak-willed excuse for a political leader. Even knowing that Jesus is innocent, Pilate caves in to the angry mob. But before agreeing to become part of the most

*Hosea 10:8

tragic miscarriage of justice the world has ever known, he cowardly tries every way possible to avoid responsibility. Let someone else make the decision, Pilate thought, as he sent Jesus to Herod. When that didn't work, and when the people tugged on the strings of his political security, Pilate tried literally to wash his hands of the matter. But Pilate condemned himself through his acts of cowardice. It was he, after all, who had reminded Jesus: "Don't you realize I have power either to free you or to crucify you?"

Have there not been times in our own lives when we joined with Pilate in the matter of what to do with Jesus? Perhaps we tried to let someone else make the decision for us. Some of us sent Jesus to our parents to see what *they* had done with him. Some of us inquired of our church as to what view it took of Jesus, without searching the Scriptures for ourselves.

Others of us have tried to ignore the issue altogether. For a time, we just washed our hands of making *any* decision. It was easy to think we could do that, because, after all, that is what most of the world does every day. They immerse themselves in work and distract themselves in play, hoping that Jesus will just go away. Through total self-absorption they don't have to think about Jesus anymore. With hardly any effort at all they can let him be the good man and wonderful teacher they've heard about. But the Son of God? That's asking too much.

If Pilate was sincerely interested in knowing the truth, the truth is that no one can walk away from Jesus with impunity. Like Pilate, each of us must answer the question: "What shall I do with Jesus Christ?"

As Christians we have taken bold steps of faith in committing ourselves to Christ. Of all people, we are the most courageous. We have defied the whole world to confess Jesus as our Lord and Savior. We have announced him in the public proclamation of baptism. And we have worn his name with confident joy!

DAY 29 WITH JESUS

FORGIVENESS

The Crucifixion of Jesus

IT IS SOMETIME BEFORE NOON WHEN THE PROCESSION REACHES THE out-skirts of Jerusalem and the crowd gathers on a craggy little hill which is known as Golgotha—that is, the Skull. As Jesus is nailed to the wooden cross and lifted up, the scene below him becomes a strange mixture of emotions. On one hand he sees the bitter sorrow of his family and followers, and on the other hand he sees the carnival-like atmosphere of the soldiers and those who have demanded his death. As he awaits his death with increasing pain and agony, Jesus speaks briefly with one of the two thieves being crucified with him. Then, seeing his mother, Mary, he directs John to care for her. By early afternoon the end is near. As unusual dark-ness covers the land, Jesus cries out his last words and gives up his spirit in death. The significance of the hour is marked by a series of miraculous events which fill the people with awe.

Mt. 27:33,34, 38 Mk. 15:23,25, 27,28 Lk. 23:32-34a Jn. 19:18 (9 A.M.- noon)	JESUS IS CRUCIFIED. LkTwo other men, both criminals, were also led out with him to be executed. When they came to the place called the Skull, there they crucified him, along with the criminals—one on his right, the other on his left. Jesus said, "Father, forgive them, for they do not know what they are doing."b MkThen they offered him wine mixed with myrrh, but he did not take it. It was the third hour when they crucified him.
Mt. 27:37 Mk. 15:26 Lk. 23:38 Jn. 19:19-22	INSCRIPTION ON CROSS. Pilate had a notice prepared and fastened to the cross. It read: JESUS OF NAZARETH, THE KING OF THE JEWS. Many of the Jews read this sign, for the place where Jesus was crucified was near the city, and the sign was written in Aramaic, Latin and Greek. The chief priests of the Jews protested to Pilate, "Do not write 'The King of the Jews,' but that this man claimed to be king of the Jews." Pilate answered, "What I have written, I have written."

bSome early manuscripts do not have this sentence.

Mt.
27:35,36
Mk.
15:24
Lk.
23:34b
Jn.
19:23,24

SOLDIERS CAST LOTS. When the soldiers crucified Jesus, they took his clothes, dividing them into four shares, one for each of them, with the undergarment remaining. This garment was seamless, woven in one piece from top to bottom.

"Let's not tear it," they said to one another. "Let's decide by lot who will get it."

This happened that the scripture might be fulfilled which said,

> "They divided my garments among them
> and cast lots for my clothing."[c]

So this is what the soldiers did.

Mt.
27:39-44
Mk.
15:29-32
Lk.
23:35-37

CROWD MOCKS JESUS. [Mt]Those who passed by hurled insults at him, shaking their heads and saying, "You who are going to destroy the temple and build it in three days, save yourself! Come down from the cross, if you are the Son of God!"

In the same way the chief priests, the teachers of the law and the elders mocked him. "He saved others," they said, "but he can't save himself! He's the King of Israel! Let him come down now from the cross, and we will believe in him. He trusts in God. Let God rescue him now if he wants him, for he said, 'I am the Son of God.'" [Lk]The soldiers also came up and mocked him. They offered him wine vinegar and said, "If you are the king of the Jews, save yourself."

Lk.
23:39-43

THIEF ASKS REMEMBRANCE. One of the criminals who hung there hurled insults at him: "Aren't you the Christ? Save yourself and us!"

But the other criminal rebuked him. "Don't you fear God," he said, "since you are under the same sentence? We are punished justly, for we are getting what our deeds deserve. But this man has done nothing wrong."

Then he said, "Jesus, remember me when you come into your kingdom[d]."

Jesus answered him, "I tell you the truth, today you will be with me in paradise."

Jn.
19:25-27

JESUS PROVIDES FOR MARY. Near the cross of Jesus stood his mother, his mother's sister, Mary the wife of Clopas, and

[c]Psalm 22:18   [d]Some manuscripts *come with your kingly power*

Mary Magdalene. When Jesus saw his mother there, and the disciple whom he loved standing nearby, he said to his mother, "Dear woman, here is your son," and to the disciple, "Here is your mother." From that time on, this disciple took her into his home.

JESUS CRIES OUT. From the sixth hour until the ninth hour darkness came over all the land. About the ninth hour Jesus cried out in a loud voice, *"Eloi, Eloi,^{e} lama sabachthani?"*—which means, "My God, my God, why have you forsaken me?"^{f}

When some of those standing there heard this, they said, "He's calling Elijah."

JESUS IS GIVEN DRINK. ^{Jn}Later, knowing that all was now completed, and so that the Scripture would be fulfilled, Jesus said, "I am thirsty." ^{Mt}Immediately one of them ran and got a sponge. He filled it with wine vinegar, put it on a stick, and offered it to Jesus to drink. The rest said, "Now leave him alone. Let's see if Elijah comes to save him."

JESUS DIES. ^{Jn}When he had received the drink, Jesus said, "It is finished." ^{Lk}Jesus called out with a loud voice, "Father, into your hands I commit my spirit." ^{Jn}With that, he bowed his head and gave up his spirit.

MIRACULOUS EVENTS. At that moment the curtain of the temple was torn in two from top to bottom. The earth shook and the rocks split. The tombs broke open and the bodies of many holy people who had died were raised to life. They came out of the tombs, and after Jesus' resurrection they went into the holy city and appeared to many people.

PEOPLE STRUCK WITH AWE. ^{Mt}When the centurion and those with him who were guarding Jesus saw the earthquake and all that had happened, they were terrified, and exclaimed, "Surely he was the Son^g of God!" ^{Mk}Some women were watching from a distance. Among them were Mary Magdalene, Mary the mother of James the younger and of Joses, and Salome. In Galilee these women had followed him and cared for his needs. Many other women who had come up with him to Jerusalem were also there. ^{Lk}When all the people who had

Mt. 27:45-47
Mk. 15:33-35
Lk. 23:44,45a
(About 3 P.M.)

Mt. 27:48,49
Mk. 15:36
Jn. 19:28,29

Mt. 27:50
Mk. 15:37
Lk. 23:46
Jn. 19:30

Mt. 27:51-53
Mk. 15:38
Lk. 23:45b

Mt. 27:54-56
Mk. 15:39-41
Lk. 23:47-49

---

^{e}Some manuscripts *Eli, Eli* ^{f}Psalm 22:1 ^{g}Or *a son*

gathered to witness this sight saw what took place, they beat their breasts and went away. But all those who knew him, including the women who had followed him from Galilee, stood at a distance, watching these things.

Jn.
19:31-37

JESUS IS PIERCED. Now it was the day of Preparation, and the next day was to be a special Sabbath. Because the Jews did not want the bodies left on the crosses during the Sabbath, they asked Pilate to have the legs broken and the bodies taken down. The soldiers therefore came and broke the legs of the first man who had been crucified with Jesus, and then those of the other. But when they came to Jesus and found that he was already dead, they did not break his legs. Instead, one of the soldiers pierced Jesus' side with a spear, bringing a sudden flow of blood and water. The man who saw it has given testimony, and his testimony is true. He knows that he tells the truth, and he testifies so that you also may believe. These things happened so that the scripture would be fulfilled: "Not one of his bones will be broken,"[h] and, as another scripture says, "They will look on the one they have pierced."[i]

The Burial of Jesus

Even in Jesus' burial a remarkable story unfolds involving two men whose names will live throughout history: Nicodemus and Joseph of Arimathea. That anyone outside Jesus' family would have sufficient courage to ask for his body would be curious enough. The real surprise, however, is that it should be a member of the very Council which had called for Jesus' execution. Yet the record notes that Joseph of Arimathea, a respected member of the Council, is also a believer, and it is he who will bury Jesus' body in his own tomb. Joseph will be aided by Nicodemus, the Pharisee and Jewish ruler who had come to Jesus by night asking how one is to be born again. Although the record of that visit did not disclose the result of their discussion, the happy ending is that apparently Nicodemus has become a believer. It is fitting, therefore, that two men whose lives have been so touched by Jesus should now express their gratitude in this final tribute.

[h]Exodus 12:46; Num. 9:12; Psalm 34:20   [i]Zech. 12:10

Mt. 27:57,58 Mk. 15:42-45 Lk. 23:50-52 Jn. 19:38a Garden near Golgotha	JOSEPH ASKS FOR BODY. It was Preparation Day (that is, the day before the Sabbath). So as evening approached, Joseph of Arimathea, a prominent member of the Council, who was himself waiting for the kingdom of God, went boldly to Pilate and asked for Jesus' body. Pilate was surprised to hear that he was already dead. Summoning the centurion, he asked him if Jesus had already died. When he learned from the centurion that it was so, he gave the body to Joseph.
Mt. 27:59,60 Mk. 15:46 Lk. 23:53,54 Jn. 19:38b-42	JESUS BURIED. JnWith Pilate's permission, he came and took the body away. He was accompanied by Nicodemus, the man who earlier had visited Jesus at night. Nicodemus brought a mixture of myrrh and aloes, about seventy-five pounds.j Taking Jesus' body, the two of them wrapped it, with the spices, in strips of linen. This was in accordance with Jewish burial customs. MtJoseph took the body, wrapped it in a clean linen cloth, and placed it in his own new tomb that he had cut out of the rock. JnBecause it was the Jewish day of Preparation and since the tomb was nearby, they laid Jesus there. MtHe rolled a big stone in front of the entrance to the tomb and went away.
Mt. 27:61 Mk. 15:47 Lk. 23:55,56	WOMEN PREPARE ANOINTMENT. The women who had come with Jesus from Galilee followed Joseph and saw the tomb and how his body was laid in it. Then they went home and prepared spices and perfumes. But they rested on the Sabbath in obedience to the commandment.
Mt. 27:62-66 (Thurs- day night, or early Friday)	SOLDIERS GUARD TOMB. The next day, the one after Preparation Day, the chief priests and the Pharisees went to Pilate. "Sir," they said, "we remember that while he was still alive that deceiver said, 'After three days I will rise again.' So give the order for the tomb to be made secure until the third day. Otherwise, his disciples may come and steal the body and tell the people that he has been raised from the dead. This last deception will be worse than the first." "Take a guard," Pilate answered. "Go, make the tomb as secure as you know how." So they went and made the tomb secure by putting a seal on the stone and posting the guard.

jGreek a hundred litrai (about 34 kilograms)

Today's Insights

Forgiveness

Is there someone in your life whom you have been unable to forgive for something he has done to you? Have you prayed about it and still find that you harbor feelings of resentment? And does your inability to completely erase that resentment leave you feeling guilty for not being able to forgive? Sometimes people hurt us so deeply that it is almost beyond our ability to forget what they have done to us and to go on with our lives, to ever recapture the good feelings we once had for the one who has wronged us.

But imagine Jesus hanging there on the cross, his life oozing away with every struggling breath, looking down at his accusers and tormenters, only to say: "Father, forgive them, for they do not know what they are doing." Can we even begin to comprehend how Jesus could think such a thing at that agonizing moment, much less express it aloud? Did they not know what they were saying when they insulted him? Did they not know what they were doing when they falsely accused him and demanded his death on the basis of trumped-up evidence? How could Jesus overlook such willful treachery?

Have you ever heard a child say to his parents, "I hate you! Go away and leave me alone!"—or worse? Yet hardly any parent would take such an attack seriously (beyond giving some appropriate discipline), because a little child does not fully appreciate the significance of what he has said. Perhaps it is somewhat like that in the case of those who taunted and killed Jesus. They didn't fully realize the broad canvas of God's providence on which their evil deeds were being painted. And for that Jesus could forgive them.

In a more personal way, Jesus was only too willing to forgive the sins of the thief who, even in the final hour of his life, placed his faith in Christ. Might *we* not have said, "Sorry, but it's too little too late"?

And what about John, who had deserted Jesus in the garden along with all the other disciples? Is not Jesus forgiving John as he directs him to care for Mary? Our own response might have been, "I'm not talking to you, John!"

If there were those at the foot of the cross who despised Jesus' forgiveness, there were also those who treasured it. The loving act of Joseph and Nicodemus in burying the body of Jesus is a wonderful response to the forgiveness they had received. Through the forgiveness of Jesus, Nicodemus had been born again. He had become a new person, rid of resentment, freed from guilt.

Have we not also been forgiven for the many ways in which we have crucified Christ afresh? Do we not also know the feeling of freedom that comes from having been forgiven? Then we should be all the more willing to forgive those who have hurt us. Jesus' example forces us to look at those in need of forgiveness at the foot of our own cross. And is there any better time than now?

DAY
30
WITH
JESUS

BELIEF

Jesus' Resurrection and Appearances

THE IMPORTANCE OF JESUS' DEATH IS SURPASSED only by the good news of his resurrection! Jesus has prophesied that he will live again, and therefore his credibility is in jeopardy if he is now unable to demonstrate power over his own death. That very claim, and its obvious implications, has already prompted the Jewish leaders to demand a Roman guard at the tomb.

The events which follow are nothing short of marvelous. They not only confirm Jesus' credibility but also provide for believers the assurance of life after death. The drama of Jesus' reappearance unfolds with initial fear, amazement, and outright disbelief on the part of the disciples, but thereafter turns to both belief and joyous celebration. His reappearance is not merely an apparition from the spirit world. Jesus eats in their presence and invites them to touch the wounds where his hands were nailed to the cross. He appears not only in Jerusalem immediately after his resurrection but also later in Galilee. Jesus' appearance is no mere figment of their imagination. This is Jesus himself!

The Gospel writers begin their accounts of the resurrection as the stone sealing the tomb is rolled away. Several of the women come to the tomb early Sunday morning, only to find it empty. When angels at the tomb tell them that Jesus has been raised from the dead, the women react with both fear and joy. At that point the chronology of events becomes somewhat complex, but it appears that Mary Magdalene runs ahead of the other women to find Peter and John, who, upon being told of the body's disappearance, rush with Mary to the empty tomb. As Peter and John go away greatly perplexed, Jesus himself appears to Mary Magdalene there by the tomb, and then to the other women who are still on their way back from the tomb to tell of the resurrection. Of course Jesus' appearance to Mary and the other women gives them even more to tell about, but when the disciples hear it, they simply cannot bring themselves to believe it.

Although there is no direct record of it, apparently Jesus makes a special appearance to Peter sometime on Sunday. The other apostles make reference to that appearance as they are discussing the resurrection later that night with a disciple named Cleopas, to whom Jesus had appeared during the same day. Finally, on this day of resurrection, Jesus will be seen to appear to all the other apostles except for Thomas, who is not present at the time. Thomas' subsequent disbelief is dispelled a week later, when Jesus again appears to the apostles and Thomas views Jesus in person. The apostles will be with Jesus on several occasions, both in Jerusalem and further north in Galilee, before he gives them their apostolic commission and parting instructions.

Sense now the quietness and anticipation on the morning of this ultimate miracle—the resurrection of Jesus the Christ!

Mt. 28:2-4 (Sunday morning)	**STONE ROLLED AWAY.** There was a violent earthquake, for an angel of the Lord came down from heaven and, going to the tomb, rolled back the stone and sat on it. His appearance was like lightning, and his clothes were white as snow. The guards were so afraid of him that they shook and became like dead men.
Mt. 28:1 Mk. 16:1-4 Lk. 24:1-3 Jn. 20:1 At the tomb (Sunday morning)	**WOMEN COME TO TOMB.** When the Sabbath was over, Mary Magdalene, Mary the mother of James, and Salome bought spices so that they might go to anoint Jesus' body. Very early on the first day of the week, just after sunrise, they were on their way to the tomb and they asked each other, "Who will roll the stone away from the entrance of the tomb?" But when they looked up, they saw that the stone, which was very large, had been rolled away.
Mt. 28:5-7 Mk. 16:5-7	**RESURRECTION ANNOUNCED.** As they entered the tomb, they saw a young man dressed in a white robe sitting on the right side, and they were alarmed. "Don't be alarmed," he said. "You are looking for Jesus the Nazarene, who was crucified. He has risen! He is not here. See the place where they laid him. But go, tell his disciples and Peter, 'He is going ahead of you into Galilee. There you will see him, just as he told you.'"
Lk. 24:4-8	**WOMEN REMINDED OF PROPHECY.** While they were wondering about this, suddenly two men in clothes that gleamed

like lightning stood beside them. In their fright the women bowed down with their faces to the ground, but the men said to them, "Why do you look for the living among the dead? He is not here; he has risen! Remember how he told you, while he was still with you in Galilee: 'The Son of Man must be delivered into the hands of sinful men, be crucified and on the third day be raised again.'" Then they remembered his words.

Mk.
16:8

WOMEN GO AWAY FEARFUL. Trembling and bewildered, the women went out and fled from the tomb. They said nothing to anyone, because they were afraid.

Jn. 20:2

PETER AND JOHN TOLD. So [Mary of Magdala] came running to Simon Peter and the other disciple, the one Jesus loved, and said, "They have taken the Lord out of the tomb, and we don't know where they have put him!"

Lk.
24:12
Jn.
20:3-10
At tomb

PETER AND JOHN VIEW TOMB. So Peter and the other disciple started for the tomb. Both were running, but the other disciple outran Peter and reached the tomb first. He bent over and looked in at the strips of linen lying there but did not go in. Then Simon Peter, who was behind him, arrived and went into the tomb. He saw the strips of linen lying there, as well as the burial cloth that had been around Jesus' head. The cloth was folded up by itself, separate from the linen. Finally the other disciple, who had reached the tomb first, also went inside. He saw and believed. (They still did not understand from Scripture that Jesus had to rise from the dead.)

Then the disciples went back to their homes...

Mk.
16:9
Jn.
20:11-17

JESUS WITH MARY MAGDALENE. Mk[When Jesus rose early on the first day of the week, he appeared first to Mary Magdalene, out of whom he had driven seven demons.] JnMary stood outside the tomb crying. As she wept, she bent over to look into the tomb and saw two angels in white, seated where Jesus' body had been, one at the head and the other at the foot.

They asked her, "Woman, why are you crying?"

"They have taken my Lord away," she said, "and I don't know where they have put him." At this, she turned around and saw Jesus standing there, but she did not realize that it was Jesus.

"Woman," he said, "why are you crying? Who is it you are looking for?"

Thinking he was the gardener, she said, "Sir, if you have carried him away, tell me where you have put him, and I will get him."

Jesus said to her, "Mary."

She turned toward him and cried out in Aramaic, "Rabboni!" (which means Teacher).

Jesus said, "Do not hold on to me, for I have not yet returned to the Father. Go instead to my brothers and tell them, 'I am returning to my Father and your Father, to my God and your God.'"

Mt.
28:8-10

JESUS APPEARS TO WOMEN. So the women hurried away from the tomb, afraid yet filled with joy, and ran to tell his disciples. Suddenly Jesus met them. "Greetings," he said. They came to him, clasped his feet and worshiped him. Then Jesus said to them, "Do not be afraid. Go and tell my brothers to go to Galilee; there they will see me."

Mt.
28:11-15

CHIEF PRIESTS COVER UP. While the women were on their way, some of the guards went into the city and reported to the chief priests everything that had happened. When the chief priests had met with the elders and devised a plan, they gave the soldiers a large sum of money, telling them, "You are to say, 'His disciples came during the night and stole him away while we were asleep.' If this report gets to the governor, we will satisfy him and keep you out of trouble." So the soldiers took the money and did as they were instructed. And this story has been widely circulated among the Jews to this very day.

Mk.
16:10,11
Lk.
24:9-11
Jn. 20:18

WOMEN TELL OF APPEARANCE. When they came back from the tomb, they told all these things to the Eleven and to all the others. It was Mary Magdalene, Joanna, Mary the mother of James, and the others with them who told this to the apostles. But they did not believe the women, because their words seemed to them like nonsense.

Mk. 16:12
Lk.
24:13-27
Road to
Emmaus
(Sunday
afternoon)

JESUS APPEARS TO CLEOPAS. Now that same day two of them were going to a village called Emmaus, about seven miles[k] from Jerusalem. They were talking with each other

[k]Greek *sixty stadia* (about 11 kilometers)

about everything that had happened. As they talked and discussed these things with each other, Jesus himself came up and walked along with them; but they were kept from recognizing him.

He asked them, "What are you discussing together as you walk along?"

They stood still, their faces downcast. One of them, named Cleopas, asked him, "Are you only a visitor to Jerusalem and do not know the things that have happened there in these days?"

"What things?" he asked.

"About Jesus of Nazareth," they replied. "He was a prophet, powerful in word and deed before God and all the people. The chief priests and our rulers handed him over to be sentenced to death, and they crucified him; but we had hoped that he was the one who was going to redeem Israel. And what is more, it is the third day since all this took place. In addition, some of our women amazed us. They went to the tomb early this morning but didn't find his body. They came and told us that they had seen a vision of angels, who said he was alive. Then some of our companions went to the tomb and found it just as the women had said, but him they did not see."

He said to them, "How foolish you are, and how slow of heart to believe all that the prophets have spoken! Did not the Christ[1] have to suffer these things and then enter his glory?" And beginning with Moses and all the Prophets, he explained to them what was said in all the Scriptures concerning himself.

Lk.
24:28-32
Emmaus
(Sunday
evening)

JESUS' IDENTITY REVEALED. As they approached the village to which they were going, Jesus acted as if he were going farther. But they urged him strongly, "Stay with us, for it is nearly evening; the day is almost over." So he went in to stay with them.

When he was at the table with them, he took bread, gave thanks, broke it and began to give it to them. Then their eyes were opened and they recognized him, and he disappeared from their sight. They asked each other, "Were not our hearts burning within us while he talked with us on the road and opened the Scriptures to us?"

[1]Or *Messiah*

Mk.
16:13
Lk.
24:33-35
Jn.
20:19

CLEOPAS TELLS OF APPEARANCE. LkThey got up and returned at once to Jerusalem. There [Jnon the evening of that first day of the week, when the disciples were together, with the doors locked for fear of the Jews,] they found the Eleven and those with them, assembled together and saying, "It is true! The Lord has risen and has appeared to Simon." Then the two told what had happened on the way, and how Jesus was recognized by them when he broke the bread.

Mk.
16:14
Lk.
24:36-44
Jn.
20:20
(Sunday
night)

JESUS APPEARS TO DISCIPLES. While they were still talking about this, Jesus himself stood among them and said to them, "Peace be with you."

They were startled and frightened, thinking they saw a ghost. He said to them, "Why are you troubled, and why do doubts rise in your minds? Look at my hands and my feet. It is I myself! Touch me and see; a ghost does not have flesh and bones, as you see I have."

When he had said this, he showed them his hands and feet. And while they still did not believe it because of joy and amazement, he asked them, "Do you have anything here to eat?" They gave him a piece of broiled fish, and he took it and ate it in their presence.

He said to them, "This is what I told you while I was still with you: Everything must be fulfilled that is written about me in the Law of Moses, the Prophets and the Psalms."

Jn.
20:21-23

APOSTLES RECEIVE AUTHORITY. Again Jesus said, "Peace be with you! As the Father has sent me, I am sending you." And with that he breathed on them and said, "Receive the Holy Spirit. If you forgive anyone his sins, they are forgiven; if you do not forgive them, they are not forgiven."

Jn.
20:24,25

THOMAS DOUBTS. Now Thomas (called Didymus), one of the Twelve, was not with the disciples when Jesus came. So the other disciples told him, "We have seen the Lord!"

But he said to them, "Unless I see the nail marks in his hands and put my finger where the nails were, and put my hand into his side, I will not believe it."

Jn.
20:26-29
(Week after
resurrec-
tion)

JESUS APPEARS TO THOMAS. A week later his disciples were in the house again, and Thomas was with them. Though the doors were locked, Jesus came and stood among them and said, "Peace be with you!" Then he said to Thomas, "Put your finger here; see my hands. Reach out your hand and put it into my side. Stop doubting and believe."

Thomas said to him, "My Lord and my God!"

Then Jesus told him, "Because you have seen me, you have believed; blessed are those who have not seen and yet have believed."

Jn. 21:1-14
Sea of Galilee
(Some later time)

JESUS APPEARS TO DISCIPLES. Afterward Jesus appeared again to his disciples, by the Sea of Tiberias.[m] It happened this way: Simon Peter, Thomas (called Didymus), Nathanael from Cana in Galilee, the sons of Zebedee, and two other disciples were together. "I'm going out to fish," Simon Peter told them, and they said, "We'll go with you." So they went out and got into the boat, but that night they caught nothing.

Early in the morning, Jesus stood on the shore, but the disciples did not realize that it was Jesus.

He called out to them, "Friends, haven't you any fish?"

"No," they answered.

He said, "Throw your net on the right side of the boat and you will find some." When they did, they were unable to haul the net in because of the large number of fish.

Then the disciple whom Jesus loved said to Peter, "It is the Lord!" As soon as Simon Peter heard him say, "It is the Lord," he wrapped his outer garment around him (for he had taken it off) and jumped into the water. The other disciples followed in the boat, towing the net full of fish, for they were not far from shore, about a hundred yards.[n] When they landed, they saw a fire of burning coals there with fish on it, and some bread.

Jesus said to them, "Bring some of the fish you have just caught."

Simon Peter climbed aboard and dragged the net ashore. It was full of large fish, 153, but even with so many the net was not torn. Jesus said to them, "Come and have breakfast." None of the disciples dared ask him, "Who are you?" They knew it was the Lord. Jesus came, took the bread and gave it to them, and did the same with the fish. This was now the third time Jesus appeared to his disciples after he was raised from the dead.

[m]That is, Sea of Galilee   [n]Greek *about two hundred cubits* (about 90 meters)

Jn.
21:15-17

PETER REINSTATED. When they had finished eating, Jesus said to Simon Peter, "Simon son of John, do you truly love me more than these?"

"Yes, Lord," he said, "you know that I love you."

Jesus said, "Feed my lambs."

Again Jesus said, "Simon son of John, do you truly love me?" He answered, "Yes, Lord, you know that I love you."

Jesus said, "Take care of my sheep."

The third time he said to him, "Simon son of John, do you love me?"

Peter was hurt because Jesus asked him the third time, "Do you love me?" He said, "Lord, you know all things; you know that I love you."

Jesus said, "Feed my sheep.

Jn.
21:18,19

PETER'S DEATH FORETOLD. "I tell you the truth, when you were younger you dressed yourself and went where you wanted; but when you are old you will stretch out your hands, and someone else will dress you and lead you where you do not want to go." Jesus said this to indicate the kind of death by which Peter would glorify God. Then he said to him, "Follow me!"

Jn.
21:20-24

JOHN'S DEATH QUESTIONED. Peter turned and saw that the disciple whom Jesus loved was following them. (This was the one who had leaned back against Jesus at the supper and had said, "Lord, who is going to betray you?") When Peter saw him, he asked, "Lord, what about him?"

Jesus answered, "If I want him to remain alive until I return, what is that to you? You must follow me." Because of this, the rumor spread among the brothers that this disciple would not die. But Jesus did not say that he would not die; he only said, "If I want him to remain alive until I return, what is that to you?"

This is the disciple who testifies to these things and who wrote them down. We know that his testimony is true.

TODAY'S INSIGHTS

Belief

Suppose a friend of yours died, and on Thursday, following the funeral, was buried in the local cemetery. You were there. You saw the body in the casket, and then the casket being lowered into the earth. Now suppose that on Sunday morning someone you trust comes to your house and tells you, "I know you're not going to believe this, but I just saw your friend walking down the street. And, what's more, he actually talked to me!"

Would you believe it? Would it help any if, for months before his death, your now-deceased friend had said on several occasions, "I'm going to die soon, but don't worry—I'll be back." Isn't it likely that you would have long since dismissed his boast as foolish talk?

Sometimes an event is easier to believe when it is printed on the pages of Holy Scripture, because it is sufficiently remote to be a story of faith around which adherents to a particular religion can rally. But it is important to remember that the scenario given above is as realistic as what happened when Jesus was resurrected from the dead. There were real people who had real doubts based upon what they felt were reasonable grounds for disbelief. Few of us in their position would have believed any more readily. Remarkably, however, they ultimately *did* believe!

Some have said, of course, that Jesus' resurrection was no more than a fictionalized story promulgated by Jesus' disciples. Yet the evidence is simply too strong to the contrary. Over the centuries many people have fabricated outrageous stories, but how many of them have actually laid down their lives in defense of those stories? How many have continued to maintain the accuracy of their stories when faced with persecution? And yet that is exactly the fate of those who have related their eyewitness accounts of Jesus' death, burial, and resurrection.

Suppose for a moment that Jesus' resurrection is a lie. Naturally, we could still accept Jesus' teaching as the grandest message ever proclaimed. But suppose the story is true—every word of it? Then we are dealing with the most important fact in all of human history! The man claiming to be God incarnate, the man who said he was the Way to fulfillment and peace, and the Truth about the meaning of our very existence, and the Life which leads to life eternal—*that man* was all the things he ever said he was!

"That man" is your friend who just walked through the door to say, "What you've been told is true! I *am* alive again. And because it's true, you can trust me when I say that you too can live forever beyond death."

As Christians we have reached out in faith and touched Jesus. We have trusted Jesus when he said, "Stop doubting and believe," for "blessed are those who have not seen and yet have believed." Have we also believed that through him we will live forever? Like Jesus himself, we will triumph over death!

ANTICIPATION

Final Instructions and Ascension

AFTER THESE WONDERFUL EVENTS, JESUS IS NEXT SEEN AGAIN WITH his 11 apostles on a mountain in Galilee. There they are given the special mission of evangelizing the world, a task to be accomplished through their personal testimonies regarding Jesus' life, death, and resurrection. Even as they are receiving this commission, some among them still have doubts about their mission. But the time is soon to come when, filled with God's Holy Spirit, each will stand strong in his faith and become a vibrant force in changing the hearts of men and women throughout the civilized world.

Some time passes before Jesus makes his final appearance with the apostles, and the scene changes to Jerusalem. There Jesus directs the apostles to remain in the city until they receive a special power which he promises will come from the Father. Later he gives them their final instructions, promises them the Holy Spirit, and then is caught up into heaven as two angels stand by to comfort the apostles with the grand promise of his second coming.

[The most reliable early manuscripts and other ancient witnesses do not have Mark 16:9-20.]

Mt.
28:16-20
Mk.
16:15-18
On mountain in Galilee

JESUS COMMISSIONS APOSTLES. ᴹᵗThen Jesus came to them and said, "All authority in heaven and on earth has been given to me. Therefore go and make disciples of all nations, baptizing them in° the name of the Father and of the Son and of the Holy Spirit, and teaching them to obey everything I have commanded you. And surely I am with you always, to the very end of the age." ᴹᵏ"Whoever believes and is baptized will be saved, but whoever does not believe will be condemned. And these signs will accompany those who believe: In my name they will drive out demons; they will speak in new tongues; they will pick up snakes with their hands; and when

°Or *into*; see Acts 8:16; 19:5; Romans 6:3; 1 Cor. 1:13; 10:2 and Gal. 3:27.

they drink deadly poison, it will not hurt them at all; they will place their hands on sick people, and they will get well."

Lk.
24:45-49
Jerusalem
(Before
Pentecost)

PARTING INSTRUCTIONS. Then he opened their minds so they could understand the Scriptures. He told them, "This is what is written: The Christ will suffer and rise from the dead on the third day, and repentance and forgiveness of sins will be preached in his name to all nations, beginning at Jerusalem. You are witnesses of these things. I am going to send you what my Father has promised; but stay in the city until you have been clothed with power from on high."

Mk.
16:19
Lk.
24:50,51
Acts 1:6-11

JESUS ASCENDS. LkWhen he had led them out to the vicinity of Bethany, he lifted up his hands and blessed them. Ac[They] asked him, "Lord, are you at this time going to restore the kingdom to Israel?"

He said to them: "It is not for you to know the times or dates the Father has set by his own authority. But you will receive power when the Holy Spirit comes on you; and you will be my witnesses in Jerusalem, and in all Judea and Samaria, and to the ends of the earth."

After he said this, he was taken up before their very eyes, and a cloud hid him from their sight.

They were looking intently up into the sky as he was going, when suddenly two men dressed in white stood beside them. "Men of Galilee," they said, "why do you stand here looking into the sky? This same Jesus, who has been taken from you into heaven, will come back in the same way you have seen him go into heaven."

Lk.
24:52,53
Acts
1:12-14
Jeru-
salem

DISCIPLES RETURN JOYFULLY. LkThen they worshiped him and returned to Jerusalem with great joy. AcWhen they arrived, they went upstairs to the room where they were staying. Those present were Peter, John, James and Andrew; Philip and Thomas, Bartholomew and Matthew; James son of Alphaeus and Simon the Zealot, and Judas son of James. They all joined together constantly in prayer, along with the women and Mary the mother of Jesus, and with his brothers.

Acts
1:15-22

CALL FOR JUDAS' REPLACEMENT. In those days Peter stood up among the believersp (a group numbering about a

pGreek brothers

hundred and twenty) and said, "Brothers, the Scripture had to be fulfilled which the Holy Spirit spoke long ago through the mouth of David concerning Judas, who served as guide for those who arrested Jesus—he was one of our number and shared in this ministry."

(With the reward he got for his wickedness, Judas bought a field; there he fell headlong, his body burst open and all his intestines spilled out. Everyone in Jerusalem heard about this, so they called that field in their language Akeldama, that is, Field of Blood.)

"For," said Peter, "it is written in the book of Psalms,

"'May his place be deserted;
let there be no one to dwell in it,'[q]

and,

"'May another take his place of leadership.'[r]

Therefore it is necessary to choose one of the men who have been with us the whole time the Lord Jesus went in and out among us, beginning from John's baptism to the time when Jesus was taken up from us. For one of these must become a witness with us of his resurrection."

Acts
1:23-26
MATTHIAS CHOSEN AS APOSTLE. So they proposed two men: Joseph called Barsabbas (also known as Justus) and Matthias. Then they prayed, "Lord, you know everyone's heart. Show us which of these two you have chosen to take over this apostolic ministry, which Judas left to go where he belongs." Then they cast lots, and the lot fell to Matthias; so he was added to the eleven apostles.

Mk.
16:20
JESUS' MESSIAHSHIP PREACHED. Then the disciples went out and preached everywhere, and the Lord worked with them and confirmed his word by the signs that accompanied it.

Conclusion to the Gospel Accounts

John's account includes this statement as to his purpose in recording the events of Jesus' ministry:

[q]Psalm 69:25   [r]Psalm 109:8

Jn. 20:30,31	Jesus did many other miraculous signs in the presence of his disciples, which are not recorded in this book. But these are written that you may[s] believe that Jesus is the Christ, the Son of God, and that by believing you may have life in his name.

Indeed, each of the other accounts unquestionably has the same purpose—the preservation of Jesus' life, teaching, and miraculous works so that all who read may acknowledge him as Lord and Savior.

John concludes his account by indicating that he and the other Gospel writers had been able to capture in written words only a small fraction of all the miracles, healings, praying, and preaching that Jesus did while on this earth.

Jn. 21:25	Jesus did many other things as well. If every one of them were written down, I suppose that even the whole world would not have room for the books that would be written.

Even with only these four brief accounts of his life, the story of Jesus has been preserved throughout the centuries for every generation, translated into virtually every language on earth, and believed by countless millions who have responded in obedient faith to God through his Son, Jesus the Christ.

TODAY'S INSIGHTS

Anticipation

Why is it that we have an irresistible urge to shake the packages under the Christmas tree? What is there about a box with pretty paper, ribbons, and bows that makes us want to guess what's inside? And why does the master of ceremonies at an awards banquet inevitably hold us in suspense before announcing the winner? It's because we love anticipation! It whets the appetite for the surprise to come, making it all the better. It dramatizes the importance of what is about to happen.

How God loves a celebration! And how he loves to thrill us with anticipation. Through the prophets of old he let the world

[s]Some manuscripts *may continue to*

"shake the package" for almost 40 centuries. A word here, a clue there. When would the Messiah come? Who would he be? What would be the nature of his kingdom? The little nation of Israel could hardly wait for those answers. In their excited speculation, many of them guessed wrong again and again. But imagine their surprise when what they had hoped to receive came in the least likely package of all!

Even his own disciples could scarcely believe the gift they had received in the person of Jesus. And now he has left them for the glories of heaven. But not without, once again, the precious gift of anticipation: "I am going to send you what my Father has promised." But when, Lord? "It is not for you to know the time or dates," he said, "but you will receive power when the Holy Spirit comes on you." But, they must have wondered, what would *that* mean in their lives?

As if this were not excitement enough, Jesus also gave them the anticipation of his return. As they looked heavenward at his ascension, they were told, "He will come back in the same way that he went." But when, Lord? Again the reply might have been, "It is not for you to know. But look for it, for I will return!"

You can almost sense the joy and excitement running through the small group of men and women who had come to believe in Jesus. On the brink of defeat, and convinced that with Jesus' death all was lost, they had been amazed by his resurrection and thrilled by his reappearance. Now they had gathered in eager anticipation of his promises, and of how their lives would be dramatically changed.

Wouldn't it be great to have been with them? To be right there, to see Jesus face-to-face, to see him ascend into heaven, and to "shake the package" of what lay ahead! We know now that when the package was finally opened, only days beyond the Gospel record, the Holy Spirit came with unprecedented power!

With the opening of that package came the promise that we can have the same gift of the Holy Spirit, working in our lives through our faith in Jesus Christ. How will God bless us today? What wonder will he perform in our lives tomorrow? Oh, the divine anticipation of it all!

The Daily Bible®

F. LaGard Smith

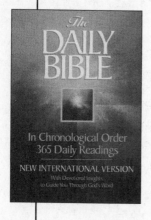

Unlike any other Bible you have ever read...

As this unique, chronological presentation of God's story unfolds before you, you will begin to appreciate God's plan for your life as never before. Reading the Bible will become a fresh, inviting, more informative experience. In *The Daily Bible* you'll find these helpful features:

- **The New International Version**...the most popular modern version of Scripture, a highly respected and understandable translation.

- **Chronological/Historical Arrangement of Every Book of the Bible**...lets you easily understand God's redemptive plan as you read from creation to Revelation in the order the events actually occurred.

- **Devotional Commentary**...leads you smoothly through the Scripture, painting the scene for what is about to be read with historical and spiritual insights.

- **365 Convenient Daily Reading Segements**... arranged so you can read all of God's Word in one year.

- **Topical Arrangements for Proverbs and Ecclesiastes**...enable you to focus on specific aspects of God's wisdom.

Meeting God in Quiet Places

F. LaGard Smith

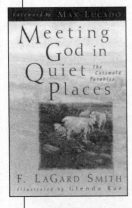

Do You Long for the Peace of God's Presence?

Imagine yourself whisked away to the beautiful English country-side—walking down quiet lanes, beside rambling dry-stone walls with spring flowers and summer grasses that reach out to touch you as you pass by.

In these inspiring parables drawn from his daily walks through the magnificent Cotswolds, F. LaGard Smith shares life-renewing insights to guide you to the very heart of God. When the daily clamor threatens to overwhelm you, these personal meditations will refresh both the eye and the soul, bringing renewed perspective to the values and qualities of life you cherish.

The Narrated Bible

**with Devotional Commentary
by F. LaGard Smith**

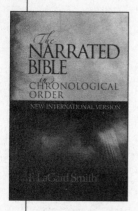

**Revolutionize Your
Understanding of God's Word**

Read the entire Bible—from Genesis to Revelation—as a single, continuous account of God's personal interaction with man! *The Narrated Bible* presents Scripture (NIV) in chronological order to provide a fascinating tapestry of God's creation, judgments, love, provision, and mercy. An insightful descriptive narrative ties events together and draws you irresistibly into the center of action and a new understanding of the glory and power of God's sovereignty. You'll experience—

- deeper insights for your own spiritual journey as the prophets and their teachings come to life in their historical, geographical, and cultural contexts.

- greater understanding of God's wisdom and encouragement through the unique arrangements of the book of Proverbs (by topic) and the book of Psalms (by sentiment).

- a deeper awareness of the life of Christ and His teachings through the harmonized Gospels.